T0277607

HARLEM WORLD

HARLEM WORLD

How Hip Hop's Super Showdown Changed Music Forever

JOHNS HOPKINS UNIVERSITY PRESS
BALTIMORE

Johns Hopkins University Press
2715 North Charles Street
Baltimore, Maryland 21218
www.press.jhu.edu

Library of Congress Cataloging-in-Publication Data

Names: Mael, Jonathan, 1992– author.
Title: Harlem world : How hip hop's super showdown
  changed music forever / Jonathan Mael.
Description: Baltimore : Johns Hopkins University Press, 2023. | Includes
  bibliographical references and index.
Identifiers: LCCN 2022046755 | ISBN 9781421446882 (hardcover) | ISBN
  9781421446899 (ebook)
Subjects: LCSH: Rap (Music)—New York (State)—New York—History and
  criticism. | Hip-hop—New York (State)—New York—History. | Harlem (New
  York, N.Y.)—History—20th century.
Classification: LCC ML3531 .M16 2023 | DDC
  782.42164909747/1—dc23/eng/20220930
LC record available at https://lccn.loc.gov/2022046755

A catalog record for this book is available from the British Library.

Book design and composition: Dustin Kilgore

For Mom, and for anyone who's ever been told "no" and did it anyway

Contents

Cast of Characters

The Cold Crush Brothers (aka Cold Crush)

Curtis Brown (Grandmaster Caz)

Carlos Mandes (DJ Charlie Chase)

Adrian Harris (Easy A.D.)

Kenneth Crump (Almighty Kay Gee)

Jerome Lewis (Jerry Dee Lewis, or JDL)

Angelo King (DJ Tony Tone)

The Fantastic Romantic Five

Theodore Livingston (DJ Grand Wizzard Theodore)

Robin Diggs (Master Rob)

Kevin Ferguson (Kevie Kev or Waterbed Kev)

James Whipper II (Whipper Whip or Prince Whipper Whip)

Ruben Garcia (Rubie Dee)

Darryl Mason (Dot-A-Rock)

Harlem World Crew

Charles Leake (Charlie Rock)

Randy Sanders (DJ Randy)

Sam Blocker (Son of Sam)

Jack Taylor (Fat Man or Fat Jack, founder of Harlem World)

The L Brothers

DJ Mean Gene

DJ Cordie-O

Wild Style *Cast and Crew*

Charlie Ahearn (director)

Patti Astor (playing Virginia)

George Lee Quiñones (playing Raymond Zoro)

Frederick Brathwaite (aka Fab 5 Freddy; playing Phade)

Sandra Fabara (aka Lady Pink; playing Rose Lady Bug)

Hip Hop Artists

Mohandas Dewese (Kool Moe Dee, part of the Treacherous Three)

Lamar Hill (L.A. Sunshine, part of the Treacherous Three)

D'Bora Meyers (DJ Baby D, part of the Mercedes Ladies)

David James Parker (Busy Bee Starski)

Luis Cedeño (DJ Disco Wiz)

Clive Campbell (DJ Kool Herc)

Joseph Saddler (Grandmaster Flash from Grandmaster Flash and the Furious Five)

Melvin Glover (Melle Mel from Grandmaster Flash and the Furious Five)

Nathaniel Glover (the Kidd Creole from Grandmaster Flash and the Furious Five)

Anthony Holloway (DJ Hollywood)

Claude Gray (Paradise Gray)

Disco King Mario

Kurtis Walker (Kurtis Blow)

Sharon Green (Sha Rock from the Funky 4 + 1)

Rodney Stone (Lil' Rodney Cee from the Funky 4 + 1)

Author's Note

The events described in this book took place more than forty years ago, and I am so thrilled that I was able to speak with so many wonderful people who experienced them firsthand. Occasionally, multiple versions of the same event were described by different people who were there. I made every effort to give an ear to everyone, to quote them, and then to piece together events based on as many sources as possible.

Although I was fortunate to have interviewed a lot of amazing people for this project, I wasn't able to talk with everyone I had wanted to reach. Some individuals opted not to provide an interview for this project, and there were others who simply couldn't be located, despite my best efforts. Luckily, the Museum of Pop Culture in Seattle has an extensive archive of oral histories from significant individuals in the hip hop genre, and I was able to use those histories extensively for this project alongside my own interviews.

HARLEM WORLD

Introduction

The Crispy Crust Pizzeria

In 1979, Sylvia Robinson was in trouble. The former soul music star turned record executive needed to find success in order to keep her R&B label, All Platinum Records, afloat. The family business, which she had founded in New York City in 1976, was involved in a large lawsuit that threatened the label's very existence, according to her son, Joey Robinson Jr.[1] The "Pillow Talk" singer needed her fortunes to turn, which happened at a birthday party thrown for her by her sister and niece at the giant New York club Harlem World. It was at that party that Sylvia would experience the music that would change her life: hip hop, which had been around New York for the previous six years but was still in its infancy. She saw the DJ delighting the crowd by spinning records and saying his rhymes over the beats, a rapping DJ, and she knew she was onto something unique.

"Seeing the people respond to it, that's where she got the idea to do a rap record," said Joey Robinson Jr. in a 2001 interview. "She said, you know, the Lord had given her this vision to do a rap record."[2]

Her interest piqued, Robinson decided that hip hop would be her label's savior. Hip hop: a new musical genre dominated by "rebellious" youth, one that had yet to break into mainstream radio. She set off to find some young men who could rhyme and get a party going—emcees—to appear on a record.

At first, Joey knew exactly who to get in touch with: an emcee friend of his who went by the name of Casper. Casper initially agreed to record with All Platinum, and Sylvia began producing the track for what would become the music industry's first rap record. But after a few days of working, Casper backed out. According to Joey, Casper's father advised him to stay away because of the pending litigation against the label.

Disheartened, Sylvia asked Joey to find someone else—anyone who could rap—to appear on the record. Joey had a friend named Warren Moore, who said he could help him and his mother meet emcees who were performing in the area. The three set off in Warren's Oldsmobile 98 to track them down.[3]

They found them at the Crispy Crust Pizzeria in Englewood, New Jersey. There they met the emcees who would become the Sugarhill Gang, the chart-topping group that brought hip hop to the mainstream masses through pop radio. These emcees were not well known among hip hop circles, which were built from individuals and groups who had honed their craft in the scene for years before being signed to a record deal. Rather, they were friends who were in the right place at the right time. That place was the Crispy Crust on a Friday night. When "Rapper's Delight," Sugarhill's debut single, was recorded, the belief among the heavyweights in the still-undefined genre was that hip hop was strictly a live art form centered around working the crowd with original and creative routines rather than immortalizing whole songs on wax. But it turned out that the novice performers who would become the Sugarhill Gang were the perfect choice for Robinson's project.

Warren had taken Sylvia and Joey to the pizza parlor to meet his friend Henry Lee Jackson, who went by the stage name Big Bank Hank. Hank rapped as he made pizzas at the Crispy Crust. "He would rap all the time," fellow Sugarhill member Wonder Mike told the *New York*

Times after Hank's death in 2014. "While he was making the pizzas, while he was slicing them, while he was serving them."[4]

That night, the three told Hank that if he was interested in working with All Platinum, he had to audition on the spot: "And I'm making pizza and Joey and his mother walks in," Hank said. "I don't know these people at all, right? And it's like somebody walking up to you and saying, 'I want you to make a record for me.' And I'm looking around going, 'did I miss something here?' Looking around going, 'yeah, it's a joke, right? Right.' No, no, no.

And they were serious! And I'm . . . picture this, I'm full of pizza dough, and I'm like, okay, they want me to come outside and audition in the car. I'm like, Ooookkkkaaaay, you know?"

Hank wanted in. He kicked all of the customers out of the pizzeria and shut it down for the night, then hurried out to audition inside Warren's car.[5] According to Joey, a commotion rose up around the car because so many people from the street were grooving to the music and enjoying Hank's rhymes.[6] By that time, Hank's friends, Guy "Master Gee" O'Brien and Michael "Wonder Mike" Wright, had gathered at the Crispy Crust. With Hank still in his work apron, sauce stains and all, the three competed for the Robinsons' admiration, even after they had left the pizzeria and headed to the Robinsons' house in Englewood, New Jersey. Hank, Gee, and Mike impressed Sylvia enough that she couldn't decide which rapper would be the best fit, so she joined the men together to form the Sugarhill Gang on the spot: "And she said, 'You know, I just came up with a new record company called Sugarhill Records,'" Hank said. "And she said, 'You all are the first group on Sugarhill Records, and we'll name you all Sugarhill Gang.'"

That was a Friday night. "Rapper's Delight" was recorded the following Monday, at a cost of $750.[7]

There's always a great deal of anticipation when needle meets wax and makes that soft, scratchy sound just before a record starts to reveal itself as it spins around its turntable. But the Sugarhill Gang's twelve-inch disc of wax created an especially memorable moment for young people across America. Quite simply, on September 16, 1979, they released one of the most important songs in music history.

When the immortal words "I said-a hip, hop, the hippie, the hippie/to the hip hip hop-a you don't stop the rock . . . " first pumped through speakers,[8] it became clear that a new genre of music—foreign to most listeners—had landed in American bedrooms and barbecues from coast to coast. "Rapper's Delight" clocked in at a healthy seven minutes and ten seconds (an extended version was almost fifteen minutes long), yet somehow, most people who bought that record when it first came out still have the entire track memorized. This was an exciting moment; it's not often that a musical genre has a "big bang"–type explosion tracing back to one song. This was clearly the first commercial hip hop record.[9] The song was everything hip hop's earliest originators intended for it to be: a clear alternative to disco, a crowd-pleaser, a little rebellious, and extremely fun and funny. Hip hop at its core was music made by the people for the masses, and even though Robinson produced the song for a commercial audience, the spirit of free creative expression runs through it.

The song's structure was unusual. There were no choruses or refrains. Three talented (albeit inexperienced) emcees simply traded verses, which included boastful rhymes like:

> You see I'm six foot one and I'm tons of fun
> And I dress to a T
> You see I got more clothes than Muhammad Ali
> And I dress so viciously
> I got bodyguards, I got two big cars, that definitely ain't the wack
> I got a Lincoln Continental and a sunroof Cadillac.

Or more sexual and risqué verses, such as:

Well, I'm Imp the Dimp

The ladies' pimp

The women fight for my delight

But I'm the grandmaster with the three emcees

That shock the house for the young ladies

And when you come inside, into the front

You do the freak, spank, and do the bump.[10]

There were mentions of wooing Lois Lane away from Superman, the feeling of eating gross food at a friend's house and having to pretend you like it, and "super sperm." The concept of "rockin' to the beat" was mentioned in about a dozen different ways. Quite simply, the lyrics were a perfect introduction to the themes of hip hop at the time. There was a bit of everything for someone who was tired of disco's monotony (and there was a large audience who felt that way).

Complete with an infectious break from Chic's "Good Times" that begged for the roller skates to come out, it's not surprising "Rapper's Delight" reached the Top 40 in the United States, peaking at No. 36.[11] It charted in Britain, Canada, Holland, and West Germany as well.[12] Decades later, *Rolling Stone* magazine listed it as the second greatest hip hop song of all time.[13]

Hank went back to working at the Crispy Crust after the recording session. That's where he heard the song on the radio for the first time alongside his customers. An up-and-coming station called WKTU had decided to air the track. Hank recalls, "The pizza shop is jam-packed with people. It was also like the prime hangout . . . you know, used to be young kids, right? And, 'we have a new record by the Sugarhill Gang.' I'm like, 'whoa man! Turn this up! You know, this is neat!' They play the record. Now you have to understand, this record is almost 16 minutes long, right? They played it in its entirety. When the record got maybe into three minutes of the record? [DJ] Paco got onstage and said, 'Our phone lines are locked. Please do not call this station anymore. We will play the record again.'"[14]

* * *

While the Sugarhill Gang is mostly remembered as a one-hit wonder, that one hit was about as important as it gets. All of a sudden, hip hop was embraced by millions of Americans who had either never heard of it before or terribly misunderstood it. In addition, hip hop's popularity meant that the African American English (AAE) dialect gained more exposure to a broad audience than it ever had before. It is still the most studied of all English dialects.[15] The music was appearing in commercials for Fortune 500 companies, and graffiti-style fonts were being used in all manner of print ads.[16] In just sixteen minutes, a movement strictly for those "in the know," fueled by word of mouth and experienced only by New Yorkers, had broken through to all corners of America.

But, as it turns out, the leaders of the movement that forged hip hop and the wider culture that accompanied it didn't necessarily want that. "He just took the rhymes like they were and he didn't change it up," said Curtis Brown, who goes by the name Grandmaster Caz on stage. "The Superman rhyme about Lois Lane, and flying through the air, panty hose? That's all my rhyme, that's all my stuff. So when that came out by them, we was like, they ain't no emcees."[17]

Caz is one of the most significant pioneers in the history of the genre, having developed much of the lyrical style that hip hop is based around. Caz was a regular performer at the Bronx club Sparkle, where Hank worked security, and the two built a friendship. Hank even managed Caz's early group, the Mighty Force, for some time.[18] Over the course of the relationship, Hank asked to look at some of Caz's legendary notebooks filled with rhyme ideas. He took a specific liking to one, which would become the basis for his first verse in "Rapper's Delight":

> Check it out, I'm the C-A-S-A-, the N-O-V-A, and the rest is F-L-Y
> You see, I go by the code of the doctor of the mix
> And these reasons I'll tell you why.[19]

Casanova Fly was Grandmaster Caz's stage name at the time. Caz didn't receive a writing credit for the song. This was breaking a code held sacred by early emcees—don't take other people's rhymes. Hank's theft was further compounded by the Sugarhill Gang's lack of experience in the hip hop scene and their snap formation by Sylvia Robinson (other crews typically rehearsed for months before even playing their first show). Many of the primary figures in the genre didn't know who Hank, Gee, and Mike were.[20]

While "Rapper's Delight" opened up previously unimaginable doors for rappers, many of the genre's originators saw it as a poor representation of the movement they had worked so hard to build up away from the eyes of the American music industry. The song was catchy, but it wasn't spontaneous, didn't feature harmonized routines, and lacked the ferocity and youthful abandon that hip hop was designed to feature. To hear hip hop like that and see the greatest shows New York had to offer, fans still had to head to the intersection of 116th and Malcolm X Boulevard to the genre's greatest proving ground and the place where Sylvia Robinson first discovered hip hop: Harlem World.

Groups like Grandmaster Flash and the Furious Five, the Funky 4 + 1, the Treacherous Three, the Fantastic Romantic Five, and many more had cut their teeth in a fight for supremacy in the New York scene. Shows at Harlem World were part rappers' convention, part competitive sport, part house party, and yes, part concert. At this cramped, loud nightclub, hip hop survived in its purest form, and through the crucible of the battles that occurred there, the genre's most important artists honed their craft well before most Americans were aware hip hop even existed. "Rapper's Delight" might have been hip hop's first successful song, but Harlem World was hip hop's first real home.

DJ Grand Wizzard Theodore at the
T-Connection, 1980. The show included the
Fantastic Romantic Five, DJ Kool Herc, and
DJ Clark Kent. Photo by Charlie Ahearn.

Chapter 1

The Sound Room

Disco. Perhaps that is the most divisive word in the history of American music. For different people, it means different things. For some, it represents the carefree wistfulness of the "Me Decade," when bubbles, glitter, and roller skates ruled the dance floor. For others, it's a synonym for the utter garbage that dominated airwaves and put skilled musicians out of business. Famously, on July 12, 1979, the Chicago White Sox hosted "Disco Demolition Night," where fans were asked to bring disco records that would be blown up between games of a doubleheader. Comiskey Park was filled well beyond capacity that night, despite the fact that the White Sox had been playing so badly that they were essentially out of contention. The explosion actually rendered the field unplayable for the second game, and the White Sox forfeited. The fans didn't care; they were most interested in following the lead of local radio personality Steve Dahl in condemning the entire disco genre.[1]

Not to be confused with funk, soul, or the Motown sound that rightfully held a place in the hearts of many Americans, what people commonly refer to as "disco" was drum machine–driven, ultra-repetitive, sterile dance-first music that its haters thought was gaining way too much traction in nightclubs from coast to coast. Songs like "Y.M.C.A." by the Village People and "The Hustle" by Van McCoy were capturing mainstream airtime and bringing in millions of dollars for record companies seeking to find the next conforming disco sensation rather than go out on any musical limbs.

Naturally, when mainstream culture gets a bit too stagnant, a counterculture will form. It has happened time and time again in American society, whether it was led by the bobbed flappers of the Roaring Twenties, the leather jacket– and jeans-wearing juvenile delinquents of the 1950s, or the flower children of the Summer of Love. Young people in America were and are constantly on the hunt for an alternative to the mainstream culture being forced upon them. In the 1970s, this was especially true in New York, where opulent Manhattan clubs like Studio 54 glamorized disco and the culture of decadence and materialism that went along with it. Diamond jewelry and expensive fur coats became just as much a part of the genre as repeating drumbeats and roller skates.

Fortunately, the perfect alternative had already been brewing in parts of New York City for a few years. Hip hop, in its infancy, had more similarities with disco than differences, but it came from a spirit of rebellion and fun that was unique. As hip hop grew into one of the top forces in American pop culture, its artists became symbols of twenty-first-century decadence and materialism. In the 1970s, though, the music was made solely for the enjoyment of those who produced it.

According to the people who helped to create the genre, the very complex idea of hip hop music can best be distilled into one core concept: taking tunes that were already known and playing them differently. "Hip hop is a sub-genre of funk, R&B, and disco. It's the bastard child of funk, R&B, and disco,"[2] explained Claude "Paradise" Gray, a noted hip hop historian and performer who was heavily involved in this era. Gray grew up in the Bronxdale Houses and would later go on to run the famous Latin Quarter nightclub, where he helped give a platform to iconic artists such as KRS-One and Public Enemy. His own group, X Clan, found success in the early 1990s.

What would become an entire hip hop culture started to form in the South Bronx, about as far away from the lavish Manhattan lifestyle as could be. The person who hosted the first documented hip hop party, therefore establishing this most American of genres, wasn't actually born in America. The legendary Clive Campbell, better known as DJ Kool Herc, immigrated to the Bronx in 1967 from Kingston, Jamaica, when he was twelve years old. He came from a quiet family and was friendly and good-natured, despite his giant stature.[3] Herc brought with him an element of Jamaican culture called dancehall, which involved an active DJ guiding the party as it went as opposed to simply selecting songs to be played. On August 11, 1973, Herc hosted a "back-to-school jam" in the recreation room of his apartment building at 1520 Sedgwick Avenue to celebrate his sister's birthday.[4]

According to Dr. Fred Collins, who grew up in the same building and was close with Kool Herc, the rec room, which still exists today, was a plain space with white walls and a small kitchenette. It measured 20 x 20 feet. "While it wasn't huge, it crammed in a bunch of teenagers," he said. Collins, now a professor at Western Washington University, also confirmed what many have argued: that there were hip hop parties *before* the famous one in the rec room, at a small church on University Avenue where the guys from 1520 Sedgwick and the surrounding streets would head on weekends. When they were put out at 1:00 a.m., Herc and company decided they needed a less controlled environment, so they reestablished the parties in the rec room where, Collins explained, "We could have a little more fun."[5]

The six-four, two-hundred-fifty-pound Herc brought his own eclectic taste in music to his parties.[6] He spun a range of soul, funk, and disco records from the likes of the Jackson 5, Kraftwerk, and Babe

Ruth, among many others. But it was the mild-mannered DJ's spinning technique that really gave rise to the popularization of the hip hop sound in the neighborhood. Herc focused on what he considered the best part of the record, known colloquially as the "break." Breaks are parts of songs where either the drummer or the bass player takes a solo and the rest of the track (most notably the vocals) drops out to put an extra emphasis on the section. Famous breaks include the bass solo from Chic's "Good Times" (which was used in "Rapper's Delight") and the drums from "Bongo Rock." While these were the parts of songs people wanted to dance to, they were often so fleeting that partygoers would just be getting into the groove when the break ended suddenly. Herc's solution was diabolically simple: use two turntables to rapidly switch between songs, only playing their breaks.[7] By starting the break on the second turntable just as the break on the first one was concluding, Herc could keep the crowd engaged and dancing for hours on end. Herc called this technique the "merry-go-round,"[8] and it allowed a whole new form of very athletic, physical, and visually interesting dancing to emerge.

"Break dancers" was the term given to individuals who came out onto the dance floor during Kool Herc's "merry-go-round." These dancers would drop to the floor, freeze mid-move, spin on their heads, and do whatever they could to dazzle a crowd. Moves like the "windmill," the "jackhammer," and the "air flare" weren't only marks of physical ability, but creativity. Most significantly, breakdancing is rebellious. It doesn't follow any of the conventions of typical dancing at a party. There's no need for nice clothes or a partner, and no break dancers stay in their own space.

Boys and girls who danced during breaks were known as "break boys" or "break girls." Eventually that was shortened to "b-boys" or "b-girls," and hip hop began its transition from a party trick to an entire lifestyle. In fact, these dancers are believed to be the first individuals to monetize hip hop, as they would take their speakers and cardboard boxes and perform for tourists in Central Park and other crowded Manhattan spots.[9]

According to Collins, after about ten parties in the rec room, it was simply getting too crowded to accommodate the growing number of fans from farther and farther away who made the pilgrimage to hear Herc play.[10] The parties weren't even heavily advertised. People simply knew where they were on a Friday night and headed over to the housing project. Collins was startled at how quickly Herc's new style of music grew in popularity. The solution Herc and company came up with was to move the party outside, to a park located between 1520 and 1600 Sedgwick. Collins claims that while the first rec room party had attracted between fifty and seventy-five revelers, the first outdoor party drew a crowd of hundreds. The power was supplied by Collins's friend "White Boy," who managed to hotwire the floodlights for the project's parking garage to redirect electricity to Kool Herc's equipment.[11]

"It was kind of funny because we were a block away from the Forty-Fourth Precinct," Collins said. "And you've got thousands of kids outside *blasting* music until four in the morning, and the cops never once stopped us. They went by, to make sure no one was fighting or whatever, but they never once came to stop it."[12]

It's a good thing they didn't, because in that earliest hip hop era, the parties were peaceful and solely about having fun. Collins and his massive brother, "Big Stan," were among a group of people from the neighborhood (referred to by locals as "the Valley") who made sure everything went according to plan, and people coming in from other blocks showed them great respect.

"There wasn't no fights, there wasn't no drama, there was none of that because people respected the Valley," Collins explained. "We didn't allow people to come down there doing all kinds of weird stuff.

That was really a huge part of the cultural dynamic of hip hop which you don't have now, that people don't talk about."[13]

It should be noted that claims of Herc being the first hip hop DJ are disputed. Paradise Gray, for example, suggested that title should go to Disco King Mario, who lived in the same Bronxdale housing project as he did while growing up.[14] Mario served as a mentor to significant figures like Afrika Bambaataa and Jazzy Jay, and specialized in the same break beats and up-tempo parties as Herc. Another New York DJ, Grandmaster Flowers (born Jonathon Cameron Flowers), opened for James Brown at Yankee Stadium in 1968.[15] Others note that Herc shouldn't receive credit as a founder of the genre because he and his contemporaries only played other artists' music and weren't making their own creations at that point. Some even suggest that hip hop culture goes further back, to the smooth-talking DJs of the glory days of AM radio. Muhammad Ali has been cited as an inspiration for hip hop, as has Malcolm X, both of whom enjoyed a spotlight dating back to the early 1960s.[16]

Theodore Livingston (known on stage as Grand Wizzard Theodore), one of the most influential DJs in history, claims that hip hop can actually be traced back much, much farther than that: "Hip hop was here since the beginning of time. We just gave it another word," he said. "You go back to the caveman days when the tribal master was around the campfire telling stories to all the kids and stuff like that around the fire, that's like the emcee. And then you've got the tribal people banging on the drums and stuff like that around the campfire, that's the DJ. Then you've got the tribal people dancing to the drums and stuff like that, that's the b-boy. And then when you go to the caves and look at the hieroglyphics on the caves, you see the language they spoke, the people that they worshipped and stuff like that, their way of communicating with each other. That's the graffiti artist."[17]

Livingston was born on March 5, 1963.[18] He was enamored with music from a young age. The eventual Grand Wizzard Theodore grew up on the corner of Boston Road and 168th Street immersed in hip hop culture even before that culture was neatly defined. A big fan of funk music and an avid watcher of *Soul Train* every Saturday alongside his family, Theodore was raised on music.

"I've always had a love of music ever since I can remember," Theodore said. "I mean, my mother played music all the time. She played music when she was cooking. She played music when she was happy. She played music when she was sad. She played music when she was about to beat our butts. When I came home and heard her playing music, I could tell what kind of mood she was in."[19] For what it's worth, Theodore said that when his mother was feeling especially energetic, James Brown would be playing.

Theodore grew up surrounded by graffiti, b-boys, and many other hallmarks of hip hop. His older brothers, Mean Gene and DJ Cordie-O, were early pioneers of DJing, along with their friend Joseph Saddler, who would soon take the stage name Grandmaster Flash. They were all eager to show Theodore what they knew. By the time the mid-1970s rolled around, Theodore was already making the transition from the little kid who carried crates of records for his brothers and Flash to a talented b-boy and then an even more talented DJ.

The young Theodore made a great discovery while fiddling with his mother's record player, which he described as looking "like a coffin."[20] He would play 45 records and drag the needle back to the break repeatedly so he could hear the "get down" part over and over again. By dropping the record player's arm on the right spot, he could repeat the best part of the song without using a second turntable. Theodore had inadvertently discovered the needle drop style that would become an important part of his and many DJs' tool kits for years to come. It involved impeccable timing, dropping the needle on the record exactly when it passed by the tone arm at the appropriate spot. In other words, in order to repeat a word on a 45 RPM record, Theodore would have to drop the needle once every one and a quarter seconds. After decades of practice, he can do it perfectly, while blindfolded and balancing a record on his head.[21]

Standing at five feet seven inches, the soft-spoken Theodore elected to continue coming up with new techniques for getting the most out of his growing record collection. He never wrote rhymes, just focused on refining his turntable skills as much as he could. Perhaps his greatest contribution to hip hop came as a complete accident. In 1975, while making a tape for a school project, Theodore was playing records on the family turntable at the maximum volume. This drew the ire of his annoyed mother, who came into the room to yell at him. In order to hear her better, Theodore put his hand on the record and rocked it back and forth while the player was still on. After the tongue-lashing stopped, he listened back to the tape, and really enjoyed the scratching sound the record had made as he moved it. He knew he had "lightning in a bottle."[22] This was a new trick that he hadn't heard before, one that allowed him to repeat the same part of a song essentially as many times as he liked.

"It was up in 63 Park, half a block away from where I lived at," Theodore said about the first time he scratched a record in public. "People was just so hyped. When I created the scratch, it wasn't like it took three, four weeks for me to actually bring it out to the public. It was like an overnight thing. The next time we came out was when I did it. Everybody was like going crazy. People were saying, 'Oh shit!'"[23]

The scratch quickly spread to other well-known DJs like Grandmaster Flash, and it has remained arguably the biggest hip hop staple of any DJing technique. At a very young age, Theodore had already started to make his mark.

*   *   *

DJ Kool Herc and Grand Wizzard Theodore were pioneers on the turntables, but soon, it became obvious that a DJ looking to really get a party going needed a good emcee, and Herc's good friend, Coke La Rock, took the bold first steps toward establishing what a "rapper" was. The term "emcee" is derived from the abbreviation MC, or master of ceremonies—a phrase that can be used to refer to anyone from a cruise director to a high school pep rally host. Coke La Rock filled both of those roles and more at Herc's parties. Initially, Rock (who also doubled as the parties' marijuana supplier) would just grab the microphone to give shout-outs to his friends or warn partygoers who had left their headlights on or double-parked someone else in. Eventually, however, Rock began using this opportunity to show off his impressive rhyming skills as he laid down lines like:

> As long as the music's not stopping,
> The rocks are dropping, the champagne is flowing,
> The freaks will be going.
> Hotel, motel, you don't tell, we don't tell. One time route nine.[24]

"Nobody was talking on the mic back then,"[25] Rock told Netflix's *Hip-Hop Evolution*. That's a disputable assertion, seeing as talking and rhyming over a beat had existed in some form for decades across genres. Radio hosts would wake their listeners up every morning with clever taglines and sign-offs. But it's evident that without Coke La Rock bringing that dimension to hip hop parties, the roles within hip hop would remain undefined. He helped make rhyming a staple of the genre rather than an additive that might or might not appear at a party.

Another major figure in the earliest days of rapping was Harlem's Anthony Holloway, who went by the stage name DJ Hollywood. Dressed impeccably in a business suit and hat that made him look like Marvin Gaye or one of Gladys Knight's Pips, Hollywood started performing his rhymes during the breaks of popular disco and funk music in the mid-1970s.[26] He pioneered the art of the crowd response. The famous "Throw your hands in the air / and wave 'em like you just don't care" rhyme that was such a bedrock staple of early hip hop can be traced directly back to him.[27]

"At the time, music was recorded A section, B section, break," Hollywood said. "The A section was the beginning of the record where there was only music. No talking. No singing. Nothing for a few bars. After a few bars it changed into whatever the artist was about. So when the artist came in, between those few bars at the beginning, a person was able to take something before the record ever started. I used to time that into 'opening the record.' I became a part of the record so far as the conversation is concerned. At that time period, nobody was doing conversation through the records because that was really an unheard-of type of thing, and a lot of clubs wouldn't go for people doing it."[28]

Initially, Hollywood claimed, he just wanted to find success as a traditional party DJ. But once the crowds heard his rhymes and responded favorably, he knew he'd found his niche in a crowded scene.

"'If I was a jug of wine, I would be old. If I was snow, I would be cold. Sister this is true, I'm right here with you, passing the time with the baddest jams I can find,'" Hollywood said when asked to recall some of his earliest rhymes, in which he attempted to emulate morning radio hosts. "And then the record would hit. It was just the coloring of the music, making it a picture that you could see what it was going into."[29]

Hollywood said that his rapping came along as a natural evolution from this, as he stopped trying to talk over the record and instead started singing. Once the technology evolved to include multiple turntables, a mixer, and a microphone as part of a DJ's kit, Hollywood started to work his rhymes into the *entire* song rather than just as a fancy accent at the beginning or end.

It wasn't until 1974 or '75, Hollywood explained, that people started to really take notice of his rhyming. While his rhymes were simple, he was able to build a following in New York City, but not among the b-boys and b-girls who were avid Kool Herc fans. Hollywood came from what he described as a tried-and-true disco background and didn't abandon the genre in favor of something new.[30] For that reason, some people don't credit him as much for his innovations in the hip hop genre.

"In order to go to a Hollywood party, you had to have a suit and tie on," Grand Wizzard Theodore explained. "If you don't got no suit and tie on, you're not getting inside. We were able to get inside there sometimes, and we would start breaking, and he'd cut the music off and say, 'We don't do that in here.'"[31]

Hollywood didn't dispute what Theodore said but didn't necessarily see that as a bad thing, claiming that his parties were designed to cater to New York's disco-loving clientele: "We were in a class by ourselves at the time. That's why I think I'm not considered to be hip hop, because I'm not dressed down. We wore suits. We were clean. The ladies, they were clean, a lot of young ladies got in the party because they were dressed appropriately. They weren't age-appropriate but they looked it. Guys started coming into the club looking real good, real sharp. They had hard-bottomed shoes. This kind of separated what was just street—meaning it cost nothing to do. I think that's what separated the two groups the most, and the age difference too.

The club situation, you had to look the part because that held down the riff-raff. Guys didn't come in there to mess their clothes up. That's why when they say 'Yo, they didn't let us breakdance in the club . . .' they wouldn't let you *in* the club. I don't know how you got to the point of you being in there and breakdancing and they threw you out. They shouldn't have let you *in*. At that time period young people did what young people do and the grown-ups kind of did what they do. They didn't mix the apples and the oranges."[32]

Even though he played to a disco crowd, Hollywood was indeed rapping. It was in his footsteps that DJs began to adopt this as part of their performances and talk over or "toast" (as it was known in Jamaica) the record. Some DJs found this multitasking to be extremely challenging and a good way to lose track of the music, but many were able to handle both responsibilities and give a dynamic performance.

*   *   *

One of those early DJ/rapper combinations was Curtis Brown, who later took the stage name Grandmaster Caz. Caz was born in 1960 in the same Bronx neighborhood as Kool Herc.[33] The Grandmaster grew up a giant music fan, even though hip hop didn't exist at all until his teenage years. Unlike Theodore, whose inspiration mainly came from his brother, Caz picked up his adoptive parents' music, like James Brown and the Jackson 5[34] (whose landmark *ABC* album came out when he was ten), as well as whatever he'd hear in his day-to-day exploits. There was only one radio station that played in the morning in the Bronx, and it had to appeal to everyone, so Brown was exposed to a very eclectic selection of music every day before heading out to school. "There was always music around me but it was—it wasn't the music that you would think," Caz said. "I used to listen to WABC AM radio. Barry Manilow and Neil Diamond and Simon and Garfunkel and stuff like that, and I picked up all of that. I got my dose of Motown and Temptations, Jackson Five and all that, too, but I was also exposed to that. That music kind of stuck with me more inside than outside. I'm a child of hip hop. I'm playing in hip hop and that's the music that I have a passion for. But the music when I go home and listen, I'm listening to Barry Manilow."[35]

Because he lived so close to Herc, Caz was kept in the loop about the happenings at Herc's early parties—which he was too young to attend—by older kids in the neighborhood, who would clear off the block, basketball courts, and playgrounds to flock to 1520 Sedgwick.[36] What he heard about excited him, as he was always on the hunt for new music to enjoy. Caz, like many other young people, didn't get a chance to experience what would become hip hop culture until Kool Herc, Afrika Bambaataa, Disco King Mario, and other influential DJs headed outside more consistently during the warmer months, where they could show off at "park jams" in their local neighborhoods alongside the stars of New York's legendary playground basketball scene. These jams served to grow a DJ's fan base by reaching crowds they couldn't at traditional house parties. Cedar Park and Crotona Park in the Bronx and Queensbridge Park in Queens were a few of the many spaces where savvy listeners could go to hear the best music from early hip hop pioneers.[37]

"It became so big because it was accessible," said Paradise Gray. "The parties at that time were for the grown-ups, but now the teenagers and the little kids got to see it. And those teenagers and little kids were Grandmaster Flash and Grand Wizzard Theodore."[38]

For Caz, finally being able to experience hip hop in person was a supremely influential turning point in his life. To not just hear about the new way music was being played, but rather to see it done in person, to feel the music pulsing through his body—it sent him down the path to becoming a hip hop legend at a very young age. In my 2021 interview with him, he smiled widely as he described what it was like to attend a park jam in the 1970s. The tall and skinny teenager with great skills on the basketball court initially performed as a b-boy in 1974.[39]

According to Caz, on a hot summer day, you could find a jam in the Bronx through word of mouth, or simply by exploring. "You'd be walking down the street and see like a caravan of people walking all walking in the same direction and you'd be like, 'That's the jam, they're going to a jam,'" Caz said.[40] "You'd be like, 'YO, WHERE THEY JAMMIN' AT?!' and somebody would be like, 'Yo, 129, so and so and so.' And then the walk to the jam, you gotta get your essentials, get your munchies and everything on your way. You get about three or four blocks away depending on the sound system and then you start hearing the music. And then you get closer and you start *feeling* the music, and then you start seeing the people and you get yourself ready to step into it. It was a whole aura about the thing. And then when you got to the jam it's like, 'Yo, I'm here, I've arrived,' and you started seeking out people. Where the b-boys at? Where the chicks at? Who's DJing? Who's behind the ropes? It was a big thing to be behind the ropes. If you wasn't down with the DJs or something, you couldn't go behind the rope, that shit was sacred."[41]

Caz was completely enamored with every aspect of the hip hop culture he watched grow in his own neighborhood. He was gifted in the four key parts of the movement. He was a good artist who drew graffiti-style art on paper with markers from a young age. He could dance, he could DJ, but where he would make his mark on the culture was with his rapping and lyricism. In fact, he gave up playing organized basketball before high school just so he could focus on his music.[42]

While the exact origin of the term "rapper" will always be disputed, it's clear that Caz was at the forefront of hip hop lyricism. Caz first built his relationship with Kool Herc on the basketball courts in their neighborhood, and Herc was the first DJ Caz actually followed.[43] Caz actively sought out Herc's park jams. While still unsure of exactly what he was doing, Caz began to grab the microphone at more and more jams and began going by his original stage name: Casanova Fly. With a booming voice and jovial personality, Caz still oozes hip hop to this day. He says what's on his mind, but hasn't lost his sense of humor and boisterous swagger. There's an electric quality that Caz carries where you never know if he's really happy or really angry, or if he's about to launch into a rap verse at any moment. When talking about people claiming he's one of the best rappers ever, he says, "I agree."[44]

"I wrote my first rhyme out of necessity," Caz said. "We were some of the first people to do this, so we just got the people that was around that had an interest in it. My first emcees, I pretty much taught them how to emcee. We sat in the lunchroom and wrote rhymes and went back and forth."[45] Caz's first squads were made up of his best friends, who needed to learn how to rhyme and DJ quickly as their buddy was already making a splash in multiple lanes of hip hop at a very young age.

The one thing Caz was missing, however, was professional-grade sound equipment. It's hard to build a following as a musical artist if no one can hear you. DJs needed two turntables, a booming speaker system, and most importantly, a mixer that allowed for records to be switched back and forth and cross-faded together with ease. As you might imagine, these items weren't cheap, so for the young, poor residents of the Bronx, they were hard to come by.

Luckily, a great opportunity would strike for the seventeen-year-old aspiring star on July 13, 1977.

* * *

A severe lightning storm in Westchester County came on the heels of a sweltering heat wave that had tormented New York for days. A bolt struck the Buchanan South Substation, shutting it down. That created a very taxing demand for other power lines in the area. As those lines shut down one by one, it caused a cascading effect that made it impossible to get power into New York City. Consolidated Edison, the power company tasked with supplying the city, wasn't able to shed enough load to save the system in time. By 9:36 that night, the "city that never sleeps" had been plunged into total darkness.[46]

"That night, I'm on the third floor, windows open. It was very hot, so people were outside, and suddenly the TV went off," said then-medical student Carl St. Martin on the "Blackout" episode of PBS's *American Experience*.[47] "The lights went off. All of a sudden, the noise outside in the street quickly stopped for a second, and suddenly you heard [*gasping*] because everybody at the same time realized something had happened."

In the World Trade Center's swanky Windows on the World restaurant, diners were given unprecedented permission to remove their jackets and ties, and every guest was offered free champagne. WABC's George Michael accidentally gave his radio listeners the wrong time because the studio's generator failed to power its clock. Thousands of passengers were stuck in sweltering subway tunnels for hours until their trains could slowly be pushed back to the nearest station by diesel-powered trains. As was typical of the time period in New York, arsonists set many buildings alight—more than 600 total over the course of the twenty-four-hour power failure.[48]

Many news stories and even current recollections about the 1977 blackout focus on the widespread looting and vandalism that accompanied the darkness. The *New York Times* described the looters as "emboldened by darkness and confusion"[49] as they used metal trash cans to break into storefronts. That same story reported 880 arrests, numerous civilian and officer injuries, and some agitated store owners taking matters into their own hands to guard their establishments. A Brooklyn ice-cream shop owner was reported as saying, "They're taking their shoes and breaking windows. They're animals. They should be put in jail, and throw the key away." There were even reports of sniper fire on West Ninety-Eighth Street on Manhattan's Upper West Side.[50]

ABC's news coverage on July 14 specifically pointed out the prevalence of looting in the city's "ghetto areas."[51] "As you know by now, a terrible thing happened to part of this city last night," ABC reporter Geraldo Rivera said. "When the lights went out, it began to devour itself in an unprecedented explosion of violence, and desperation, and lawlessness. Poor people who are ordinarily average citizens began turning on their own neighborhoods and consuming them. It was awful, and it was uncivilized."[52]

Needless to say, Rivera's reporting was reactionary, racially charged, and rife with errors and assumptions. The catastrophic portrayal of events fed into dangerous stereotypes. (It was, unfortunately, part of a pattern: in 2015, nearly four decades after the blackout, Rivera made headlines himself by saying "Hip-hop has done more damage to young African-Americans than racism in recent years" while discussing an awards show performance by Kendrick Lamar.[53])

The *Times* made it clear that the blackout of 1965 was more festive and peaceful when contrasted with the looting and vandalism of the 1977 version.[54] But they failed to point out that the looting could at least partially be attributed to the tensions that had been building in the city's more minority-heavy neighborhoods for years, tensions that would continue into the 1980s. That same Geraldo Rivera report that described the events on July 13 as "uncivilized" disparaged New York's African American residents but highlighted some of the issues that plagued many urban areas around the country in the late 1970s. An economic downturn, an energy crisis, and horrible wealth inequality led to, as President Jimmy Carter so eloquently put it two years after the blackout, a "crisis of confidence" in America.[55] On the street level, however, that crisis manifested itself as hot-blooded frustration.

"The way things are, with everybody on welfare, we ain't got no goddamn jobs, right?" shouted a local woman to Rivera, with an approving crowd at her back. "The little bit that we got, for us, it was worth our while. I feel like this: God closed off the lights for one night. He let us have the opportunity to get back for all the times that we have been beat. For all the time that we have been oppressed, for all of the months we've been in this neighborhood and we don't have Pampers for our kids' behinds. But we've got Pampers now, baby."[56]

The blackout was terrifying for many New Yorkers and allowed for racial prejudices to fly out in the open, but for cash-strapped young emcees or DJs in desperate need of equipment, it was a godsend. Among the looters, whom one officer described as a "swarm of locusts,"[57] was Grandmaster Caz. When the lights went out and tensions started rising, he headed over to the Sound Room, a Bronx electronics store.

"They were pulling the gates down, so I went over and helped them pull the gates down, got it down, they broke the window, and we went inside," Caz said on an episode of *Hip-Hop Evolution*. "And then the cops came, and they had flashlights, so everyone was like, 'Shhh, get down, get down.' Everybody was down on the floor until the flashlights disappeared, and then we got up, and then we ran out. I had a Clubman Two Mixer, and that's what I got away with."[58]

For the seventeen-year-old Caz, the blackout was a great win, one that let him begin to get serious about performing. He was far from the only young emcee to take advantage of the looting. "I have a theory. Before that blackout you had about maybe five legitimate crews of DJs," said Disco Wiz, a pioneering Latino DJ. After the blackout, "you had a DJ on every block, everybody hit every electronic store imaginable. Every record store. Everything."[59] The influx of new equipment did have a palpable effect on the hip hop scene, as it allowed well-supplied DJs and emcees to start building crews. Soon, the parks would be vibrant on weekends, filled with talented men and women using their brand new equipment to bring never-before-seen levels of funk to the streets. Finding someone with a sound system was no longer an issue, so pioneers like Grandmaster Caz and Grand Wizzard Theodore (who already had a setup) could focus on the next steps to building a musical genre: the performance.

The Fantastic Romantic Five (minus Whipper
Whip) over the Cross Bronx Expressway, 1981.
From left to right, Rubie Dee, Grand Wizzard
Theodore, Dot-A-Rock, Master Rob, Kevie Kev.
Photo by Charlie Ahearn.

Chapter 2

———

Routines

In the late 1970s, especially after the influx of new equipment from looting during the 1977 blackout, hip hop grew exponentially. DJ Hollywood refers to it as the "hip hop explosion."[1] During the summers, parks and blocks rang out with booming speaker systems, and fans could be selective about who they wanted to party with. Still, nobody used the phrase "hip hop" to refer to the scene. Everything was still advertised as a "disco party" or "disco dance." This new music was still essentially considered disco, just disco that was played in a different way and for a younger crowd that was more open to new things.

At the time, the DJ was the big draw in hip hop, and people would come out to dance and enjoy the music their favorites could dig up. It wasn't until the DJs who followed in the footsteps of the genre's originators got their hands on the equipment that hip hop was elevated into more of an art form. "The next generation who came in after Herc and Afrika Bambaataa were the ones who started scratching and DJing," Paradise Gray said. "Herc and [Bambaataa] couldn't DJ to save their lives, they were record players. They played records, they had no skills."[2]

Regardless of technical skills on the turntable, the best thing a DJ could do at a park jam to grow their audience was bring exciting music that people hadn't heard before. The DJ who had the best record collection would expand their following the fastest. DJ Kool

Herc and many of his contemporaries who specialized in that art went to great lengths to keep their finds private, including covering up or coloring over the labels on their records so rivals couldn't figure out what was being played[3] (although that did cause an issue later on when they needed to find particular records in their collections). The ultimate goal for a DJ playing at a block party or park jam was to build up enough popularity to have a place to play when the weather turned colder and the parties moved inside. Such was the case for eleven-year-old Theodore Livingston, who took on the name DJ Theodore. He joined forces with his older brothers, DJ Mean Gene and DJ Cordie-O, to form his first group—the L Brothers—which, after many lineup changes, would eventually become the Fantastic Romantic Five.[4]

"We started doing parties ourselves and going around to different projects around the area and going to different parks and playing music, letting everybody know that we was out there," Theodore said. "Back then, all the DJs had to do block parties to let everyone know that they were around. So when the wintertime comes and it gets real cold and you start handing out flyers for your parties, people would say, 'Okay, these guys did block parties, the music was nice, I had a good time, let's go check them out.'"[5]

Indoor parties eventually led to DJs charging admission for their shows. Paradise Gray says the initial prices were around one dollar for men and fifty cents for women.[6] Although the Bronx is typically regarded as the birthplace of hip hop, according to Gray, the first flyers that actually used the phrase were advertising parties in Brooklyn.[7] DJs in Queens and Harlem also were building their followings and growing in popularity, but no one was able to make a profession out of hip hop at that point. It was mainly thought of as fun new music to experiment with—an undefined trend that was picking up steam.

"We spread hip hop from block to block like Johnny Appleseed back then," said Gray. "We had to break open a light pole to get electricity; we also had to cut the wiring and rewire everything so we could plug shit in. A lot of resourceful men and women lived in our community. I learned Ohm's law when I was ten years old."[8]

During this very early era of hip hop (ending in 1979), people outside of these communities had no clue where to go to find a jam. It was impossible to enjoy or even discover the music if you weren't from (or connected to) the neighborhoods where young people were creating it.

"How would anyone know any of this?" asked pioneering filmmaker Charlie Ahearn, who was instrumental in exposing hip hop to a wider audience with his film *Wild Style*. "The only way to know is to go [to the neighborhoods]. It was not something in magazines, never, ever, never. It wasn't discussed, it wasn't in the clubs."[9]

* * *

A major shift in hip hop occurred when DJs started assembling crews who elevated the genre by performing with different roles in a synchronized group. DJs could put on a great party for people who wanted to dance, but the party and park jam crowds craved something more: a performance. Specialized emcees began to hone their craft and plan out their performances; they worked directly with their DJs to ensure the show was of a high quality. The park jams—in addition to letting DJs build their own followings—allowed them to find new emcee talent behind the microphone, seeing as anyone who could rhyme and had some guts could come up and give it a shot. This led to the formation of some of the greatest groups of all time.

The L Brothers went through several different iterations before becoming the Fantastic Romantic Five. A 1979 flyer for a jam at 308 E. 166th Street advertised the crew as the "L Brothers 79" with the "Fantastic 4 MCs." Those emcees are listed on the flyer as "Kevie-Kev,

Robie-Rob [sic], Rubie-Dee, and Star-Ski."[10] The three L Brothers—Theodore, Mean Gene, and Cordie-O—topped the bill. Star-Ski is shorthand for the playful, hilarious, tank-topped Busy Bee Starski, who shows up in virtually every documented hip hop show in the late 1970s and early 1980s. In fact, he earned his nickname "Busy Bee" because he was everywhere and involved in everything.[11] Unfortunately, this also meant that his time in groups was short-lived. He was really more of a solo emcee. The other three emcees on that flyer would remain with Theodore for years.

Robin Diggs (known on stage as Robbie Rob, and later Master Rob) and Kevin Ferguson (Kevie Kev, and later Waterbed Kev) were born in January 1961 and March 1963 respectively to a doting mother who always made sure her kids looked good.[12] They grew up to be great-looking guys, and they knew it. Brimming with confidence from a young age, they walked the streets of the Bronx like they owned the place. Kevie Kev, with his tight braids, designer shirts, and charming personality, was a third-grade classmate of Theodore's.[13] Robbie Rob was so gifted that by the time he had been with Theodore's group for a year, he had already switched names to Master Rob at the urging of Busy Bee Starski.[14]

"For him to look at me as a master, that must've meant that I commanded the microphone," Rob said. "My presence on that microphone made me be the master, and he looked at me that way and everybody respected me as the master. I said since I had that title, I've got to be my best self."[15]

When Kev saw his old classmate Theodore performing at a block party with Gene and Cordie-O, the fourteen-year-old asked if he could try to show off his skills for the L Brothers' crowd. The three DJs didn't perform with emcees at that time.

"Kev came and asked me, 'Can I get on the mic?'," Theodore said. "And I was like, 'Wow, get on the mic?' So I asked my brother Mean

Gene and said, 'Hey, this is Kevie Kev, we went to school together, do you wanna put him on the mic?' He was like 'Nah! We don't put nobody on the mic! No!' My brother, he was mean. I was like, 'Well, let's see what they can do, maybe they can be a great asset to the crew.' Once I finally put Kev on the microphone and he started saying some rhymes and I started chopping up some breaks, they loved him. The girls loved him. Everybody loved him. So I invited them to the house, they talked with my brother and stuff like that, and he became our emcee."[16]

After a few shows with the L Brothers, Kev asked Theodore, Gene, and Cordie-O if his older brother Rob could join the crew as well. They were happy to bring him aboard.[17] The L Brothers now featured two emcees and three DJs.

The third emcee found his place in the group by sheer coincidence. Ruben Garcia (stage name: Rubie Dee) was born in 1960 in Rio Piedras, Puerto Rico.[18] After moving to New York when he was five, he was raised in the Bronx by his mother's stepmother alongside one of his cousins. Standing only five feet, two inches, with an athletic build, Garcia had long hair that would've fit in beautifully at Woodstock or during the Summer of Love. After skipping two grades in elementary school, Garcia moved back to Puerto Rico for middle school. There, he completed eighth grade by age twelve before moving back to the Bronx to attend Monroe High School, where he graduated (eventually) while working on the side.[19]

The young Garcia wasn't patched into the hip hop scene much as a young kid. Even to this day, he considers himself the "Drake of the salsa music scene," a reference to the days when he used to teach dance classes in New York. A lover of Latin dance and a skilled baseball and softball player, the man who would eventually take the stage persona Rubie Dee found hip hop completely by chance. Despite living in such a diverse neighborhood and having many African American friends at school, he hadn't been exposed to much Black culture: "I had a lot of African American friends. A lot of them. Good friends, but I didn't call you to go out like, 'Hey let's go have a beer, smoke a joint,' I didn't call you to do that. You stuck to your own kind."[20]

According to Garcia, he was playing baseball one day at St. Mary's Park near his apartment. Even though it was getting dark, he could hear booming music coming from across the grass. A jam was clearly underway. The music wasn't enough to pull him from his game, but when a young Black woman who he was enamored with walked by the field and headed toward the sound, he immediately forgot about the game. Given the cultural divide in the neighborhood, his buddies weren't into the idea of following a Black girl to a jam. Garcia replied by saying, "You don't see what I see." When they said they were apprehensive, he said, "There's fifteen of us. With baseball bats!"[21] Undeterred by his friends' unwillingness to join him, Garcia took off alone.

He trailed this young woman all the way to the front of the party. When the girl noticed he was following her, he awkwardly told her he had done so after seeing she was headed to the park jam. She smiled. Nothing ever came of that bit of flirting, but something more significant took place. Soon, Garcia was dancing to James Brown's "Funky Drummer." He was awed by how the DJ was able to extend the break; he'd never heard anything like that. After seeing him dancing and having a great time, the DJ bestowed on Ruben the honor of allowing him behind the ropes, which immediately meant that the crew was down with him and gave him status at the party. However, Garcia was still green in terms of hip hop knowledge.

"We're introducing ourselves to each other and I asked him a dumb question, 'Are you a DJ?', and he said yeah," Garcia said. "He was (rest in peace) Kool DJ AJ."[22]

Loving what he was hearing, Garcia invited his new friend to play at the community room in his building, which could fit seventy-five people. They decided to charge one dollar per person; AJ would keep everything. Three days out, after the party had already been advertised, AJ canceled due to a conflicting gig. Disappointed but with no real solution to the problem, Garcia took a walk across the borough all the way down toward Boston Road, hoping to stumble upon a DJ. After never hearing hip hop for the first seventeen years of his life, he heard the "boom" for the second time in a couple of weeks. He followed the sound to his second-ever jam. This time it was a group with three DJs and two emcees: the L Brothers.

Emboldened by his first jam experience a couple of weeks prior, Garcia approached Mean Gene with a proposition about playing the gig in three days.

"I went to Mean Gene and I told him about the event," Garcia said. "I said, 'Money has been collected, flyers have been put out. We need you,' and he came. Kevie Kev and Robbie Rob did not come. He came, the party was great, and I liked it. I made friends with Mean Gene, I became kind of a friend with Mean Gene on a professional level."[23]

After attending a few more L Brothers parties, including some "hooky parties" they would throw during school hours to hide from class, the seventeen-year-old Garcia seized on an opportunity offered to him because Kev and Rob were away. While Cordie-O was plugging the mic in for a sound check, Garcia picked it up and started the typical procedure ("Testing one two three") that was required. His voice was squeaky and quiet back then, so the mic needed to be turned up louder. Suddenly, the music came on! Garcia was caught holding the mic when the Whole Darn Family's "Seven Minutes of Funk" pumped through the speakers.

"Everyone was dancing and I was grooving and Cordie looked at me and I still had the microphone in my hand," Garcia, who took on the name Rubie-O at the very outset of his career, said. "He just pointed at me like, 'Go ahead.'"[24]

Garcia performed the rhymes Kev and Rob would've done if they had been there. He knew the rhymes because he had recorded a tape of the emcees performing, which he blasted from his boombox as he walked around the city. He had his back to the audience the whole time and only had about three rhymes memorized, but he performed to the best of his ability and he liked the feeling. The crowd liked him, too. The L Brothers had found their third emcee. At the urging of Master Rob, Garcia soon changed his name from Rubie-O to Rubie Dee (not to be confused with the legendary actress Ruby Dee). Busy Bee Starski, who had worked with multiple groups and built his own reputation as a great party-starting emcee, began his short tenure soon after.

DJ Theodore, alongside his brothers and the four emcees, performed at local high schools and community centers in the winter and park jams and block parties in the summer. Sometime in late 1979, Theodore and the emcees decided to split away from his brothers to form the Fantastic Four (kids in the neighborhood made fun of the name because of the comic book series).[25] Kevie Kev said the move was amicable and had to do with a difference in the long-term aspirations of the group: basically, the Fantastic Four was thinking bigger than Mean Gene and Cordie-O. Along with the new-look group (so called because the lineup had been newly revamped), the emcees decided that the name "DJ Theodore" would no longer cut it. Theodore wasn't too keen on being a "grandmaster," as some DJs like Flash and Flowers were calling themselves, but the members of the group were fans of "The Grand Wizard" Ernie Roth, a popular Jewish pro wrestling figure. Roth had adopted the name as a slight to the Ku Klux Klan, whose leaders go by "Grand Wizard."[26]

"That's when we said we'll go with 'Grand Wizard,' because I played my music differently than anybody else," Theodore said. The second "Z" didn't come into being until the early 1980s, when other DJs were beginning to call themselves "Grand Wizard" as well.[27]

It's no surprise that the first strong pre-planned hip hop acts were groups, considering how thoroughly Black popular music at the time was dominated by Motown products like the Jackson 5, the Supremes, and Smokey Robinson and the Miracles. In fact, before rapping existed, groups of boys would harmonize on the streets of New York and compete against one another to see who the best singers were.[28] Although some DJs could rap from behind the turntables while leaning into a mic on a stand, many preferred to outsource that work, allowing them to focus on blending records and isolating beats.

There were also some practical reasons that made performing with crews the way to go. For one thing, having extra hands around made transporting the DJ's equipment easier. For another, while the DJ maintained the power in the group, it was still critical to have safety in numbers to protect the whole crew from street-level violence in the city. According to Paradise Gray, "You better have a crew because if you come outside without a crew and you don't have no reputation, you're not going to come back home with anything. They're going to take your equipment, they're going to take your records, they'll kick your ass and take your money, take the clothes off your back and send you home in your underwear and your socks. You better have a crew. Stick-up kids would roll up on you with a shotgun and take everything you've got. We're talking about the South Bronx."[29]

A nice fringe benefit of working in a group was that these crews started to generate more sophisticated music than that of the first DJs in the early and mid-seventies. While they weren't making records, the groups—for the first time—began to practice their routines with the goal of perfecting them rather than joining up together at park jams and working off the cuff. With party prices rising higher and higher through the 1970s and '80s and groups drawing larger and larger crowds at community centers, local schools, and block parties, the pressure was on to deliver a stronger product.

Grand Wizzard Theodore and the Fantastic Four were on the cutting edge in that area, especially after Busy Bee Starski left to focus on his solo career. Theodore, Rob, Kev, and Dee decided to add two more emcees, Dot-A-Rock and Prince Whipper Whip, to round out their group.[30]

The journey for the two new emcees to get to the point of spitting rhymes in front of Theodore's turntables was a long, winding odyssey.

* * *

James Whipper II (known as Whipper Whip onstage) is a fascinating individual. He split his time growing up between his birthplace in the South Bronx and his family's country of origin, Puerto Rico. Once, in elementary school, his father told him and his siblings they were going on a vacation to Puerto Rico. That trip turned out to be unusually long—six months, in fact. His father even took a job there.[31] Eventually, the family got a house, and their stay was extended for a couple of years. Once his father and stepmother split up, his mother came down to the island to get him back. She wanted him to return to live with her in the Bronx and see his old friends. It was an offer he couldn't refuse.[32]

Whipper's love of playing music didn't start by hearing records at a Kool Herc party or listening to his first rapper in the park like Rubie Dee but rather from his time at the now-closed Edward W. Stitt School on 164th Street. "It was in sixth grade when my teacher put a saxophone in my hands, is actually where I started," he said. "And I was like, 'What is this?' I didn't even know what it was called! 'I'm supposed to play this?' I started playing."[33]

Whipper was a natural. He came from a musical family that embraced both their Black and Puerto Rican heritage. In fact, growing up, he thought everyone spoke Spanish, partially because of his upbringing in Puerto Rico and partially because he lived among so many Puerto Ricans in the Bronx.[34] His father was a gifted guitarist who spoke seven languages, a result of his time in the military. For his part, Whipper was a natural with the saxophone. He said he was composing his own music within a year of first getting the sax in his hand.[35] He wasn't much of a disco fan (with the exception of the song "Dancing Queen"—he used to make out with a girl named Carmen from across the street, and that was their song). Much like Curtis Brown (aka Grandmaster Caz), Whipper grew up listening to WABC in New York, which he said played "pretty much everything" from the Rolling Stones to Stevie Wonder. In fact, Whipper and Curtis Brown met when they were both fifteen after being introduced by a mutual friend named Smiley Smile, who lived across the street from Caz and heard the music pouring out of his first floor window.

"I was just in the right place at the right time," Whip said. "I grew up in a cool part of the Bronx where shit was happening and it became a movement. It became us, it became our movement."[36]

* * *

By late 1977 or 1978, DJ Casanova Fly and his high school classmate DJ Disco Wiz (aka Luis Cedeño) had refined their act and were making some noise in the Bronx. Casanova Fly was an expert at getting the party going, although he hadn't committed to writing rhymes as much as he would later.

"Caz played a lot of disco," Whipper Whip said. "He played a lot of good disco hits, and Caz was just a showman on the turntables. Caz'll get on and he'll dance while he plays and do little tricks and all this and other stuff, he had his little razzmatazz with him. And the crowd loved it. The crowd really, really loved it, and he had a big following all throughout the Bronx."[37]

Disco Wiz targeted a smaller crowd and focused on heavier beats. "My thing was always the beats," he said. "I used to just cut the beats. Every beat, just back and forth, and that was my thing. The b-boys used to be fidgeting on the sidelines and always used to say, 'Wiz, when you getting on? Wiz, when you getting on?'"[38]

"Cutting up a record" refers to the act of pulling pieces out of a song to make it as energetic as possible for hip hop dancers to show off their moves. It also involves switching between different songs to keep the dancing going as long as possible. Disco Wiz was known for his aggressive style of hard switches between beats that had b-boys showing off their best moves in the center of the dance floor.

Whipper joined up as an assistant in the Mighty Force Crew with Caz[39] and Disco Wiz (who was part of the group until he was incarcerated for attempted murder in 1977).[40] Toward the end of a 1977 jam in the park at 188th Street and Webster (a location that he has since dubbed "Whipper Whip Park"), Whipper asked for a chance to make an announcement about future parties, and Caz and Disco Wiz obliged. For the first time, the good-looking young man with an afro puff and a sharp, high-pitched voice stepped to the mic. Whipper did some brief rhyming using an "echo chamber" trick that was popular at the time; the effect involved repeating the same syllable at the end of words so they trailed off. The crowd loved it. Whipper realized he might have a bright future in music beyond the saxophone.

"It was so cool, you know, everybody was like, 'Whoa,'" he said. "I was like, 'Man, I gotta start writing, I need something more to say.'"[41]

And he would need a lot to say. Whipper Whip was the only pure emcee in the Mighty Force Crew at that time and he would often need to keep a party rocking from 10:00 p.m. to 4:00 a.m. That was unsustainable, and he knew he'd need a partner—a second emcee. The number of talented emcees in the Bronx at the time was totally unknown, so the crew held open auditions.[42]

Whipper Whip found his partner out in front of the Police Athletic League at Webster and 183rd Street. He was a serious-looking young man with a chiseled jaw wearing a flashy outfit and pink sunglasses. It was Darryl Mason, who went by the name Dottie Dot at the time.[43]

"Dot was always a cool character," Whipper Whip said. "He was one of those guys like if we had five dollars, that means he had two-fifty and I had two-fifty. We were Frick and Frack like that. We'd come home from school and get a little tre bag [a very small bag of pot] and a couple of Coors and we straight."[44]

Despite his love of fun, Mason was very reliable and dedicated to his job. According to Whip, no matter how late they were out giving their parties the night before, he'd be at his job at 6:00 a.m. the next morning.[45] He worked alongside his mother at a local rehabilitation facility, and he would hold that job from the time he was in high school until his retirement shortly before his 2015 passing. Whipper Whip described Dot as being extremely down-to-earth and happy to hang out with anyone. This was the partner that Whipper Whip was looking for; luckily, he was able to convince Dot-A-Rock to join the Mighty Force.[46]

With Caz behind them, the duo played everywhere together and were inseparable. The two emcees took on the nickname "Salt & Pepper" and were a formidable tandem in the New York scene.

The Mighty Force, keen on growing as quickly as possible by playing as often as they could, began roping off their DJ setup to prevent anyone from coming up and grabbing the microphone. This was their first giant step toward converting the open mic–style jams and block parties into what would eventually become full-fledged concerts. Many of the most popular and influential crews of the time had started engaging in this practice, including the one headed by Grandmaster Flash.

* * *

The group that would eventually become Grandmaster Flash and the Furious Five started with just the DJ, Joseph Saddler, aka Grandmaster Flash, and three emcees: Melle Mel; his brother the Kidd Creole, who in 2022 was sentenced to sixteen years in prison for a fatal stabbing; and Keef Cowboy, who passed away in 1989. They elevated the performance aspect of hip hop through their decision to position the emcees in front of the DJ on stage and shift the focus of the audience. "They were the ones that made you really pay attention to what the people were rapping," Paradise Gray said. "The rappers were just accessories or the DJ would rap before that."[47]

A lover of technology and anything that rotates (including dryers and bicycle tires) growing up, young Joseph Saddler was the perfect innovator to take DJing from playing records to controlling the turntables and using them as instruments. He innovated the best technique yet for extending the breaks in songs when he had the epiphany that putting his hand on a vinyl record would stop it from playing, and rotating it counterclockwise would pull the record back to the part he was seeking. To make sure he landed at the perfect break each time, the man who would take the stage name Grandmaster Flash marked the breaks on records with a crayon and made sure to wind the record back to the correct spot. Looking like a mad scientist behind the turntables, he could manipulate the record without having to touch the tuning arm. It was a giant leap forward.[48]

D'Bora Meyers, a Bronx resident and the future DJ for the groundbreaking Mercedes Ladies, remembers seeing Flash perform at a local school park in 1977. She was blown away.

"I started, as I was getting older, getting immersed into R&B," Meyers said. "I got into R&B and from there, I just went out to hang out with my girlfriends, and they said 'Let's see this guy named Flash.' I was like 'Who's Flash?' but we went out and saw him and I was like 'Oh *my god*' and that was it. How he was cutting up the record, how they were emceeing to it. Just his whole demeanor on it, watching how the crowd was reacting. I was thinking 'Damn, could you imagine if a girl did that?'"[49]

From that day on, Meyers decided she wanted to be the female Grandmaster Flash. Although her boyfriend at the time was dismissive (even though women have been involved in hip hop since its earliest iterations), she took on the name DJ Baby D and joined up with the Mercedes Ladies. The first all-female hip hop crew, the Mercedes Ladies were the sister group to Theodore's L Brothers for a period of time; the performers would hang out, learn from one another, and often share the stage.[50]

What was as equally important as Flash, however, was the work of his emcees Mel, Creole, and Cowboy. They transformed the act of talking into a microphone from a complimentary condiment to the main course of any hip hop performance. Whipper Whip saw this early version of what would eventually become the Furious Five at a club in the Bronx called the Black Door.

"The way Mel would rock a crowd . . . each one of them had their own aura," he said. "Mel was just an incredible writer, and Kid Creole, he just rocks that echo chamber like no one else can, he was like, 'Creole ole, solid gold gold, the prince of soul soul, playing the role role.' It was just incredible. And then Cowboy was the guy who just hyped up the parts, 'Say ho!' and had everybody scream, and so each one of them had their own little thing."[51]

Flash, Mel, Creole, and Cowboy influenced many notable figures in the genre with their presentation, which was far beyond Whipper Whip and Baby D. Because of this, Flash and Co. became hip hop's original trendsetters. Whatever they did was suddenly cool. Crews started to send their emcees to the front and give them more clout over the audience. They would even perform on elevated stages when possible, like performers in other genres.[52] Where the first generation of DJs were more centered around getting people up and dancing, the next wave of crews focused on delivering a complete musical performance more in line with other popular genres at the time.

"We were heavy into talent shows in our community, and everyone wanted to be Michael Jackson," Paradise Gray, who was exposed to hip hop from a very young age by living in the Bronxdale project, said. "I would say Michael Jackson and James Brown are the two greatest influences in the history of hip hop. They were those dudes."[53]

* * *

By 1979, there had been major shifts in the lineups of many of the founding hip hop groups. For example, the Force Emcees broke up, although Whipper Whip and Dot-A-Rock carried on with their Salt & Pepper act as a duo. They did this with a fair amount of success, but they knew that in order to take their careers to the next level, they'd need to be in a larger group, since that was the trend for the most successful acts at the time.

One night, Salt & Pepper were invited by Kool Herc to perform in front of him at a local show. According to Whipper Whip, at one point in the routine, Dot-A-Rock said, "Yo, Charlie Chase, yo,"[54] to shout out his friend (born Carlos Mandes), a talented DJ in attendance that evening. That shout-out would be very consequential.

Born in 1959, Mandes, like Whipper Whip, Rubie Dee, and Disco Wiz, is Puerto Rican. With thick black hair and piercing eyes full of conviction, Mandes looked intense, and he had the personality and musical skills to match. He found it initially difficult to gain acceptance in an art form dominated by African Americans, considering no Puerto Rican DJ had enjoyed breakthrough success prior to him coming on the scene (Wiz was a contemporary of his).[55] A bassist growing up, Mandes played in a merengue band and earned his first money from live performance at age fourteen. Mandes's friends who played drums and keyboard in the band also DJed parties at local colleges on the side under the name Tom and Jerry. Around the beginning of 1975, Mandes watched them practice on the turntables for the first time, and it intrigued the self-described technology nerd to the point that he started studying under them and tagging along to their gigs.[56]

Around the same time, Mandes discovered hip hop at the local community center. On a winter day, as Mandes was heading inside to meet his friends to play ping-pong, he walked past a room where some of the older kids were having a party.

"I'm hearing music coming out of there, but I'm hearing music that I'm familiar with," DJ Charlie Chase said. "I stopped to look through the window and it's dark as hell, you can't see anyone in there. All you could see is one light on at the very end of the room. It was a lamp with no shade."[57]

Chase saw some kids he knew so he went inside, still unsure exactly what he was hearing. He'd been to plenty of parties before to play, but he'd never seen someone cutting up breakbeats and using drum parts to get the party going like the hip hop DJ was doing. He also recognized the songs, specifically one by Trans–Europe Express, but he had never heard it played in that style before.

"I go to the front and I see it's my friend Ronald," Chase said. "I said 'Yo, Ronald, what's going on?' and he said, 'We're just jamming here,' and I'm like 'Yo, this is crazy, what are you guys playing?'"[58]

Ronald explained to Chase that they were just taking the breaks from popular disco songs and playing them back to back. He gave him a whole crash course in the scene, speaking over the thump of the music: how there were crews around the Bronx, how DJs and emcees and b-boys all came together for the jams. Chase was hooked and sought to carve out a niche for himself in hip hop. He initially struggled to even find records that had breakbeats on them, partly because the DJs he spoke to weren't eager to divulge their secrets.

Chase turned to rock music, which he loved, and used beats from the likes of Cheap Trick, Queen, Aerosmith, and Rush. He would also cater to requests from Latinos for salsa or disco.[59] He claims he was the first crossover hip hop DJ.

When he hung out with Tom and Jerry, Chase would often get a chance to play some records after the dance floor cleared out while the other two crew members went to flirt it up at the bar.[60] Before he had heard hip hop beats, he was happy to play songs like "The Hustle." But after practicing and getting advice from some of his friends from the community center, Mandes was ready to unleash something different at a Lehman College party with a majority Latino audience: "The place is packed, the place is jamming," he said. "All of a sudden, the floor clears out again. Now this time I have my arsenal of breakbeats, so I get on and I start jamming and I'm just going and going and jamming and jamming and people are liking it. And people come back out on the floor and they're not dancing 'The Hustle' or anything like that. Now they're just dancing freestyle, dancing the way we Latinos do, it's picking up, man, and Tom and Jerry come back and they're like, 'Oh, great!' Boom, they knocked me out of the box. Although they took me off the turntables, I felt a real huge sense of satisfaction, like I accomplished something. That was my first time rocking something."[61]

Mandes stayed for about a year with Tom and Jerry before going out on his own. He also adopted the name Charlie Chase around that time because he felt as though he was always chasing something: the top spot in the city, the best breakbeats, or, more tangibly, Grandmaster Flash.

Chase first started to form the crew that would become the Cold Crush Brothers in 1978. His friend RC introduced him to a high school classmate named Angelo King, who went by DJ Tony Tone on stage. Together, Chase and Tone made plans for a new group. It was around this time that Whipper Whip and Dot-A-Rock gave them the shout-out, and they talked about linking up as a foursome. After a quick meeting, the two came aboard.[62]

"The emcees that had a falling out with Caz and decided to leave, they would come with me," Chase said. "I don't know why but that always happened."[63]

The same flyer advertising the 1979 L Brothers show that was scheduled to take place at 308 E. 166th Street mentioned that "The Chase Crew!" would be the other matchup in the hip hop battle. That group featured three DJs, Chase, Tone, and Mighty Mike, alongside emcees Whipper Whip, Dot-A-Rock, T-Bone, and Easy A.D. (aka Adrian Harris). Just underneath the Chase Crew's lineup is the phrase "Cold Crush Crush Crew."[64] The Cold Crush Brothers name had clearly started to take shape, but this flyer shows that they were still working on the exact wording. According to Chase, Tony Tone tracked him down at an arcade across the street from Chase's building to suggest the Cold Crush Brothers name. There, Tone presented Chase with his source of inspiration: a red and white flyer that read "Another Cold Crush Product" at the top. Tone originally wanted the word "Crew" in the name, but Chase suggested a single amendment: to change "Crew" to "Brothers" to show how serious the group was in their attempt to rise to the top of the New York scene. They were, in his eyes, family.[65]

The early hot spots for the Cold Crush Brothers included local parks in the Bronx and schools like 118 Park, 129, and 63, according to Whipper Whip.[66] Chase and Tone were (and remain) talented DJs, and their emcees were both energetic and innovative. Whipper Whip and Dot-A-Rock continued writing and performing, but in this era of Cold Crush, the stage could get a bit crowded and there wasn't always enough microphone to go around. Despite the group's growing popularity, the duo formerly known as Salt & Pepper decided to leave their crew behind. According to Chase, they were only part of the Cold Crush Brothers for about two weeks before they left the family.

"We told Charlie, like, 'Yo, man, you know, we just want us on the mic, we don't want no other emcees,'" Whipper Whip said. "He was like, 'Well, yo, y'all, I got my boys, I know it's business, but they're friends too.' I was like, 'Well, you can't mix friends and business, yo, this is business.'"[67]

*   *   *

Whip and Dot quickly started looking for their next endeavor. As Salt & Pepper, they played a venue locals had nicknamed "Duck City" because of the need for people (even five-foot-five Rubie Dee) to duck as they moved between different rooms. In one of those rooms, the two encountered Grand Wizzard Theodore.

Theodore didn't need much convincing to help them out. According to him, "I remember the day that they approached me and said, 'Yo, Theodore, we would like to audition so that we could be a part of your crew.' I was like, 'Wait a minute, I never thought about that. I never thought about adding two more emcees to the emcees that I already got.' I was like, 'Wow, you know what? I think you guys would be a great asset to the crew.' I went to Kevie Kev and Robbie Rob and was like, 'Yo, I think Whipper Whip and Dot-A-Rock would be a good asset to the crew. They have their own crowd, we have our own crowd, and we can mash the two crowds together,' because people who came to our parties didn't go to Whipper Whip and Dot-A-Rock's parties and people who went to Dot-A-Rock and Whipper Whip's parties very rarely came to our parties. I figured we put them down with us and see what happens."[68]

Initially, Theodore's idea of adding two more emcees was met with resistance from Kevie Kev and Master Rob. They argued that three emcees were enough and they didn't know who Whipper Whip and

Dot-A-Rock were.[69] Theodore, the group's founder, overrode them and brought the Salt & Pepper emcees onboard, taking the total number of group members to six and ushering in a new group name: Grand Wizzard Theodore and the Fantastic Five Emcees.

*   *   *

Although Whipper Whip and Dot-A-Rock's separation from Cold Crush was amicable, it still left the group two emcees short, so Chase and Tone immediately went on the lookout to find replacements. Their most coveted target was a good friend of Chase's who had recently changed his stage name from Casanova Fly to Grandmaster Caz. Caz's Mighty Force Crew had gone through many iterations, including the Force Four and the Force Five. He would continually bring on (and mentor) new emcees to fill out the spots only for them to leave the crew and try to make it on their own.

That finally changed when Caz's crewmate and longtime friend Jerome Lewis, who went by Jerry Dee Lewis (JDL) on stage, convinced him to stop cycling through new members and just continue on with Tone as the "Notorious Two."[70] JDL was fiery, he was energetic, he was a bit nuts. Whatever adjectives are used to describe the ultra-talented emcee, they all seem to involve his intensity both on the mic and off it. Sporting very '70s sideburns and a goatee, JDL wouldn't rap into the microphone so much as pour his heart out into it. In the early days, he wore a big, flat Pittsburgh Pirates–style baseball cap like his partner Caz. He smiled while he was performing, but it almost seemed like a front designed to mask the unbridled passion that was brewing inside. "I didn't like JDL," Chase said. "He was crazy, he was always getting high, he was irresponsible, he was just one of them guys."[71]

Although they were now a two-man act, Caz and JDL became widely known as one of the best emcee combinations in New York.

The enthusiasm that JDL put into each performance was unmatched, while Caz's creativity was the engine that made the duo go. A surviving tape of the pair rapping over the disco classic "Got to Be Real" by Cheryl Lynn in 1979 shows their incredible coordination in a remarkably advanced routine.

The two traded verses and harmonized for four minutes without a hiccup as Caz also handled duty at the turntables:

> I'm Jerry D, the best emcee, rockin' the mic for you
>
> I'm Grandmaster Caz, I got a lot of class, and we are the Notorious Two
>
> Two grown brothers from around the way, and we know just what you like
>
> Notorious on the turntables
>
> Notorious on the mic
>
> And we got rhymes galore to keep you on the floor
>
> And you can bet your bottom dime
>
> We go the first of the year to the end of December
>
> Without saying the same rhyme.[72]

Even though the Notorious Two were finding success, Caz felt bogged down by having to split the DJ responsibilities with JDL. He didn't like hauling his own equipment, which he believed wasn't up to snuff compared to that of the other hip hop acts in town. Caz really wanted to focus on his work as an emcee; hip hop was transitioning to a more rapper-focused style, and he didn't want to be left behind.[73] Though Cold Crush had a reputation for being a crew that emcees came into and out of rapidly, Caz was intrigued by the idea of joining up with Charlie Chase and company. When Chase approached him initially about helping to fill the spots abandoned by Whipper Whip and Dot-A-Rock, though, he was noncommittal.[74] He'd been friends with Chase for years, but the two had never worked together.

Chase and Tone decided to hold open auditions for the Cold Crush

Brothers at South Bronx High School. Chase prepared for the auditions by trying to come up with a conniving scheme to get Caz, one of the best emcees in the city, on his crew. He invited Caz to help him and Tone pick new members to join the group. The opportunity arose after the crew had enjoyed the audition from Kenneth Crump, who went by Almighty Kay Gee onstage. Chase invited Caz, who then invited JDL, to take a "test drive" alongside existing emcee Easy A.D. (Adrian Harris) and Kay Gee. In the empty high-school auditorium, the four really clicked, and Chase and Tone knew they had the makings of a great group.[75] However, getting Caz to join was still a tough sell. Chase grabbed him and took him to a quiet spot in the school, where he spoke in a hushed, urgent voice.

"I had him cornered, like you have in boxing," Chase said. "I said 'Caz, I know I've been telling you about getting down. I'm *telling* you, I am planning something big. I want to do something big. I know what it takes to make this big. If you join us, I promise you, I feel it in my bones, we are going to be one of the biggest things that ever hit this fucking city.' He saw the conviction in my eyes."[76]

That was enough to compel Caz to join up with the Cold Crush—on the condition that JDL could come with him. Chase originally said no (as mentioned before, he wasn't a JDL fan), so Caz said that if he couldn't bring JDL, the whole merger was off. Thinking quickly and weighing his options, Chase gave in and welcomed JDL to the group alongside Caz.

Unbeknownst to Chase at the time, Caz had a vision of the future of hip hop. He knew that he'd need to join a larger group to realize this vision, so the invitation to join Cold Crush was actually much more welcome than he thought. "By the time it became an emcee-oriented thing, I figured that's the route I wanted to go," he explained. "For Cold Crush, I don't have to DJ or nothin'. We got two DJs, they've got the sound system. I could finally just rap, I could be an emcee.

The tide had kind of turned at the time and the emphasis was on the emcee and the emcee group. My job getting down with the Cold Crush Brothers was to whip the emcees into shape. To be the captain of the four. That was my main job. So I put DJing to the side. I put flyer making to the side, and I put taping parties to the side because there were other people to do those things now. I didn't have to do everything now."[77]

Caz would end up being the most impactful addition Chase and Tone ever made to their group, but they also discovered a gem in Almighty Kay Gee. He wasn't well connected to any Cold Crush members at the time, but he was an incredible talent who would become a staple of the group.

In one of the earliest pieces of footage ever captured of a hip hop party, Charlie Ahearn shot some video at Harlem's Celebrity Club during a 1980 "emcee convention" hosted by Kool DJ AJ. Performing after Caz, Kay Gee whipped the crowd into a fervor as if he was Led Zeppelin.[78] Wearing sunglasses in what was already a dimly lit room, the handsome, short-haired, and skinny Kay Gee spat out syllables with a dexterity and speed that was extremely rare at the time. He was a perfect fit with Caz and the other emcees. He could keep up and sometimes outpace them. When watching the footage, it's hard to identify when he breathes.

After locking down Caz, JDL, and Kay Gee as emcees, Chase and Tone had a complete crew, which they believed had enough firepower to rival any squad in New York.

* * *

One of those rival squads was just starting to make their presence known in the city. The Fantastic Five was gaining popularity, but there was so much more to be done to turn them into a truly special group. Grand Wizzard Theodore, Whipper Whip, Dot-A-Rock, Rubie Dee,

Master Rob, and Kevie Kev had the idea to set themselves apart by adding elements previously unseen in hip hop routines, like dance steps, vocal harmonies, and matching outfits. Those elements turned simple call-and-response routines or short, DJ Hollywood–style raps into elaborate performances that could last a half hour or more. But with so much going on during a performance, there were more opportunities for disaster, and Theodore and company were unwilling to allow for that. That meant the Fantastic Five would need to get serious.

"We spent a lot of time together," Theodore said. "We practiced sometimes like seven days a week. And our girlfriends used to get mad: 'You guys are spending too much time together.' It was really crazy."[79]

Synchronized from dance steps to outfits, the Fantastic Five brought Vegas-style showmanship and Motown-style sex appeal to the stage. That wouldn't have mattered if their music wasn't sublime. According to Theodore, it would only take ten to twelve records to build up a full twenty-five-minute routine for the Fantastic Five, and he relied on his instincts to determine what to play. The lyrics would come first, and Theodore knew how to compliment them with the perfect beats to get the crowd dancing.

"My job is to make sure that I have the right music to fit the words," Theodore said. "And everything came together so beautifully. I'm pretty good at that. I can do a party and look at the crowd and know exactly what they want to hear."[80]

The Five also knew how to keep the show fresh and interesting if New Yorkers came out to see Fantastic multiple times. Theodore would often repeat records that called for the same dance steps so his crew could stay synchronized, but the emcees were constantly writing new lyrics or bringing new routines to the table. For example, Whipper Whip and Dot-A-Rock would still perform their Salt &

Pepper routine while the other emcees left the stage and whipped the crowd into a frenzy before the whole crew reassembled.[81] Sometimes Fantastic would create an entirely new show with all-new records from Theodore's collection. Their act took off, especially among a specific subset of hip hop fans.

"Fantastic were more like a singing group," Paradise Gray said. "They were more polished and less rough than the Cold Crush and those guys. Cold Crush was talking street shit. Fantastic was talking to the women. They reminded you more of someone who was an entertainer than someone who was a rapper. They had an understanding of the fact that if you packed the place with women, you'd have a better chance of making money and a greater chance of not showing up at a place with a bunch of stick-up kids and b-boys dancing."[82]

The words that come up most when discussing the Fantastic Five are "tight" and "nice" because their performances were rehearsed so consistently and they were one of the first groups to treat hip hop like a performance art. For example, Theodore cut up "Daisy Lady" by 7th Wonder while Whipper Whip and Dot-A-Rock synched up for a portion of their old "Salt & Pepper" routine.

> Well I'm the D-O-T-A-ROCK
> When you hear me rock the mic you're guaranteed to wanna stay
> Relax and listen to what I say
> Now when I rock your body to the break of day
> We're gonna rock your mind, we're gonna shock your mind
> Cuz Salt & Pepper Emcees are gonna drop a dime
> Yes, I'm the Whipper Whip and I'm a superstar, we're gonna rock your
> monkey ass no matter who you think you are
> And then you listen to our voice woo-ha we sound good when Salt &
> Pepper's in your neighborhood

Rock to the beat everybody because we're number one
We just want the party people to come and get some[83]

These were standard themes at the time for any crew, well rehearsed or not. What set the Fantastic Five apart was their impeccable presentation and resemblance to the Jackson 5 and other superstar pop groups. They included intricately layered vocal harmonies and a dynamic stage presence that would have been the envy of the earliest innovators, like DJ Hollywood and Coke La Rock.

* * *

While Fantastic was making an impact around the new hip hop genre, the revamped Cold Crush Brothers focused on coming in hot. According to Grandmaster Caz, they practiced for a full year before the new lineup of himself, Chase, Tony Tone, Easy A.D., JDL, and Almighty Kay Gee started playing shows.[84] The resulting chemistry propelled the six-man outfit into city-wide stardom when they first surfaced and began performing. Their dance steps weren't as crisp, their outfits weren't coordinated, and they didn't have the same following among the ladies as Fantastic, but Charlie Chase's crew could make incredible music.

Cold Crush's routines included disco elements but called in from all other genres and showed more lyrical dexterity than any of their predecessors, which can be partly attributed to Caz's diverse taste in music growing up. The first routine Cold Crush debuted was actually set to the melody of Queen's "We Will Rock You."

Well it's one, two, three, four
Cha-Charlie Chase and C.C. Four (and the Cold Cold Crush, the Cold
    Cold Crush)

I'm Grandmaster Caz

Jerry Dee

Easy A.D.

And my name is emcee Kay Gee

We're down with Chase, we gonna rock the place

You try to mess with us and we'll dog your face

Singing *"We're the Cold Crush emcees"* (with Charlie Chase)

Say *"We're the Cold Crush emcees"* (we gonna rock the place)[85]

When Charlie Chase blasted out a Brian May guitar lick taken from the record, it ignited the crowd and kept the party roaring. As disco began to die in mainstream America in the late '70s and early '80s, Cold Crush helped keep hip hop from suffering that same fate by bringing in fresh ideas. The genre was starting to shift from an alternative to disco music (or even an extension of it) to something much more original and creative. The potential for hip hop was never higher, despite the fact that it was brewed in the cauldron of one of the unlikeliest places an art form has ever emerged from: 1970s New York.

Fishing for coins in the South Bronx Streets, 1980. Photo by Joe Conzo Jr.

Chapter 3

New York, New York

If you were living anywhere in America other than the Bronx, events like Ronald Reagan's 1980 visit, coupled with the way the media covered the area, would have you believing that the borough was among the worst places in the world.

The race for president in 1980 was hotly contested between Jimmy Carter, the incumbent Democrat from Georgia, and Republican challenger Reagan, the former governor of California. Carter had stumbled through a horrible 1979 that had drawn the ire of many Americans. The country was still plagued by high energy costs stemming from the oil embargo of the mid-1970s. The Iran hostage crisis showed what many citizens perceived as a weakened America on the world stage. Inflation was at 13.5 percent,[1] and perhaps worst of all for Carter, he had lost copious amounts of good political will through his "Crisis of Confidence" speech, in which he outlined the lack of unity in the country and called on everyday Americans to help solve the issues plaguing the nation.

For the progressive Carter, these issues were further compounded by a surge of conservative energy that would come to be known as the "Reagan Revolution." The challenger was an immensely skilled politician and communicator. He used the slogan "Let's Make America Great Again" to great effect. His promises to increase military spending while also lowering taxes,[2] which were scoffed at by many economists, were smash hits with rank and file Republicans. However, Reagan had limited success with liberal voters, especially minorities. The "Great Communicator" sought to bridge that gap as much as he could. He figured a visit to the South Bronx would do the trick. This led to perhaps the most unusual campaign stop in the history of presidential politics.

On August 5, 1980, Reagan stood in a vacant lot on Charlotte Street amid 90-degree heat and high humidity to deliver remarks about how his opponent wasn't fulfilling his promises to the urban poor.[3] Carter had stood in that same lot in 1977 and promised aid to help rehabilitate the area; now, Reagan pointed out that the lot was, in fact, still vacant. This visit came on the heels of Reagan's morning speech to the National Urban League and hours before he met with Jesse Jackson and the editors of *Ebony* and *Jet* magazines.[4]

In those remarks at the National Urban League, Reagan spoke about how he was unfairly labeled as being anti-Black and anti-poor because of his party affiliation. He asked those in attendance to look past labels and instead consider him as an individual. He called upon John F. Kennedy's famous 1960 speech to Houston-area Protestant ministers in which he shook off the labels that had been placed on him because of his Catholicism. According to the *New York Times*, Reagan received only a smattering of applause from the audience, which was largely Black people. Reagan said in the speech that there were "perceived barriers between my political beliefs and the aspirations of Black Americans. Those barriers are false. What I want for America is, pretty much, what the overwhelming majority of Black Americans also want."[5]

That received no reaction from the crowd.

Later that day, Reagan emerged from his limousine clad in a tan summer suit, waving to a crowd who was eager to boo him. News cameras captured residents screaming "HELP US!" at the candidate as his loafer-clad feet strutted over piles of rubble and garbage, his Secret Service detail imploring locals to get away from him. A large police presence watched over barricades separating residents from Reagan as he spoke.[6]

Standing in the rubble-strewn lot, where the nearest building was graffitied with the word "decay," Reagan made one of his most notable remarks of the entire campaign. He said of the South Bronx that he hadn't "seen anything that looked like this since London after the Blitz."[7]

The comment comparing the urban decay in an American neighborhood to the terror inflicted by the Nazis in 1940 turned many heads. Although Reagan likely was trying to show sympathy in that moment, the remark is remembered as being tone-deaf. His follow up comment wasn't much more empathetic.

"I'm impressed by the spirit and determination of these people to save what they have,"[8] he told reporters.

Truth be told, Reagan's description of the area was at least somewhat accurate. There were parts of the South Bronx that had been completely leveled and left as nothing but piles of bricks and dirt. Other parts were abandoned, the buildings covered in graffiti tags, the black paint standing out against the tan bricks. To outsiders, graffiti didn't carry the same cultural meaning that it did inside the neighborhoods. Promises of funding to build new housing projects had gone largely unfulfilled. An industrial park had been approved, with $4.3 million in government funds, but that didn't come close to the $55.6 million Carter had promised standing on Charlotte Street in 1977.[9] However, the Bronx wasn't—and still isn't—so singular that it can be defined by one vacant lot on Charlotte Street. The borough was defined by nuance rather than stereotypes.

A photo from the next morning's *New York Times* showed Reagan visiting a group of mainly Black protestors who had gathered across the street, chanting "Go back to California!" In the image, Reagan's sweaty face is reflected in the mirroring of a scally cap–clad man's sunglasses. He was facing a skeptical crowd, but that didn't stop him from trying his best to advocate for himself. As he spoke about Carter's broken promises, he was interrupted by a woman shouting, "What are *you* going to do for us?"[10] After several attempts to get the crowd to quiet down (including trying to count down from three), he screamed out, overloading the microphones held by the newsmen following the campaign. His voice comes across as ear splitting on recordings.

"I'M TRYING TO TELL YOU! I know now there is no program or policies that a president can make that the Federal Government can come in and wave a wand to do this."[11]

Reagan's voice was hoarse and the chanting drowned out his arguments. News footage shows how he was growing visibly frustrated with the locals, his face red and his expression deeply set, when he said, "Look, if you will listen—I can't do a damn thing for you if I don't get elected."[12]

Reagan continued to spar back and forth with locals by promoting his policies of tax incentives for private industry and relying on the grit of citizens to get things done. He said what was happening in the Bronx was "a disgrace" and that the problems couldn't be fixed overnight, and that he wouldn't make any promises he couldn't keep.[13] Some locals were receptive to Reagan's ideas and thanked him for his time.[14] Many others continued voicing their displeasure until he returned to his waiting wife to be whisked away in his limousine. Many shouted "We need jobs!" as Reagan walked through a crush of humanity. It was a moment of political history not seen since (even though Ted Cruz tried to replicate it in 2016 and was unceremoniously shouted out of the neighborhood).[15] This was a real back-and-forth, substantive debate between the urban poor, many of whom lacked shirts and shoes, and the leading conservative of his era. Reagan opened eyes as to what could possibly be done to revitalize desolate parts of New York.

Sadly, however, nothing ever came of his promises. The visit, along with the summit with Jesse Jackson and the speech to the NUL, ended up being remembered as little more than a publicity stunt. Carter received 83 percent of the African American vote in 1980 and Reagan claimed only 14 percent.[16]

* * *

In 1977, a special episode of *CBS Reports* entitled "The Fire Next Door" investigated the factors that led to the Bronx becoming the "arson capital of the world," as host Bill Moyers described it.[17] He pointed out that in the previous ten years, more than 30,000 buildings were burned and abandoned, many of them "built to last hundreds of years."[18] In the documentary's opening scene, a team of firefighters responded to a small blaze in an abandoned apartment, and a twenty-two-year firefighting veteran explained the process that leads to buildings becoming abandoned as smoke rushed out of an open door on the fifth floor of a brick building on Popham Avenue: "They start the fires in the vacant apartments. Before you know it the whole wing, then the building. People move out. The landlord starts to cut back on his maintenance because he's not making any profit. More and more apartments become vacant and it becomes less profitable for the landlord. Before you know it you have a block with no one living there. It becomes a wasteland like the South Bronx."[19]

The most shocking claims made by the special were that an occupied apartment building in the Bronx could be purchased for $1,000 and that the city had a tax moratorium at the time that allowed landlords to collect rent and pay no taxes. These factors disincentivized building owners from maintaining their buildings properly or providing services like heat and running water unless they were caught by the city.[20] After fed-up residents finally cleared out of the building, landlords would hire an arsonist to burn the property down and then collect on their federally mandated fire insurance policy, making a quick profit of more than $70,000.[21]

Other motivations for arson included a city policy that stated that people on welfare whose apartments were burned were moved to the front of the line for consideration to be transferred to a different public housing project, so impoverished residents frustrated by their living conditions would often burn down their own residences. Moyers recounted one story of a woman with three children who moved her belongings to a relative's place before having her nephew come in during the early morning hours to start the fire.[22] Sometimes, kids in the neighborhood started fires in abandoned buildings just for fun.[23]

That report also revealed the heart-wrenching stories of residents who remained in the neighborhood even as their blocks were literally burning down. One woman shared how she needed to stay in her otherwise abandoned building because she couldn't find an apartment that would accept her three dogs (she said she had six before teenagers threw the other three off the roof). She had no running water, electricity, or heat, and said she was scared of being alone.[24] A woman who was identified as "Ms. Barkley" was surrounded by her children as she explained why she hadn't unpacked most of her furniture, saying that the mice were running rampant around her apartment and she didn't want to risk damage to her new bed. "As soon as I get the place, I'm just going to move," she said. It's shocking to see Barkley, draped in a red head wrap and a black leather jacket, show Moyers how her bathroom was missing a ceiling and recount stories of bags of garbage being thrown into the streets, flying past her window on the way down. She claimed to have joked with a neighbor about how they needed to move "before the garbage piles up to the third floor."[25]

But of course, the story of the Bronx is far more complex and meaningful than the stereotype of it as acres of smoking ruins that gets perpetuated about the neighborhood to this day.

* * *

While the Bronx became synonymous with urban decay and misery during the disco era, that was not always the case. Europeans first settled the mainland areas just north of Manhattan Island in the mid-seventeenth century, led most famously by sea captain Jonas Bronck, who lent the future borough his last name.[26] It wasn't until 1898 that New York City consolidated the five boroughs together, pulling them out of their separate counties.[27] From that time on, the Bronx enjoyed a period of immense growth, bolstered by a wave of Italian immigrants and the post–Civil War Great Migration of African Americans fleeing the segregated South.

The Bronx was largely an agricultural area for a long portion of its history, until the first subway line to Manhattan (the Third Avenue Elevated line) was completed in 1906. The El allowed for a quick commute and drew more people from sweltering, overcrowded Manhattan tenements into what was essentially a country suburb.[28] Eastern and Central European Jews made up the largest group in this initial move. It was around this same time that the New York Botanical Garden (1891) and Bronx Zoo (1897) first opened for visitors. Yankee Stadium opened in 1923, during a period of rapid economic growth. Massive blocks of buildings were developed on previously vacant land and everything from tailor shops to department stores to opera houses were erected quickly in the booming borough. Between 1900 and 1930, the population of the Bronx grew from 200,507 to 1,265,258.[29]

While the Great Depression ravaged many parts of New York, the Bronx was comparatively spared. President Franklin Delano Roosevelt's New Deal programs allowed for the building of new parks, streets, post offices, and a jail. At this point, the Bronx was nearly 50 percent Jewish but also home to strong African American and Puerto Rican populations.[30]

"It was great, it was absolutely great," said John Braithwaithe, who moved from Manhattan to the Bronx with his family in 1945, when he was two. "I don't know [why] the Bronx has gotten a bad rap. Back in the '40s and '50s it was a real nice place to live. Parents looked out for one—the children in the neighborhood, there was always somebody watching over who's—what's going on in the neighborhood."[31]

Much like the kids from generations who came after him, Braithwaithe played street games with his friends to pass the time. "In the daytime there was of course marbles, and skully, and spinning tops and roller-skating, and they would draw in chalk a track on the street and that would become a roller derby rink and you'd be knocking one another about. And so—in the hot summer they would direct the—open a hydrant and direct the flow of water with either a cut off can or even a milk carton."[32]

After World War II, the demographics in the neighborhood shifted dramatically. Hundreds of thousands of New Yorkers were kicked out of their homes in Manhattan and other parts of the Bronx in the name of "urban renewal" and many of them resettled in the borough in a wide variety of neighborhoods, such as Morrisania near Yankee Stadium, or the West Bronx. This campaign disproportionately affected New Yorkers of color.

At this time, the country was beset by white flight, a gradual migration in which white residents of many major US cities left their increasingly multicultural neighborhoods for homogenous suburbs (most famously Long Island's Levittown, which was built beginning in 1947). It can be argued that "flight" is a misnomer for this type of relocation because many whites were openly hostile to minorities at the time and even acted violently in an effort to keep neighborhoods segregated. This discriminatory departure was compounded by racist practices such as redlining and mortgage discrimination, which further worked to segregate major cities like New York.

The other major factor behind the Bronx's demographic shift was a massive wave of immigration from the Caribbean in the 1950s and 1960s. According to the Library of Congress, "In 1945, there had been 13,000 Puerto Ricans in New York City; in 1946 there were more than 50,000. Over the next decade, more than 25,000 Puerto Ricans would come to the continental U.S. each year, peaking in 1953, when more than 69,000 came. By 1955, nearly 700,000 Puerto Ricans had arrived. By the mid-1960s, more than a million had.[33] A wave of immigration from the Dominican Republic and Jamaica also took place in the 1960s after the Hart-Celler Act eliminated archaic immigration quota laws.[34] Along with its thriving Black community, the Bronx was further diversified by many cultures which would play an instrumental role in developing hip hop.

*   *   *

Soon after the Bronx experienced its major population boom, a construction project began that would ultimately be the single greatest contributing factor to both the community's local issues and outsiders' negative perception of the neighborhood. The Cross Bronx Expressway, which was built mainly between 1948 and 1963, bifurcated the borough, separating neighborhoods with a six-lane highway.[35] The brainchild of notorious urban planner Robert Moses, the expressway cost many people their homes and devalued the housing of those who remained. Additionally, the Cross Bronx caused people to think of the Bronx in terms of north and south, with the

South Bronx regarded as the poorer, more desperate area.[36] Advocates like Jane Jacobs used the impact of the Cross Bronx Expressway as their main arguments against building similar highways in major cities around North America.[37]

Around the same time the Expressway was being built, the borough's largest public housing projects opened. These included the Bronx River Houses (which first opened in 1951), the Forest Houses (1956), and the Bronxdale (1955), which has since been renamed for former resident and current Supreme Court Justice Sonia Sotomayor.

"For its failings, the New York City Housing Authority works in terms of public housing. That's something that can't be said for many cities across the country," said hip hop historian Kevin Kosanovich. Kosanovich stressed how the families who first moved into these housing projects had the kids who would develop the hip hop genre during their teenage years.[38]

"There are these pockets of not so much financial stability or upward mobility, but ways for the community to come together," Kosanovich said. "The community endures, people are able to hang out outside, they're able to have a sense of continuity, enough so you have a foundation to piece together this world vision."

Kosanovich added that, despite the Bronx's reputation as a desperate area, the socioeconomics of the neighborhoods were really more nuanced than outsiders believed. For example, DJ Kool Herc's documented 1973 party at 1520 Sedgwick Avenue took place in Mitchell-Lama housing, a West Bronx public housing campus that served "moderate and middle income families,"[39] while Grandmaster Flash came from the Forest Houses in the South Bronx, which mainly served lower-income families.

"Kool Herc rented out the rec room and threw a nice back-to-school party, primarily so he and his sister Cindy could get some new clothes before school starts," Kosanovich said. "It's as simple as that. The fact that his dad has a good system, is a fan of music . . . it's very innocent. 'We have a need, we want to look great with our back-to-school outfits, and of course we're able to do it in our building, and our block.'"[40]

According to Dr. Stephen Payne, the archivist at the Bronx County Historical Society, the media was largely responsible for the borough's nasty reputation in the 1970s and '80s. But the journalists who created a strong narrative around a small neighborhood got many crucial details wrong. The area that was commonly referred to as the South Bronx in major media outlets, for example, was actually not the southernmost area of the borough, but rather a ten-block radius near Fox Street where the desolation looked especially thorough, mainly due to the open expanses of space where buildings once stood.[41]

"That's where the most dramatic scenes of burnt-down buildings and empty lots were," Payne said. "Naturally, if you're a member of the media looking for a juicy shot of the Bronx in the 1970s, you're going to go there. There's a narrative in there that is present both in the news stories and obviously still persists today."[42]

Payne explains that condescending interviewers looking for residents quick to blame their fellow Bronx neighbors further fueled the national perception that the borough was in rough shape. In reality, however, much of the Bronx was a decent place to live, according to the majority of locals who have contributed one of the hundreds of oral histories the Society has collected.[43]

*   *   *

Another good example of the disconnect between the media portrayal of the Bronx and what was happening on the ground relates to how different people perceived graffiti. To some, graffiti was a public menace and something that should be eradicated. To others, it was a lovely art form that beautified the area and told the story of the struggles faced by residents.

Graffiti has come to be perceived as synonymous with hip hop culture. But much like the music it's become associated with, the definition and main stylistic aspects of this form of street art are complex and hard to categorize. For example, Sandra "Lady Pink" Fabara, one of the finest graffiti writers in 1980s New York and a costar of *Wild Style,* says that real graffiti must be done illegally to vandalize property, while "graffiti style" art can be made on paper, canvas, or any other medium. She believes that the actual act of writing graffiti needs to include an element of danger and delinquency; these subversive aspects transform it into something different from just squiggly letters in spray paint.[44]

Fabara, who immigrated to New York from Ecuador when she was seven, took on the name Lady Pink because of how beautiful the word "Pink" looked when spray painted with precision.[45] Pink was always passionate about all sorts of visual art. When she was still in high school, she began showing her work at local art galleries—a far cry from the art she'd do after dark. According to Pink, she was the only woman known to be able to compete with men in the graffiti world when she first started.[46] As an adult, her work has been added to collections at the Met and Boston's Museum of Fine Arts, among other notable institutions.[47]

While tagging buildings with people's names in plain black paint might not mean much to the average passerby, this type of graffiti does carry cultural significance. However, the sort of masterful work Lady Pink and her group were doing when she was young went far beyond that, becoming the impetus for films like *Beat Street* and the inspiration for all sorts of Fortune 500 ad campaigns. The most famous canvases for serious graffiti writers were New York subway trains, which had the blank space needed for giant murals and also functioned as mobile billboards for various artists, who could display their work all over the city. But according to the diminutive Lady Pink, no graffiti writer would ever start with the giant undertaking of doing a train.

"Everything was taught master to apprentice," Pink said. "Learning how to do style in books is a must. You have to practice and practice and get the style just right. It takes a long time of schooling before you can bring it out into prime time. Before you tag on the wall you have to have style. Before you can go painting with anybody on a train you have to have style and know how to do it. There were lots of girls in my school who did that on paper and in books, but then to have [spray] can control and skills to exercise a great big piece of what you just did on paper real small, that's a whole new level of learning, and you have to graduate onto that. I didn't just pop out of the woodwork and start painting on subway trains."[48]

Whereas hip hop, in its earliest days, was completely wide open and anyone could grab a mic and work the crowd, graffiti was a much more regimented world, one that dates back well before Kool Herc and Mario's first parties. Sneaking around pitch-black train yards in the dead of night and trying to paint giant murals before the police found you wasn't the sort of work that could be completed in an ad-hoc way if everyone was going to remain safe. According to Lady Pink, the "adrenaline rush" that comes with breaking the law is one of the reasons that graffiti on trains and in the streets rose to a higher level than legal graffiti-style art. She tagged her first train at fifteen years old; the feeling, she says, was "adventurous, exciting, thrilling, all of those things that kids like."

"I was looking over my shoulder, I was scared, I was excited, everything," Pink said. "It came out straight for being so nervous, the letters came out straight, it went well for the circumstances, I was pretty happy about it."[49]

One of the surprising revelations from Pink was that graffiti and hip hop weren't as intertwined as the popular narrative today would suggest. For example, she was always a fan of disco and rock music, but didn't actually listen to much hip hop. She also pointed out that graffiti had a major head start as an art form and was already a very organized subculture by the time hip hop arrived. According to Pink, hip hop was more "regional," while graffiti was widespread throughout the city. She estimated that 40 percent of all graffiti writers had nothing to do with hip hop.[50]

"It's a disservice to lump everyone together as a stereotype when that is not so," she said. "Graffiti writers are so focused on their work that nothing else intrudes in there. It's got nothing to do with dancing, we've got no music intruding, we work in silence. Only in certain neighborhoods did that cross over."[51]

Graffiti was a powerful way for teenagers to express themselves while being rebellious and sticking it to the man at the same time. In that way, its story mirrors hip hop's. Graffiti's impermanence, though, makes it a very different art form. Some of the train murals, for example, would only last for a few hours before another crew painted over them or the city buffed the paint out, although others would stay for months. Lady Pink is particularly proud of a Beatles tribute she completed after John Lennon's death in December 1980 that stayed up for an unprecedented four years.[52] Other graffiti would never be completed at all, as a train would sometimes pull out while artists were in mid-spray. That was especially heartbreaking.

*   *   *

Like generations of Bronx residents before him, Grand Wizzard Theodore has many happy memories from his childhood, including heading to the cinema at 42nd Street to watch his beloved karate movies or going to the Casita Maria Center for Arts & Education at 928 Simpson Street, where he played pool, basketball, and ping-pong with a group of kids that represented the diversity of the Bronx. He had Jewish, white, Asian, Latino, and Black friends. "We all lived in the same neighborhood," he recalled. "I think that was good for us to be able to interact with each other. I really enjoyed going there. We played and played and played and it didn't really matter what color you were."[53]

Despite this, Theodore said his experience in the Bronx more closely aligned with the decaying vision the media tried to perpetuate. Growing up on Boston Road, he bore witness to the more challenging aspects of urban life. Even though he had a great time as a child, he was aware of the issues plaguing his neighborhood: "It was rough, but if you're in your own neighborhood you didn't have anything to worry about or anything like that. If you wander off into other neighborhoods, you had to know somebody. You have to understand the Bronx was plagued with gangs; every neighborhood you'd go into it was gangs. Not only Black Spades, you had Savage Skulls, Savage Nomads. I mean, that's why they made the movie *The Warriors*."[54]

But for many Bronx residents in the '70s and '80s, having an identity tied so closely to their neighborhood meant that there wasn't much shame about where they lived. It was home, no matter what the outside world was saying about it.

Perhaps Paradise Gray put it most succinctly when talking about the misconceptions that the outside world has about a childhood in the Bronx of that era. He described a phenomenal childhood, one where music coursed through the streets, played either by live bands or (once hip hop took hold) DJs. Another magical thing about the Bronx back then was that you could find current and future NBA players on the local courts. Most importantly, perhaps, the kids had the run of the neighborhood when they got home from school, as the vast majority had two working parents who didn't return until later.[55]

"We're out in the street," Gray, who grew up in the Bronxdale projects, said. "We took care of each other. We didn't murder each other, we gave each other fair fights. If you came from somewhere else and you wanted to fight, you could get a fair fight in my community. Even if you won you could walk away without getting jumped. We didn't pull weapons on each other. We didn't pull guns on each other. The older dudes on the corner would not allow us to smoke cigarettes or drink beer with them. If you wasn't a street kid they didn't even allow you *on* the corner. In those days, men ran the streets, and us children, we ran the parks."[56]

Joe Conzo Jr., Cold Crush's photographer and a lifelong Bronx resident, expressed similar sentiments, focusing on the positives of his living situation. "As kids growing up in this era, we made the best of what we had," he said. "I always tell people you can't miss a house with a white picket fence and a backyard and a swing if you never had one. These abandoned buildings and these lots were our playgrounds and we made the best of it."[57]

Conzo's photographs captured a vibrant, eclectic community rich with culture and music. A sign advertising Newport cigarettes in Spanish sat alongside graffiti tags for the Uptown Wales Crew on a brick facade at Wales Avenue and 152nd Street.[58] A street vendor sold plantains out of a shopping cart across the street from La Primadora Cigars and Reilly Electronics on 149th Street and Third Avenue.[59] Another photo depicts a young boy running a string down a storm drain, presumably to fish for money, with dark graffiti adorning the brick wall behind him with phrases like "THE MUGS," "TONY 82," and "SONIA."[60]

Adorned with a giant "Angela Davis afro," as he described it, the Puerto Rican Conzo was obviously a child of the seventies, often wearing three-quarter-sleeve baseball-style T-shirts and bell bottom jeans. He would later go on to work as a firefighter and EMT, including during the September 11, 2001, terrorist attacks. His father was a close confidante of the legendary bandleader Tito Puente and music was king during his childhood, but he was drawn to photography from the time he got his first Minolta camera.[61] A self-described non-athlete who lacked the gift of gab, Conzo focused on photography after picking it up from his stepfather. He took photography classes through junior high, high school, and three semesters at New York's School of Visual Arts.[62] As a kid, his parents allowed him to build a darkroom in the downstairs bathroom, where he would spend hours smoking marijuana and listening to cassettes.

For the kids in the neighborhood, Conzo's unique skills stood out. "It became a love and passion of mine," Conzo said. "It set me apart from the kids in the neighborhood pretty much. It was cool because I could run upstairs and develop a roll of film and show them a contact sheet of their photo, or an 8 x 10. I even became *popular* so to speak. People became popular because they were a star high school basketball player, baseball player, or from writing graffiti, b-boying, breakdancing, so many different things, and my lane was photography."[63]

Conzo photographed just about everything in the Bronx, but when he first discovered hip hop music, it sent him on a trajectory toward making his eventual mark on the culture. He first saw Charlie Chase play at the North Bronx's T-Connection club. Conzo was awestruck that Chase was able to play the music he heard at home, including James Brown and the Jackson 5, but in a new way. "I was just like,

'Oh shit.' That's what I wanted. It was something different."[64] Soon, he would become Cold Crush's photographer, and his photographs would be among the first to appear on hip hop flyers.[65]

Conzo's positive attitude about the neighborhood is shared by many of hip hop's major early figures. The setting he captured in his photos was actually a phenomenal petri dish for a new art form to spring up because the focus needed to be placed on what *could* be done rather than what was impossible. Hip hop, like the world it was created in, relied on craftiness and working with what was around you. Even the music itself is made of upcycled scraps of other songs. While there might not have been much wealth around, money was replaced by youthful exuberance and resourcefulness.

"Think of the aspect of jury-rigging a fucking light pole. The word that comes to mind is DIY," said Sule Holder, a hip hop archivist at the Rock & Roll Hall of Fame discussing a method DJs used to get power to their systems for park jams. "Hip hop was a DIY art at first. It's like punk in that way, looking back to London and the Sex Pistols and all that. No one else was going to do it for you, you had to steal equipment and steal fucking electricity to have a party."[66]

Grand Wizzard Theodore began practicing that skill at a young age. Like Paradise Gray, he was adept at rewiring the inside of a light pole to power his equipment at whatever park jam or block party he was performing at.[67] The young Theodore's DJ skills actually gained him quite a bit of clout in the neighborhood. He first performed publicly at eleven years old and traveled with the L Brothers as an equal, not a little helper or assistant. Even the local gang members and stick-up kids took note of his skills. He was so celebrated around the Bronx, he never had to worry about getting mugged.

"The older generation, the kids that were eighteen, nineteen years old, that were able to come to the parties—when they see me in the street they recognize me and know who I am," Theodore said. "If I was to go to a different neighborhood and you've got the stick-up kids and the drug dealers and all of these people on the corner, they look at me like, 'He's OK, let him pass, that's the DJ.' I might be going to see a girl and walking through the hallway and maybe there are the drug dealers or a bunch of people using drugs or a bunch of mean people just standing around bothering everybody, but when I come they're like, 'That's the DJ, let him through let him through, make way, that's the DJ,' that's one of the reasons why I never got jumped or anything like that."[68]

For Theodore, it also helped that his brother, DJ Mean Gene, was the "neighborhood bully." Even though he was a similar size to Theodore, he carried a reputation that he was not to be messed with.[69]

Grandmaster Caz's childhood was defined by "art and basketball," the latter of which he played every day growing up. The lanky and lean Caz said basketball was his first love. "If I didn't do hip hop, I'd probably have tried to play ball or something," he said.[70]

"By the time high school came around, I was into the music. The music became my main focus so I was never on organized basketball teams. That took up too much time. Too much commitment. My commitment was basically hip hop. I was a street ball player."[71]

Even though the neighborhoods in the Bronx where hip hop first developed might have *looked* desolate and troubled to outsiders, to many of the young people who grew up there, they represented a happy and nurturing home. It so happens that those young people would be the most significant figures in the next wave of hip hop's expansion. Theodore and Dot-A-Rock, among others, have cited their parents as being among their biggest supporters. Paradise Gray spoke the same way about elders like Disco King Mario, who provided a positive example and good advice to the young people in the neighborhood.

* * *

While the Bronx gets most of the attention when looking back at New York poverty, just across the river in Harlem, people were struggling as well despite the myriad of positive works of art and culture being produced in the neighborhood. The 1970s was one of the worst decades in Harlem's history. A 1991 *New York Times* article stated that Harlem lost many residents beginning in 1970, leaving behind an impoverished area as the city turned its attention to programs in the Bronx and other boroughs. The same article stated that, as of 1991, nearly two-thirds of neighborhood residents made less than $10,000 per year.[72]

Photographs of Harlem taken in 1970 by Jack Garofalo for *Paris Match* magazine show urban scenes that could've been easily mistaken for the Bronx. In one image, a steel trash can spits fire high into the air as a young girl rides her bicycle past it, looking back as if mesmerized by the flames.[73] Another shows a family of six belonging to local butcher "Billy" playing in one room of their two-room apartment, with two boys riding Big Wheel tricycles around the living room.[74] There were also shots of beautiful women sporting reddish-orange afros and men dressed in traditional African garb or impeccable double-breasted suits.[75] The neighborhood is famed for its glory days in the Roaring Twenties, its role in the 1960s civil rights movement, and its reputation as a general hub for groundbreaking Black thought and culture. According to Paradise Gray, 1970s Harlem wasn't defined by its impoverishment like the Bronx because it grew notorious for other reasons.

"The stories are being told, but they're being overshadowed by the street element," he said. "*American Gangster*. When you have Nicky Barnes, and you have Frank Lucas, and you have Pee Wee Kirkland, and Bumpy Johnson. When you have those guys, that's hard to fucking top. That's the story of Harlem. All of those Vietnam veterans were returning with opioid addictions. Harlem was the epicenter of the epidemic of those drugs."[76]

"Harlem is just like any other place in the sense that every city has its own hood, but if you have the All-Star Game in that city, they're gonna make sure you don't see it," said Lamar Hill, who went by the stage name L.A. Sunshine as a part of Harlem's Treacherous Three. "The Apollo Theater was four blocks away from where I lived, and everybody that gathered at the Apollo wouldn't gather four blocks away. There was dilapidation and drug infestation and things of that nature. It's just a matter of what side of the street you're on."[77]

It should be noted that drugs were a major issue throughout New York during this time period, and the popularity of different drugs ebbed and flowed. The specific Harlem figures who became famous then may have led to an association between the neighborhood and drug issues, but throughout the 1970s and '80s, New York as a whole was gripped by this problem.

The front page of the *New York Times* on July 16, 1982, touched on the drastic measures the city was taking to deal with its drug crisis. The piece, entitled "City Seeks to Dislodge Drug Trade by Demolishing Tenement Havens," discussed how the Lower East Side of Manhattan had become a premier marketplace for heroin and cocaine.[78] City-owned tenement buildings had been turned into, as the article put it, "fortresses" by enterprising drug dealers, about twenty to thirty of whom controlled the massive industry. The city's solution was simply to tear the buildings down, giving the dealers nowhere to operate.[79]

While that approach may seem drastic, some buildings allegedly grossed $20,000 per day. The buildings' physical structure was essential to the trade: the article described sophisticated drug dealers working like "bank tellers." They accepted users' money through a crack in a brick wall before sliding the drugs out, so the two individuals never saw each other.[80]

"It is the No. 1 growth industry on the Lower East Side," claimed Andrew J. Stein, the Manhattan Borough president at the time.[81] A five-year-old girl was able to capture the desperation of the issue more succinctly. "See, over there," she told the reporter. "That's the place where they stick bad needles in you."[82]

While the *Times* was interested in this massive Manhattan industry, drugs like powdered cocaine were mainly being sold in large quantities to out-of-towners. With a price well over $120 per gram in 1982,[83] powder was an exclusive drug for the wealthy, and it became associated with the glamor of disco parties and clubs like Studio 54. In 1982, the Fantastic Five even referenced "Always sniffin' blow" as part of a braggadocious rap in their Christmas routine, set to the tune of "Jingle Bells."[84] For many local New Yorkers, though, heroin was a cheaper option, and one that overran Harlem in the '70s and '80s.

The development of crack cocaine in the early 1980s was especially impactful on the lower-income neighborhoods where hip hop was flourishing. Crack originated when a glut of powder on the market emanating from hotbeds like the Bahamas caused the price of cocaine to drop by more than 80 percent. The solution many of the major cocaine dealers came up with was to cook the pure cocaine into a substance that could be sold in much smaller quantities at the street level and smoked, rather than snorted.[85] "Crack" gained its name from the crackling sound it made when it was smoked. It wasn't considered a party drug, but rather an addictive lifestyle changer. Crack cocaine didn't start gaining national publicity until around 1985, but it had been in American cities well before that. In a 2000 interview with PBS's *Frontline*, a crack dealer and addict from the Bronx who identified as "Paul" said he first became addicted to the drug in 1983.[86]

"[Crack] caught on a lot. And that began like in 1983, 1982, around there," Paul said. "But like everybody knows, that [cocaine] been around forever, but back then it was a high-class drug. Only people like movie stars and sports, they used stuff like that. But when it got past that state and into the street, people was like, wow, overwhelmed."[87]

New York's drug issues spilled into the hip hop scene; Caz, Theodore, and many other early figures in the genre described drug dealers and users as being common sights in the neighborhood. Gang violence, poverty, and many other problems plagued the environment, but they were initially issues happening *alongside* hip hop, rather than being interwoven into the music. The music and culture were a form of escapism that allowed partiers to throw away their cares, at least for the night. In fact, Joe Conzo spoke of how park jams and block parties unified different neighborhoods. Hip hop "just brought the neighborhood and other neighborhoods together. You'd meet different people. You'd meet girls. You'd meet guys. You'd see b-boys, b-girls, graffiti artists. You'd want to see who was on the mic, who was saying what, who was DJing. The Bronx was very territorial at the time so it wasn't advisable to go on your own to different parts. You'd go with a group. And nine times out of ten it was just bonding with other people from other parts and even other boroughs."[88]

The Cold Crush Brothers at the Hoe Ave
Boys Club, 1981. Photo by Joe Conzo Jr.

Chapter 4

—

Hip Hop's Great Poet

Young Curtis Brown, even as a second grader, stood out among his peers at the now closed Sts. Philip & James School on East 213th Street. Brown's teacher noticed that while the class was supposed to be practicing their print letters, he was already copying the model cursive letters displayed above the chalkboard—a task the teacher hadn't even gone over yet.

"I started with the script," Grandmaster Caz said. "They was like, 'Yo, we're not doing that yet,' and I was like, 'I'm sorry, I'm past that shit already, this is how I write now.' From an early age, my pen game was dope."[1]

Always a fan of art—especially graffiti, although he never sprayed trains or buildings[2]—Caz used his steady hand and excellent penmanship to fill thousands of notebook pages with lyrics. Many of his journals remain legendary items in the history of hip hop: the equivalent of the Federalist Papers or the Betsy Ross flag. Caz's words flow across the page with minimal cross outs or edits.[3] They look like the stream of consciousness of a true artist adept at his craft. Caz elevated hip hop by moving past the classic braggadocious rhymes or call-and-response party routines into storytelling with a full narrative structure, all presented over a beat and impeccably cleaned. His rhymes read like beautiful poetry at a time when poetry and rap weren't compared regularly, and the routines he developed for Cold Crush remain relevant and iconic. Caz seems to have a rhyme for everything.

"When I start a thought, I pretty much go all the way through it. I used to, so my books reflect that," Caz said. "Nowadays I'm a little more 'Write a little, come back to it.'"[4]

As one of Caz's famous lines states, he's "six-one and a half, no good at math, saying rhymes to myself while I'm taking a bath."[5] The tall, sturdy Caz would bounce between an afro, long braids, or shorter hair. He often wore a serious, furrowed expression on stage, but he would smile as well below his black moustache, especially when the crowd vibed with him. Nearly every one of Joe Conzo's Cold Crush performance photos shows Caz drenched in sweat. A fan of James Brown and Mick Jagger, Caz was, like them, a hard-working man (although the fact that the parks and other venues didn't have air conditioning definitely contributed to his perspiration).

"Back then," Caz said, "I was totally into the craft, and I wasn't just writing for myself, I was writing for the group as well so *we* had to be dope. I know *I'm* dope but *we* got to be dope. So that's another set of consciousness that you have to put in it."[6]

Joe Conzo said that the words flowed freely out of Caz onto the paper while he worked. He pointed out how Caz is referred to by many as the G.O.A.T., or Greatest of All Time. While the "G" commonly stands for "Greatest," Caz, in keeping with his brand, morphed it into "Grandest."[7]

"Even today, you put a mic in Caz's hand and he can hold his own against the top guys today, the best of them," Conzo said. "That goes to him being immersed in what was going on at the time, using simplistic bars. They were simplistic enough that so many people across the board—no matter what color you are, race, creed—can identify with [them], and that just gives Caz the edge."[8]

Prior to joining Cold Crush, Casanova Fly was already deep into the process of transforming into Grandmaster Caz. In hip hop, Grandmaster was a title reserved for those who have achieved a certain level of greatness. There are grandmasters in chess, golf, and martial arts, but not every kid that puts on his first white belt is a grandmaster. It takes years of hard work and sacrifice. It was in that spirit that DJs such as Grandmaster Flowers (who predated what is generally considered the "hip hop era") and Grandmaster Flash took on that title. Technically, Caz's stage name is simply "Caz," much like Grandmaster Flash's name is just "Flash," without the important distinction placed in front of it. Not everyone in hip hop took the title of Grandmaster, though; "Almighty," "Notorious," "Funky," "Master," and many other titles have been bestowed upon emcees, DJs, and even dancers.

Caz didn't give himself his title; rather, he was "anointed" by a crowd one night when he was DJing alongside his buddy Disco Wiz. As Caz continued cutting two records back and forth faster and faster, Disco Wiz hyped up the crowd more and more. Caz struggled to keep up the pace. As Disco Wiz kept saying "FASTER," he started to rhyme it with "GRANDMASTER," and the crowd went along.[9] From then on, Caz went by "Grandmaster Casanova Fly." Show flyers reveal that he shortened his name to "Caz" around mid-1980.[10]

* * *

While he did the vast majority of the writing and then assigned parts to his fellow emcees, Caz had a real gift for taking elements or ideas from the other Cold Crush brothers and building routines off of them. Whether he drew from a tune from a pop song or just a few rhymes, Caz's creative juices flowed steadily and he would immediately put his penmanship to work (although he does admit that some of his lyrics are, in fact, rewrites).

"Let's say Kay Gee had a catchy tune or something, like 'Young ladies isn't he the sure shot?/Fly guys isn't he the sure shot?' I'll run with that. I'll take that. All right, boom. You come in, you put in a four [bars] or an eight, this and this and that, and then come back to 'Young ladies . . . ' and then we make a whole routine out of that shit. Basically this is what I've got but that's all I need."[11]

For someone who initially had to teach his high school buddies how to rhyme, Caz now had so much talent to work with on stage, but the gift of emceeing and working the crowd didn't always translate to writing, especially at the level Caz was achieving. For some of his best work, Caz would take extended solos, most famously in his "Yvette" verse, which was a part of many of the best Cold Crush shows and appeared in the movie *Wild Style*. Here, he tells a complete story with a plot, gets the crowd to go wild at the end of certain lines, and comments on something relatable to a large audience (getting caught in the bedroom with a lady by her parents). On one tape, he even asked the Harlem World audience, "Have y'all homeboys ever been caught in the bed with a girl by her parents?" Cheers erupted from the crowd. That could've been because the verse was famous at that point, because that situation had happened to many people, or both. Caz claimed that it really happened to him and bragged that he was still alive to tell the tale before launching into one of the hottest two-minute verses ever rapped:

> It was a long time ago but I'll never forget
> I got caught in the bed with a girl named Yvette.[12]

Caz's gritty, high-pitched voice wailed over the crowd on the tape of that verse, but there were audible laughs on lines about getting a call from Yvette and being at her door before she hung up the phone. The story followed a narrative arc with a clear beginning, middle, and end. It was funny, and was delivered with an urgency that resembled heavier rock music. In an era still dominated by "throw your hands in the air" routines, Caz was making his audience laugh and think. He would always receive a thunderous ovation when he finished.[13] Not every emcee could tell such an elaborate story in a rhyme, and Caz's love of language and writing set him apart in those early days.

"Everybody's not a writer, and when I write, I would have to write for my guys [as] if I was them, and they were me," Caz said. "It's coming from my pen, I'm writing it, but I'm writing it for JDL if JDL could write like Caz. I'm writing it for Kay Gee if Kay Gee could write like Caz, but everything has to reflect them."[14]

What's even more impressive about that verse is that, unlike most of Caz's rhymes, it's completely fictitious and all built from imagination. There was no girl named Yvette, and he definitely wasn't caught in a bed with her by anyone. Instead, he generated the narrative concept from scratch and built the story up from there, writing everything in beautiful penmanship in his notebook.[15]

"You create a narrative," he said. "You get to the point where you're like, 'Well, what's this going to be about?' It's going to be about getting caught in bed with a girl. And then you create a narrative and you start somewhere and you build towards that point, that climax. Everything I was saying in that thing, like 'It was me, the L, the A, and the All,' it was me and my crew. There's things I really used to do. I used to hang outside my school, with my boombox, with people around and shit, so I built the scenario out of that, that led to me getting caught with this girl."[16]

* * *

When Cold Crush came together in its final form, it was comprised of the "old" members—DJs Charlie Chase and Tony Tone, and emcee Easy A.D.—and the "new" additions, Grandmaster Caz, JDL, and Almighty Kay Gee. There was some difficulty in the beginning in terms of the two factions getting on the same page.[17] Each member had so much performance experience themselves (or with some members of the outfit), but that didn't necessarily help the whole combination gel together. After a few small parties where Caz and JDL performed some Notorious Two routines and Easy A.D. brought out some old Cold Crush staples separately, everyone agreed that there needed to be more cohesion. The group members didn't really hit their stride and blend in perfect harmony until they dedicated a year to practicing together.

"We had no synergy together, until they was like, 'You know what? Fuck that, y'all, we're tired of getting upstaged by these n*ggas every time they get on,'" Caz said. "'They've got routines' . . . so *they* went and started to put together a few routines and stuff like that and then I saw that and I was like, 'OK, now, that's what I'm talking about!' That made me say, 'OK, now, let's work, *now* let's work.'"[18]

When Cold Crush reemerged from their year of clandestine practice and performed as a group once again, Caz was nervous about showing the new and improved crew off to an expectant crowd because the crew had essentially gone underground. They hadn't shared their routines with anyone for a full year. It took a bit of time for the six to find their flow, but the routines kept improving as the Cold Crush played more and more shows. Some of those brand-new routines would become classics (such as the original "We Will Rock You" routine, which is one of the earliest examples of a hip hop group successfully using a rock melody). After a few shows, they were spandex-tight and could practically finish each other's sentences.[19] The name "Cold Crush" started moving higher and higher up flyers advertising big shows, and the four emcees became a can't-miss product in the Bronx and beyond. Nightclubs had also grown to be the prominent showcase spots for hip hop, usurping community centers and recreation rooms, so the parties grew bigger—the expectations from the crowds higher. As time went on, Cold Crush developed too many routines to fit into one show, so some very good numbers needed to be cut from the performance.

"We got a lot more routines than what you hear in a cassette tape or one of our shows," Caz said. "That's because over time I see what works, what's a little corny, and then we take the strongest stuff and that's what we roll with. If we're gonna battle, we're not gonna do the 'It's You, Babe' motherfuckin' routine. We're not doing that."[20]

Cold Crush was always up for trying new things at block parties to see how they'd play, but if the crowd was dead for a few performances in a row, the routine would be scrapped. Caz blames himself for most of those flops. He had a tendency to write something with himself in mind, and it was sometimes difficult for the rest of the Cold Crush to understand what he was going for. Some of the routines looked like "Chinese arithmetic" to the other three emcees.[21]

Some routines "didn't come out the way I wrote it or the way the flow is supposed to go. It's like, 'No, we're supposed to sound together,'" Caz said. "If somebody can't do something they'll be like, 'No, fuck it, I'm gonna do it this way.' All right then, you fucked up the whole concept of the thing now because you're the one person who wants to do it another way, so a lot of that shit had to fall by the wayside."[22]

An interesting aspect of Caz's story is that his writing was so far ahead of its time that it didn't always earn him the adulation it would in later years. Early hip hop culture was centered around loving groups, not individual performers. In modern rap culture, the opposite holds true, as emcees are the emphasis and DJs and producers have faded into more background roles.

"He was the best rapper, but I didn't look at him as the leader at the time," said Paradise Gray. "I appreciated his style and everything but as a DJ, for me it was Charlie Chase and Tony Tone, and the Cold Crush. It was a whole soup, not just the ingredients. Caz was the writer that wrote most of the stuff. In hindsight, Caz was that dude, but we didn't look at it that way back then."[23]

"We were a fucking well-oiled machine dude," Charlie Chase said. "Think about this for a second: 2021, to this day Cold Crush never had a hit record, but our shows were so fucking bananas that they've stood the test of time to this day and people are still talking about it and still revere us as one of the greatest groups ever. At this point I call ourselves the Rolling Stones of hip hop."[24]

* * *

As Cold Crush was rounding into their top form, the Fantastic Five were gaining followers by the day. A driving force behind their ascent into the top tier of New York crews was the sheer talent of Grand Wizzard Theodore. By the time he, Rubie Dee, Master Rob, and Kevie Kev broke up the L Brothers, Theodore had drawn the stark and somewhat egotistical conclusion that he was put on this earth to play records and make beats. He was a natural in the truest sense of the word.

While he never wrote rhymes[25] (except for two lines he had to say during the basketball court scene in *Wild Style*), Theodore has continually fought tooth and nail to be the best DJ in the world, a title many say he still deserves in his sixth decade at the turntables. He still teaches hundreds of students each year at New York's Scratch Academy, but his style is so unique and challenging, many exquisite DJs never come close to his level. Grandmaster Flash is known for his speed and efficiency in switching between records and breakbeats, but Theodore is peerless when it comes to being smooth and playing the equipment like an instrument.

"Finesse. Theodore had finesse," Paradise Gray remembered. "Theodore had hand-eye coordination and dexterity. Theodore was more precise than a lot of the DJs that came before him. With Flash it was all about how fast he was like 'BAM BAM BAM BA-BAM BA-BAM';

Theodore was 'WICKY WICKY WICK WICK WICKY WICK WICK.' Theodore was what we called 'nice.'"[26]

What exactly made Theodore an elite DJ? He definitely was lucky to grow up in the same house as some of the first hip hop DJs ever, but that doesn't explain what made the young kid so special. Even Theodore himself has trouble explaining it. He simply considers himself blessed with a special talent. At five foot seven, he didn't have lavish basketball or football dreams. He just had the right DJ equipment in his house, found that he had a knack for music, and ran with it.

"It's a lot of practice; God has given me this gift," Theodore said. "If I had to do an hour set at midnight I'd probably get there at 11:00 so I can look around at the crowd and see what the crowd is about. I can look at the crowd and tell exactly what kind of music they want to hear just by looking at them. I know music and I know BPMs [beats per minute] and stuff like that, which is very important. Transitions are very important, too."[27]

When Theodore plays at the turntables, he looks more like a classical musician stroking the keys of a piano than a rebel playing "dangerous" music. He moves smoothly over the mixer and never puts his hands in the wrong spot. He even has good footwork, slide-stepping from one table to another while keeping one arm pressed to his left headphone so he can hear his beats over his emcees' microphones or the roar of the crowd. He is a technician who moves flawlessly (and throws great parties) to this day, but Theodore claims that the most important attribute a great DJ can have is a sound mind: "One of the things I teach at the Scratch Academy, when I'm with those kids, I tell them DJing isn't just physical, it's also mental. Number one, when I'm playing behind emcees, my transitions have to be very smooth, because I have emcees rapping over me cutting up breaks. Number two, I have people dancing on the floor. You might come to the party with your girlfriend, you have some drinks, y'all want to dance, you want to party. I need to make sure my transitions from one song to the next is a smooth transition so I can keep everybody on the floor dancing."[28]

Theodore's emcees in the Fantastic Five knew they had one of the best in the world behind them. That made for hassle-free performances, because they could concern themselves with their rhymes and harmonies. Kevie Kev partly attributes that to the group's incessant practice schedule. During the group's heyday, Kev said, they could whip up something heavy and show-ready in about six minutes.[29]

Master Rob, Kev's older brother, claimed that in the 1970s and '80s, you'd be hard-pressed to find another DJ approaching Theodore's level. The knowledge that they had a world-class DJ behind them led to Fantastic's steadily rising confidence.

"Absolutely, we trusted Theodore," Rob said. "When we were on the microphone, we trusted Theodore on them turntables to know exactly what to do. Theodore was so good at what he did that he knew our rhymes and he'd know when to bring the music down for the awesome part and he'd bring the music back up. We had 100 percent chemistry with Theodore."[30]

Still a teenager, Theodore was a sought-after teacher for aspiring DJs in the know. For Baby D, whose boyfriend laughed her out of the room when she told him she wanted to be the next Grandmaster Flash, Theodore's tutelage was invaluable. She had messed around on a friend's turntables a couple of times and discovered some natural ability before she met the Grand Wizzard at a party where they both performed DJ sets. After the party, future Mercedes Ladies member DJ RD Smiley introduced her to Theodore; the two hit it off right away.[31] Theodore helped Baby D catapult to the next level: "When I met the Grand Wizzard Theodore, that was a whole new ballgame for me. He taught me how to scratch, and it was a wrap."[32]

The Fantastic Five were hitting their stride with one mission in mind: to be the best crew in New York. According to Kevie Kev, they improved with every practice, becoming tighter and tighter, more and more polished. It was very cheap to get into hip hop shows at the time, but the crew insisted on giving a show that made people feel like they'd paid twenty-five dollars for a ticket. Part of this attitude comes from Kev's father, Robert "Bobby Starr" Ferguson, who was in a singing group, the Intruders, that regularly performed in world-famous venues like the Apollo.[33] The brothers were actually in a group of their own, the Deflections, as teenagers before joining Fantastic.[34]

Because of this passion for performing, Fantastic was one of the top draws in the city. Theodore's name appeared at the top of flyers advertising parties at clubs like the T-Connection (which became Fantastic's unofficial home),[35] the Celebrity Club, and the Ecstasy Garage, as well as high schools, roller rinks, and community centers. Word of the polished, good-looking, synchronized emcees playing in front of Theodore spread fast, and the group became household names among the hip hop faithful. At Fantastic's first performance since dropping the L Brothers moniker in 1979, they participated in an emcee contest at the Webster Center on 183rd Street, where they came in first place.[36] It wouldn't be their last competition.

"We were like ghetto superstars, more or less," Master Rob said. "The Bronx, Manhattan, Queens, Staten Island, Brooklyn, all five boroughs, we conquered it."[37] According to Kevie Kev, he started to realize the group was onto something when girls tried to buy his and Rob's phone numbers off of their friends.[38]

"More unity," Kevie Kev said of the key to Fantastic's success. "We just started staying tighter, getting closer, and more lyrics. We'd practice anywhere, we'd go across the street and bang on the top of a car just to get the sound and the rhyme. We didn't care who saw nothing. We had to figure everything out for ourselves."[39]

According to Kev and Rob, the group took their work so seriously that if a member was late to rehearsal, they'd be docked their pay at the next party.[40] Coming from a competitive basketball background, the brothers knew what needed to be done to reach the top spot, and they were determined to help lead Fantastic there.

* * *

Besides Grand Wizzard Theodore, Dot-A-Rock was the most integral member of the Fantastic Five. Although he passed away in 2015, Dot-A-Rock's old group members still speak of his greatness. It's clear that he wrote many of Fantastic's best-known and most energetic routines.

"Dot-A-Rock wrote pretty much 75 percent of all the routines we had," Theodore said. "Dot was good with the pen. All he had to do was write the rhymes and I'd fit the music to the rhymes. I'm sitting there and I'm watching him write all these rhymes, I can figure out 'Oh, this break would go good with that routine, and this would go good with that.' And everything pretty much worked out. Sometimes Dot-A-Rock would say he wrote a rap to a particular record and I was like, 'OK cool, let's play the record and you do the rap to the record,' and we'd see how it sounds. It was really cool to be creative with them."[41]

Darryl Mason adopted the name Dot-A-Rock from an old candy called Mason Dots. He was a part of Mighty Force and Cold Crush before finally landing in Fantastic, where he claimed he could make one hundred dollars per performance.[42] While he identified Kevie Kev as the "captain" of the crew, Dot-A-Rock touted himself as the storyteller and writer.[43]

Dot-A-Rock and company would use their constant practice and drive for improvement to continually expand their catalog of routines, as well as bring in some other elements never seen in hip hop, such as humping the floor mid-song.[44] Theodore had a trick where he would place himself in handcuffs and continue DJing for the crowd.[45] Along with showmanship, it was also important for Kevie Kev to have a good "knuckle game," as Dot-A-Rock put it, because the crew didn't have a manager and were often in some pretty dangerous situations. According to him, the crew brought guns right up to the stage with them in case something should happen.[46] Kevie Kev and Master Rob recalled how, during a Fantastic party at the T-Connection, a gunshot went off in the crowd, sending the club-goers scattering in every direction. To the crew's astonishment, the man who was shot was left lying on the floor, bleeding badly.[47] After the police and paramedics came in and took the wounded man away, someone wiped up the blood from the dance floor.

"They said, 'OK, y'all can put the music back on,'" Kevie Kev said. "We did, it was our party. They said 'Do it' and we didn't know the n*gga that got shot or the n*gga that shot him."[48]

Despite occasional tragic moments, the vast majority of Fantastic shows went off without a hitch, giving the crowd their money's worth and then some. Rob, Whip, Rubie, Kev, and Theodore all stressed the importance of having people leave happy. Despite not having a record out, they knew how to work a crowd, whether it was with a choreographed dance routine, a crowd-participation bit, or a quick ad-lib. Whatever it took to get people on the floor and ready to party, that's what they did. If Caz was a lyrical genius, all of the members of Fantastic were party geniuses. One of their finest routines was rooted in Theodore's masterful cutting of 7th Wonder's "Daisy Lady." The beat oozes energy and drew partiers to the dance floor like a magnet. Add in flirtatious and fun lyrics and an ultra-fast tempo from the five emcees, and you have a masterpiece. The routine also incorporated a tease from Wild Cherry's "Play That Funky Music," along with, of course, many nods to the ladies:

Let's turn it out
Let's turn it out
We'll make you scream, we'll make you shout
We're the five emcees that'll turn it out
We don't go to Tampa, we don't go to Atlanta
We got more chicks than Colonel Sanders

. . . .

We don't got no Rolls Royce, don't have a diamond ring
We bet you fifty dollars we can make your body sing.[49]

Whipper Whip and Dot-A-Rock did a remarkable job incorporating their Salt & Pepper routines into the full group performance instead of doing a separate show within a show like when they first joined up with Fantastic. But the real star was Theodore, who moved from "Daisy Lady" to Rick James's "Fire It Up" and finally Gaz's "Sing Sing," which generated audible screams from the audience. Theodore knew exactly what to play to get each audience partying, but the most complicated routines—at times, the emcees would alternate individual words—required a synchronicity that only the tightest crews had mastered. The Five's top writer loved the theatrics of great performances like that.

"We were stage people, you know," Dot-A-Rock said. "We liked to perform and to put on shows, and you know, just go to different parties, and party, and drink, and have fun, and be with the girls."[50]

It's lucky that the Fantastic Five liked to be with girls, because throughout their careers the girls certainly liked being with them. The screams of their lady fans bounced off the walls at many of their strongholds throughout the Bronx. However, the best hip hop venue in the world was across the bridge in Manhattan, and both Fantastic and Cold Crush would make it their fiefdom: Harlem World.

The Fantastic Romantic Five practicing

Chapter 5

Harlem World

Decades before hip hop was created, jazz, with its energetic solos and danceability, quickly became a favorite in the speakeasies peppering Prohibition-era Harlem. During the 1920s and early 1930s, Harlem was home to many integrated clubs where Black and white partiers could guzzle down illegal booze side by side. There, Black bands played for integrated audiences, widening jazz's fan base.

Lois Long, a white nightlife reporter for the *New Yorker* during Prohibition who wrote under the pen name "Lipstick," penned sparkling reviews of the exciting music she was being exposed to for the first time. When describing the revue at the still segregated Cotton Club, which was performed at 12:30 a.m. and again at 2:00, she chastised the audience.

"I cannot believe that most of them realize that they are listening to probably the greatest jazz orchestra of all time, which is Duke Ellington's—I'll fight anyone who says different," she wrote. "It is barbaric and rhythmic and brassy as all jazz ought to be. It is mellow as music ought to be. There are throbbing moans and wah-wahs and outbreaks on the part of the brasses, and it is all too much for an impressionable girl."[1]

Music was only one sliver of the incredible work coming out of Harlem in that era—Long's use of the word "barbaric" was meant to be complimentary. Major advancements were made in poetry, playwriting, and visual art as well. For more than a century, if there were beautiful pieces of Black artwork, scorching and delightful Black music, or riveting Black thoughts, they were likely influenced in some way by what was going on in Harlem. Of course, hip hop falls into all three categories, so it's no surprise that there would be no hip hop without Harlem.

While its importance has carried over well into the twenty-first century, this northern Manhattan neighborhood enjoyed a particularly fruitful era in the 1920s and '30s, when progress and culture were moving at breakneck speeds. Deservedly so, this flourishing of African American art and scholarship is referred to as the Harlem Renaissance. The Renaissance was partly fueled by the Great Migration—the mass exodus of African Americans leaving the South looking for better work and safety in northern cities while also leaving behind violent racism and the legacy of enslavement. As so many African Americans moved north, they brought elements of southern Black culture to a northern audience.

Harlem became so synonymous with Black excellence that when Abe Saperstein formed a barnstorming basketball team in the Midwest, he named them the Harlem Globetrotters, even though they didn't play anywhere near New York until decades later.

"The name Harlem was so big at that time . . . so even though it started in Chicago, the name [O]riginal Harlem Globetrotters had much— a, a better ring to it because Harlem was so dominant at the time," said former NBA player Jerry Harkness. "It was the Renaissance and Duke Ellington, all these guys, again, you would see, and with Sarah Vaughan. And it, it was just the epitome of Black talent. And, and not only we're talking about music talent but also poetry and painting and things. It was all of that all there together. So if you wanna have athletics, you wanted to be a part of that Renaissance."[2]

What made the Harlem Renaissance even more remarkable is that it took place during a time when white supremacy was on the rise nationwide. *Birth of a Nation*, the cinematic racism-palooza supplied by the Ku Klux Klan, debuted in 1915. The KKK saw its membership top out at between three and eight million during the 1920s.[3] Despite that, Black culture continued to push forward toward more crossover success. Trumpeter Louis Armstrong, singers Billie Holiday and Marian Anderson, Duke Ellington, and boxer Joe Louis were all massive stars.

Home to Marcus Garvey, W. E. B. Du Bois, and many other influential figures, Harlem was also a political hotbed as much as it was a cultural one. In 1926, Du Bois even wrote an article in *The Crisis* entitled "Criteria of Negro Art" in which he famously stated that "all art is propaganda" in the fight for Blacks to gain equality.[4]

Even decades after the Renaissance's heyday, Harlem held a great influence. The Harlem Writers Guild wasn't founded until 1950, when a few writers met above 125th Street and Lenox Avenue. Soon, the group began attracting talents like the legendary Maya Angelou. Angelou followed the advice of Guild founder John Oliver Killens, whom she met after one of her performances as a singer. The Guild members were serious in their critiques of one another. During their monthly meetings, the discussions were spirited, and led to the creation of some of the best literature in American history.

"You would have to say, before you left one month, you'd choose a person for the next meeting and she or he would read from the current work," Angelou said. "And they were ruthless. They had no 'ruth.' But they helped me to become a better writer."[5]

* * *

Harlem's reputation as the Black creative capitol of America was firmly established by the work of elite creators and thinkers, but for many residents, it was still an underprivileged neighborhood.

"You had a room, you had a bed," said 1930s resident Gloria Toote. "If you were lucky, you had a sink that you could wash up in. But the toilet and the tub were seldom on your floor, but you certainly had to share it. That is that heyday in Harlem. They talk about the days of the Renaissance. It was a renaissance of the mind, a renaissance of the spirit and the soul. But not of the housing accommodations. Very, very poor. Nothing unusual for a mother, a father, and a child, maybe up to three children in one room."[6]

A common thread throughout oral histories from residents growing up during the 1920s and '30s involves families putting on their Sunday best for church, which served as a cornerstone for the community. "On Sunday, everyone went to church," Toote said. Just about everyone. And well dressed, clean. Oh, Sunday was a great day. It's like Easter. We looked good on Sunday and the churches were packed. But because we made so little in income, that was all we could afford."

Donnie McLurkin, who would go on to become a successful gospel artist, said he'd heard stories about congregants distancing themselves from his maternal grandmother because she was pregnant at age thirteen in 1933.[7] "[My mother] grew up walking up to the Cotton Club or walking up to the restaurants and seeing Duke Ellington or Mahalia Jackson or Cab Calloway or Ella Fitzgerald or Billie Holiday sitting at the front window so that all the kids could come by and see them and throw coins out to them," he said.[8]

For a long time, the dichotomy in Harlem of seeing famous people walking down the street while locals lived in poverty was commonplace. Decades after the neighborhood's Prohibition heyday, it was clear among residents and outsiders that drugs were an issue in Harlem. Around the early 1960s—while great work was still being produced in the neighborhood—there was a noticeable increase in people showing the symptoms of hard drug use, most notably heroin. A *New York Times* article from July 17, 1965, chronicled how local mothers crowded to take in the NYPD's mobile display on narcotics addiction, which sat in a thirty-foot-long bus.[9] The photo accompanying the article shows a crowd of young boys standing with Police Commissioner Vincent L. Broderick, eyes glued to the display.[10]

The article went on to say that mothers in Harlem were worried about their young children becoming addicted to drugs, and that the police were distributing a pamphlet that gave the women a series of symptoms to look for. Some supposed symptoms are ridiculous ("has he stopped being interested in sports or the opposite sex?"), but others, such as emaciation, paleness, blood spots, and glassy or dilated eyes were genuine signs of drug use, and parents took them seriously.[11]

Public health nurse Nancy Bowlin recalled when drugs first intruded into the neighborhood's daily life, coming in on the heels of free cigarettes that were given at nightlife venues such as the Renaissance Ballroom. "Drugs came in. They came in free first," she said. "And then once you got hooked, you had to pay for it, you see. And then I saw the downfall of Harlem as a public health nurse . . . you used to see men and women stand up like statues because they were frozen because of what the drugs did. I would go in for a newborn inspection of a baby, and the mother would be out because of the drugs."[12]

The drug issues in Harlem were widely chronicled by the mainstream media in the 1960s much in the same way "urban decay" became a theme in news coverage of the Bronx a decade later. A 1965 *New York Times* review of writer Claude Brown's autobiography, *Manchild in the Promised Land*, carried the headline "Coming of Age in Harlem: A Report From Hell"[13] and relayed stories from Brown's upbringing, which involved multiple trips to reform schools and a school for the "emotionally disturbed." The review claimed that most of Brown's peers didn't make it out of the neighborhood and fell into lives of drug addiction, incarceration, or prostitution.[14] A particularly poignant story from the book that the review harped on involves an older Brown returning to the neighborhood. There, he runs into a girl he knew when he was younger. She asks to borrow money and offers to "turn a trick or two." While he refuses her offer, he docs give her some money, only to watch her buy heroin with it.[15]

The whole article is meant to tug at the heartstrings and present a dystopian vision of how the once-mighty Harlem had fallen into the depths of despair. While it's true that many individuals in the neighborhood had fallen on hard times, it remained a vibrant and compelling place, despite how some outsiders may have perceived it.

One of Harlem's most famous thinkers ever was active around that same time as Brown, and he had a different view regarding the suffering that had befallen many in the neighborhood. Malcolm X spoke to a Harlem crowd packed into a street. Young Minister Louis Farrakhan sat on stage behind him, watching intently.

"The white man brings [drugs] in," X said. "The white man brings it to Harlem. The white man makes you a drug addict, the white man then puts you in jail when he catches you using drugs. Who is it that controls the prostitution in Harlem? It's the white man. Who controls the sale of whiskey and wine? It's the white man. . . . Who gives you the deck of cards and the dice you use to gamble with? It's the white man. And after he sells them to you, he'll catch you with them and put you in jail for using them."[16]

Malcolm Little was born in 1925 to a father, Earl Little, who was a dedicated follower of Marcus Garvey and the president of the Omaha, Nebraska, branch of Garvey's Universal Negro Improvement Association. The family moved around often when Malcolm was young. In Lansing, Michigan, where the family moved in 1928, their house was burnt down by what Malcolm later claimed was a white supremacist group. In 1931, Earl Little was killed, according to his son, by the Ku

Klux Klan. Malcolm's mother Louise was committed to the Kalamazoo State Mental Hospital in 1938, where she would remain until 1964. After that, Malcolm and his siblings moved between different foster homes until he decided to settle with his half-sister in Boston's Roxbury neighborhood.[17]

In 1946, Malcolm was sentenced to eight to ten years in prison for larceny, breaking and entering, and firearms-related charges. He served six years in various institutions in Massachusetts. While in prison, he discovered the teachings of Elijah Muhammad, the leader of the Nation of Islam.[18] When he was released in 1952, Malcolm grew closer with Muhammad and replaced his "slave name" Little with "X" to represent the traditional African family name he was deprived of. In 1954, after moving up in the ranks of the Nation of Islam, X was appointed chief minister of Harlem's Temple Number Seven and became the Nation's spokesman and leading public face.[19] Using that platform, X became a major figure in the national civil rights movement, taking a more aggressive approach than the Reverend Dr. Martin Luther King Jr., who offered a message of nonviolence. X famously adopted slogans like "by any means necessary" or "the ballot or the bullet" and built a relationship with heavyweight world champion Cassius Clay, who would convert to Islam and adopt the name Muhammad Ali in 1964.[20]

Malcolm X and his contemporaries ushered in a new era of cultural significance for Harlem. While he wasn't an artist, his messages about Black nationalism and self-reliance were fresh, and he energized a young base of Black men and women who were disillusioned with tactics such as pursuing court cases or holding sit-ins or marches to get the point of the movement across. Until then, the civil rights movement had been largely based in the South. Harlem, which represented progress in thought, seemed like a natural fit for extending the movement's message to the North. Given the neighborhood's history, it's unsurprising that it would be at the forefront of the growing hip hop genre. In fact, Malcolm X's manipulation of language and his remarkably poignant and catchy turns of phrase would influence early hip hop lyrics.

*   *   *

For lifelong Harlem resident and hip hop aficionado Troy Smith, the Bronx and Harlem weren't much different from one another during his 1970s childhood. Both neighborhoods had their advantages and drawbacks. He'd often party in the Bronx and walk back to Harlem.

"If some girl was calling my house, my mom would always say, 'He ain't here but I can take a message,'" said Smith. "The girl would say to me, 'You ain't never home, you're always outside, what's outside?' 'The world is outside! Girl is you crazy?!' It was a lot of fun. We didn't feel like the Bronx was burning because parts of Harlem was burning."[21]

Given its close proximity to the Bronx and progressive history with Black art and culture, Harlem was a great environment for hip hop to grow. Giants in the genre like Spoonie Gee, the Treacherous Three, and Kurtis Blow grew up there.[22] Almost as soon as park jams were becoming go-to summer events in the Bronx, they were popping up in Harlem, and Harlem emcees were just as strong as their Bronx counterparts. In fact, Dr. Fred Collins and some of the earliest hip hop fans knew that Harlem was the place to go in the early 1970s for late night parties indoors, which the Bronx couldn't offer because of the limitations of its venues.[23]

"The Bronx was the absolute Mecca but there were a couple of spots in Harlem where they had after-hour[s] parties and whatnot," he said. "I always look back at that time and say 'How is it that kids fourteen, fifteen, sixteen years old can go to parties at establishments that serve alcohol and stay until 4:00 in the morning and that's OK?' Nobody asked questions, nobody's checking IDs, nobody's doing nothing. There were a couple spots like that in Harlem that we might go to occasionally and you'd see a couple of cats from the Bronx there. We didn't have *that* in the Bronx. Later on that started happening but early on, you'd go to Harlem for that."[24]

The venues that Harlem boasted for performers to take their acts were far ahead of the Bronx because of the area's long and storied history with the performing arts. Later on, the Bronx would boast clubs like the Black Door and T-Connection, but so many shows took place at high schools, community centers, and parks. In contrast, Harlem had legendary rooms that held plenty of cachet among members of the Black community and signified a degree of success for any group that touched the stage. That included the site of X's 1965 assassination.

"We partied in the room where Malcolm X was killed, the Audubon Ballroom," Paradise Gray said. "And you could still see the bullet holes in the wall and in the podium. Flash would rock in there, too."[25] A flyer from the pre-Fantastic era advertised the L Brothers with DJ Theodore as part of a "disco history" night at the Audubon taking place in two separate rooms, complete with directions for how to reach the ballroom by train from the Bronx.[26]

Of course, the Audubon was just one of many venues that housed some of hip hop's greatest parties. For the hip hop genre, the most legendary club in the area was Harlem World.

Originally the brainchild of Jack Taylor, who went by "Fat Jack" or "Fat Man," Harlem World opened in 1978.[27] Taylor was known around the neighborhood as a significant figure, partly due to his work dealing drugs. The new venue occupied a massive space on 116th Street and Lenox Avenue (which has since been renamed after Malcolm X) that would later become a Conway department store. It was located on a desolate corner and surrounded by mostly abandoned buildings, with a mosque across the street.[28] The one thing the location did have going for it, however, was its proximity to a subway station just feet away. On July 8, 1978, *Billboard Magazine* reported that the 30,000 square foot club was built almost entirely by Harlem residents. It also listed the owner as Earl Washington. He is believed to be a clean front man whose name didn't carry the heat behind it that Fat Jack's did.[29] The article stated that Washington's business history "has come in diverse areas such as lumber and real estate" and that he had successfully brought 100 jobs to that corner.[30]

Washington pointed out Harlem's history as a primary selling point for the new club. "No matter where you go in the world, people have heard of Harlem," he said. "But up to now there has not been any place for visitors to come."[31]

He argued that people from out of town didn't typically venture to the Apollo and that those who frequented the Cotton Club didn't explore the neighborhood; a new venue that attracted outsiders seemed essential. Washington told the magazine he expected Harlem World to be a direct competitor to Studio 54 and the other major Manhattan discos. There is no mention of hip hop in the article.[32]

A few months after opening, a young graduate of nearby Martin Luther King Jr. High School named Charles Leake (stage name Charlie Rock) entered what was then exclusively a disco venue for the first time. Rock claimed that "all of the pimps and players" were among the club's regulars in its early days, which can be partly attributed to the club's owner, Taylor, being such a major street figure at the time.[33]

"A couple other guys from around Harlem also got down and invested some money with [Fat Man]," said Rock. "Some were politicians and some were street cats. The thing about 'Fat Man' was that he was a master of people. He could talk a dude into bathing himself in gasoline and stepping into a fire, and tell them that they were freezing cold, and they'd believe him. He really couldn't read or write, but he knew how to handle people."[34]

The giant club—it held upwards of one thousand people—operated in the red for most of its life,[35] and Fat Man had to devise some unique solutions to zoning issues that stemmed from the venue's proximity to religious institutions and schools. The *Billboard* article mentioned resistance from community leaders who "feel that a disco is the wrong kind of business for that corner."[36] The official name of the venue was the Harlem World Cultural and Entertainment Complex, which allowed the club to remain in the neighborhood because of its suggestion that the space would be used for community-building and charitable activities.[37] Fat Man also skirted the law by using his political connections to procure temporary liquor licenses every weekend the club was hosting parties, rather than applying for a full license.[38]

Despite the club's cash flow problems, Fat Man and his employees, including Charlie Rock and the other young men who would become the Harlem World Crew, continually expanded the club to make it even bigger and better. The unpaid crew added a third floor with a VIP lounge, as well as an underground portion of the club that hosted separate parties with DJs during the bigger shows. The crowd there would be alerted when the major acts were up on stage. The lower level also doubled as a space for drug dealers to operate and for dice games to be played. The crew was actually allowed to live at the club, staying in converted office space that they had transformed into what were essentially dorm rooms. You had to be a superstar (or lady friend of one of the residents) to gain access to that part of the venue.[39]

"Nobody really knew this except our closest friends, the girls we slayed, and a couple of the top hip hop boys like maybe Caz, Love Bug Starski, Jekyll & Hyde, and Busy Bee," Rock said. "There was only a handful that knew. And they knew only because they were like the underground superstars, so we allowed them behind the scenes on the third floor where others didn't get to go. We did not care if they knew because Harlem World was the place to be at that time. Some of them actually thought it was kind of cool, because come Friday night when we turn on the lights, our living room was a whole night club. There were a lot of virginities lost on those nights upstairs at Harlem World."[40]

Like many other major hip hop venues, Harlem World started out as a strictly disco club and eventually expanded its offerings to include hip hop as the genre gained more traction in New York. Even after hip hop began making its way into the club, it was heavily influenced by the disco culture at the time. A March 13, 1980, flyer advertising a "A SHOOT OUT" at the club included a mandate for proper dress.[41] According to Charlie Chase, it was tough to get in the door, even for a star DJ like himself (he liked to go on his off nights). You had to carry yourself a certain way and dress to impress to get into Harlem World. But once you made it into the building, you were treated to a space unlike any other in New York. A flyer for the 1980 All State Wide Christmas Rappers Convention claims the club is "The Worlds [sic] Largest Disco Ever Created/45,000 Sq. Ft. Of Computerized Lights & Sound."[42] While that may be hyperbolic, it certainly was an impressive venue. Charlie Rock claimed the club was among New York's first to have a lit dance floor, as well as other features that reflected the hallmarks of a disco paradise.

"The club was very plush," he said. "Chandeliers. Thick, wall-to-wall, gold shag carpeting. Mirrored walls, and a one-of-a-kind, one-hundred-foot lightning bolt–shaped bar. It was definitely plush, and that was [Fat Man's] vision. To create a super gigantic plush environment for people to come and enjoy themselves."[43]

Other parts of Harlem World were spacious as well. The dressing room upstairs was expansive and gave crews all the space they needed to add any finishing touches to their shows.[44] From there, performers would descend a staircase onto the stage, which was decorated with a gigantic backdrop depicting a space scene that may have been inspired by Afrika Bambaataa's 1980 hit "Planet Rock." Joe Conzo's photographs show the Cold Crush performing in front of murals of scantily-dressed disco dancers frolicking on clouds with a UFO—light beams and all—hovering above them.[45] For some R&B and soul shows, tables and chairs were brought in,[46] but for hip hop the club was standing room only. A club of Harlem World's size only naturally would have a gigantic disco ball hanging overhead.[47]

Charlie Chase was struck by how spacious the former department store was, and also by the sheer sensory overload of all the lights on the dance floor. His descriptions of the people, however, really shed light on the club's atmosphere.

"People were always dancing," Chase said. "They would party hard. They would party real hard. Remember, it was still the club mentality as in a disco kind of thing but now it's different because we're doing a hip hop sort of thing with it. The girls are still looking *fly*, wearing dresses, not like today. They're wearing beautiful skirts, they're looking real cute. Some dudes are still showing up dressed up. Some dudes are showing up in nice expensive jeans and sneakers. A lot of us used to iron our jeans. Puerto Ricans took it to another level. People had their A game on."[48]

For the Harlem World residents, these sort of parties were a near nightly occurrence. DJ Hollywood, for example, played the club every Wednesday night for "Wild, Wild Wednesday," and Eddie Cheeba "owned" "Terrible Tuesdays" (which were, by all accounts, not). There were even kids' discos on Sunday afternoon.[49] As time went on and the club continued to grow, it strayed away from disco to more of a hip hop focus.

"It was actually a disco club and disco and soul and R&B groups performed there like Eartha Kitt, Dramatics, Delfonics, there's actually flyers for it," said Harlem-born Troy L. Smith, one of the country's foremost collectors of hip hop cassette tapes and memorabilia. "I guess what happened is similar to the T-Connection with Richie T: there was more money in hip hop than disco. Come to think of it, I'm surprised, because now when I talk to these disco DJs, they were charging ten, twelve dollars for their parties and hip hop was only charging three, four, five dollars. I don't understand why a promoter didn't lock down T-Connection. The thing is that Harlem World got more popular as time went by with hip hop shows as opposed to disco hip hop shows."[50]

Charlie Chase has memories of rock concerts in the club as well. He said the room was one of his favorite places to play with Cold Crush, so much so that he and the rest of the guys would spend time there whenever they could, even when they weren't performing. The group's front man has repeatedly described Harlem World as his venue of choice.

"Harlem World around 1980 was the showplace for hip hop groups back in the day," Caz said. "Towards the end of that era, towards the next generation of hip hop, the groups got smaller. And you didn't see like four-man groups anymore, five-man groups anymore. So Harlem World was that one venue where groups could really get their shine on. For us, it was home, we made Harlem World our home. So for me, Harlem World is one of the tightest venues and the place we did the most damage back in the day."[51]

It may not have had the staying power of the Apollo, but for a while Harlem World boasted a similar level of significance for the hip hop community. For the Treacherous Three's L.A. Sunshine (known as Lamar Hill offstage), a lifelong Harlem resident, the venue meant more to him than just a place to party—it was a way to escape daily life for a bit.

"From my family experience," Sunshine said, "I wanted to stay out of my house as much as possible. I knew I had a safe haven because that was a secondary home after laying all the groundwork that we did. I could go into Harlem World anytime I wanted to. I could walk in and totally be comfortable. I knew the owners and they knew me so I think having that perspective made it easier for me. It was always a second home to me and all of the fans at the time. The partygoers become part of the family. Part of that hip hop family. I go in and I hang with the same girls I saw last weekend. Remember that for the most part if you were from Harlem and were part of the hip hop circle, you were revered. You were held in high regard. Being a pseudo-celebrity in Harlem World paid dividends because it gave me the freedom to be able to be comfortable, to not have to be a celebrity, if that made sense."[52]

In addition to Hill, in the early 1980s, the Three also boasted one of the finest emcees in the world. Mohandas Dewese (Kool Moe Dee onstage) was a creative writer and thinker on par with Grandmaster Caz. Moe Dee was fearless, rapping faster than any other emcee at the time and deploying a sharp tongue with brilliant wordplay. The first word L.A. Sunshine used to describe Moe Dee was "cerebral." His thoughtful rhymes at the helm of the Treacherous Three established the group at the forefront of Harlem's hip hop scene. The Three made Harlem World their second home.

*　*　*

Harlem World lucked out with its timing: its opening coincided with the first commercially successful hip hop record, *Rapper's Delight*. With a massive assist from Caz's lyrics, the album's hit single peaked at No. 36 on the Billboard Hot 100 in November 1979 while reaching No. 4 in Holland and No. 1 in West Germany and Canada.[53] While the Sugarhill Gang weren't significant figures in the hip hop scene that had been growing organically in Harlem and the Bronx, the success of that song unquestionably brought hip hop to a larger national audience.

Bill Adler, for example, who was working at the *Boston Herald* as a pop music critic at the time, became enamored with the sound, even more so when he moved to New York in the summer of 1980.[54] Working as a freelancer, Adler wrote some of the first lengthy profiles of hip hop artists (and some of the first positive stories about the movement) in mainstream publications. He would eventually become the publicist for the iconic Def Jam record label that propelled groups like Run-D.M.C. and the Beastie Boys to international superstardom.[55]

"I would say pretty generally, the period before rap ended up on record was pretty much an underground period," Adler said. "As I think about it, it had nothing to do with business. It was folk art. Very few people I think outside of New York City had any idea what was going on under the umbrella of what would be called 'hip hop' until those first records came out in '79."[56]

Of course, Adler was referring to "Rapper's Delight," which exploded onto the scene in the fall of 1979 and swept across the country. Despite its incredible popularity—or perhaps because of it—the song was controversial among the hip hop community. Many young fans lauded the chance to finally hear rapping on the radio and to be able to buy a wax record with a party preserved for eternity. The need to go out and experience hip hop live—which for many younger fans was a barrier to hearing the genre—went away practically overnight. However, the older hip hop innovators who cut their teeth in the parks and clubs well before the Sugarhill Gang was formed were split.

"Once the records came out, more people in the projects got

involved. People were singing 'Rapper's Delight' in the classroom. It was OK; I didn't see the big idea of it. I knew the words because I heard it so much. In actuality, today, you can say it's a beautiful song because it's catchy. It's easy to decipher the words. Caz wrote the record," said Troy Smith with a laugh.[57]

"The masses loved it but hip hop could've taken it or left it," Caz said. "The average person liked 'Rapper's Delight' because the average person wasn't [a] rapper."[58]

The record took some time to gain its status as a classic, but it's proven to have remarkable staying power. In 1999, twenty years after its release, the Sugarhill Gang opened for *NSYNC—then the biggest group on earth.[59]

"You can't take away the history, you can't take away the reality that it was Sugarhill that had the idea to take this phase of music, this kind of music, and take a chance and put it out on wax and record it," said Joey Robinson Jr., who was a driving force in putting the group together. "[We never] said we invented rap. You know? But we did start rap. We did start rap, and made it mainstream for the world to know what rap is."[60]

Seemingly overnight, hip hop had the attention of record executives. Corporate America embarked on a frenzied search for the next rap stars and the hottest aspects of hip hop culture in general. Graffiti-style lettering graced advertisements for Fortune 500 companies. In classic "This is something cool—let's wreck it" fashion, novelty records designed to capitalize on the hype appeared on shopping mall shelves, such as comedian Rodney Dangerfield's *Rappin' Rodney*, which told the story of an old, white, crotchety attorney rapping from the courtroom. It was the exact opposite of the spirit of hip hop: corporate, old-fashioned, safe, and stale. The cultural appropriation was palpable and obnoxious. "Repper de Klept" by Amsterdam's Danny Boy sounds like a nervous five-year-old on the mic (even though it has a kickass sample). Shawn Brown's "Rappin' Duke" is the answer to the question, "What would a bad John Wayne impersonator who just found out what rap was on the way to the recording studio sound like?" Brown slowly stumbled through "artistic" verses like the following:

> Sure I rustled some cattle and tended the sheep
> But my main concern was rapping to the beat
> I don't bother nobody I'm a real nice guy
> Kinda laid back like a dead fly.[61]

The rise of these spoof records was a result of the people in power in the music industry dismissing hip hop as a passing fad—an interesting novelty that the kids were into that would surely be swept away by the next trend. Obviously, that didn't happen, but the shift from a club scene to radio did prove to be long-lasting. Unfortunately, the music on the radio only somewhat approached the real experience of attending a party and hearing a routine from Fantastic, or Cold Crush, or the Furious Five.

To be fair, there were some great things to come out of that rush to buy up and commercialize hip hop, most notably, the emergence of Kurtis Blow (born Kurtis Walker). A Harlem native, Blow was the first rapper to sign with a major label—Mercury—which he did shortly after "Rapper's Delight" hit the charts. A student at New York's City College at the time of his debut,[62] Blow was a more experienced emcee than anyone in the Sugarhill Gang. He came up through the same park jams and clubs that groups like Fantastic and Cold Crush did. Blow's first single was a party record in the same spirit as "Rapper's Delight," but his was tied to a certain time of year. "Christmas Rappin'" remains legendary in the annals of hip hop history. Not only did it sell well but it was rooted in the hip hop culture that had been developing since

1973. Even so, it was far more commercial in content and sound than what groups from the streets were aiming for.

"My interest was perked up by 'Rapper's Delight' in the fall of '79 and then at Christmas of '79, here comes Kurtis Blow with 'Christmas Rappin',' and that was a remarkable record just because there were so few rap records at the time," said Bill Adler. "What was so astonishing was that in Boston there was exactly one Black station, WILD, and they played that Christmas record into April just because it was such a phenomenon."[63] Blow's next single, "The Breaks," was a massive seller and competed on the Billboard R&B charts alongside songs by the likes of Michael Jackson, Diana Ross, and Rod Stewart.[64]

"'The Breaks' was a rap song, and it kind of exemplified the disco era, you know, the DJ Hollywood era, and shit like that, he was more of an emcee's emcee," Caz said.[65]

*   *   *

Before Adler could get his ink in print, hip hop was flatly disrespected by the national media on the heels of "Rapper's Delight" and "Christmas Rappin'." Even in New York City, the mainstream papers thought it was a waste of time that had captured the imagination of punk teenagers and graffiti writers, not a musical revolution. A *New York Daily News* article from February 1981 described rapping as "improvisatory a capella jive-talkin' of the first street corner harmonizers."[66] A 1981 *New York Times* article described rapping as "street corner jive talk"[67] while actually attempting to compliment Sylvia Robinson's Sugarhill Records on its ability to compete with the giant established labels of the era. Another 1981 *Times* article talks about a school social worker trying to reach students by "rapping."[68] What the *Times* didn't report on at all, however, was the presence of groups like Cold Crush and Fantastic that were racking up the reputation and gravitas that all of the early hip hop groups dreamed of at the time.

"Who read the *New York Times* or watched network TV?" noted Paradise Gray. "We had a whole different culture and lifestyle. We were superstars in our ghettos. We wasn't going to see Michael Jackson walking down the street, but we loved Michael Jackson. And he loved us, because he was incorporating our culture into what he was doing in pop music and extending our reach."[69]

The idea that a rap group could even think about a record deal wasn't a part of the hip hop mentality until the Sugarhill Gang came out of nowhere with their hit. In fact, Grandmaster Caz gave Big Bank Hank his rhymes willingly, thinking that a record deal was an absurdity, especially for unknown emcees, according to Ben Ortiz from Cornell University's Hip Hop Collection.[70] The goal was to be famous in the streets, to be "ghetto superstars," as Master Rob put it.[71]

"'Rapper's Delight' made the Sugarhill Gang radio famous, but not street famous," Joe Conzo said. "They're friends of mine and they have a place in history, but the story is that they were all each doing a different thing at the time and were put together to do this recording, and kudos to them. But they didn't have the same street cred as the Cold Crush Brothers did, or as Caz did. That at the time was what you aimed for, so after 'Rapper's Delight' came, you were aiming for record deals. If you had a dope routine and a dope DJ and a dope record collection and a dope sound system and you went from borough to borough or neighborhood to neighborhood, that's how you developed your street cred."[72]

Even the term "hip hop" itself was used in a derogatory way for a while. It was seen as a lesser art than disco, so those who breakdanced or rapped were seen as "hip hoppers" who couldn't hack it in disco. Of course, there was also a racial component to the criticism—the idea that this new artform created by African Americans and Puerto Ricans was unsophisticated—and an ageist component as well because the pioneers of hip hop were so young. What was difficult for the young hip hop artists to accept was the lack of support they were receiving from some of the top artists in other genres.

"We didn't care about the mainstream," said Paradise Gray. "We made music for us. What we did care about was our own elders and ancestors in R&B and jazz and how they disrespected us. Larry Blackmon from Cameo, Wynton and Branford Marsalis, and James Mtume were some of the most vocal elders that we worshiped who were anti-hip hop. James Mtume wound up coming around because Biggie (Smalls) sampled his song for 'Juicy' and he made more money off that one sample than he did for his entire career. What held us up and made us good was that James Brown, Bootsie Barnes, and George Prince embraced us."[73]

The origin of the term "hip hop" itself is disputed, but according to Paradise Gray, one of the most popular stories is that Keef Cowboy, who would later join Grandmaster Flash and the Furious Five, first used it in part of a performance for a party for his cousin, who was leaving for the army. The late Cowboy used "hip" and "hop" to mimic the sound of a drill sergeant ordering recruits to march in a certain cadence.

> Hip, hop
> Hip hip, hop . . . [74]

And the crowd dug it. Soon, the two words would be manipulated by many DJs and emcees into standard basic routines like the "hip, hop, the hippie, the hippie / to the hip hip hop" that started off "Rapper's Delight."

In fact, years later, it was Keef Cowboy's group, the Furious Five, who set the stage for one of hip hop's greatest nights by actually stepping away from the city. A major changing of the guard in hip hop took place when, in the wake of the success of "Rapper's Delight," Sugarhill

Records made a rush to sign other hip hop acts as quickly as possible. The Furious Five was one of their first additions. In 1980, the group consisted of Flash, Mel, Cowboy, Raheim, Scorpio, and Kidd Creole. That year, they released their debut single, "Freedom," on the Sugarhill Records label. In the song, the word "party" is used seven times in the first forty words. The single sold 50,000 copies.[75] Like most of the earliest hip hop singles, the song is essentially just a recorded, shortened version of a party that Flash fans might experience in a club with call-and-response lines and a recorded crowd in the background (it also featured some very impressive kazoo work). Despite its rudimentary subject matter, the song was the best attempt yet at capturing the energy and authenticity of a live show. The success of "Freedom" led to more singles, like "It's Nasty" and "Flash to the Beat."[76]

Soon, the Furious Five made an unprecedented move for a hip hop group and booked a tour that would take them, along with the recently signed Funky 4 + 1, out of New York for an extended period of time. According to the Funky 4's Sha-Rock, the worldwide tour covered fifty-two cities.[77] It made sense that Flash's crew would bring their music elsewhere as they were unquestionably the most popular hip hop group not named the Sugarhill Gang, who were already on their own tour, opening for major acts such as Parliament Funkadelic.[78] Flash's crew was ahead of the pack thanks in large part to their savant of a DJ, coupled with the leadership of Grandmaster Melle Mel—who is regarded still as one of the great lyricists of all time, alongside Caz. The group had been the biggest draw at clubs like the Black Door, Audubon Ballroom, Celebrity Club, T-Connection, and Harlem World for years, so a tour seemed like the next logical step. They could build upon the success of "Rapper's Delight" and "Christmas Rappin'" by bringing their show around the globe.

What was indisputably the top hip hop crew in the city departed New York in the summer of 1981, leaving a gaping hole at the top of the hip hop scene. There was only enough room at the top of the flyer for one act. The vacuum needed to be filled, and there were two crews jockeying for the top spot. A clash of giants was on the horizon.

The Cold Crush Brothers performing at
Manhattan's Club Negril, 1981. *From
left*, Charlie Chase (in background),
Almighty Kay Gee, Easy A.D., JDL, and
Grandmaster Caz. Photo by Joe Conzo Jr.

Chapter 6

Collision Course

Joe Conzo's photos reveal just how quickly the Cold Crush Brothers were growing in presence and stature among New York's hip hop scene. In his photos from 1980 and 1981, the crowds were clearly multiplying, and more and more venues were hosting the four emcees.[1] Conzo's camera documented shows at the Skatin' Palace, the famous downtown Club Negril, Disco Fever, and during Norman Thomas High School's annual senior class boat ride on the Hudson River. The crew also saw its spot on flyers changing. According to Charlie Chase, they started to find themselves at the top of the billing for whatever lineup they'd be a part of.

"It was at the point," Chase said, "when we were headlining everything. It didn't matter what it was. Every now and then we'd throw an audible [a last-second change depending on circumstances] in there. It got to a point where the promoters would have so many acts that by the time we got on, the crowd was dead. We could have thrown a kitchen sink at them and it wouldn't matter. So the audible was that we'd tell the promoter we didn't want to go last. We knew then that the crowd was ripe and ready for us and wouldn't be dead when we got on. They'd give us whatever the fuck we wanted."[2]

As they claimed top billing and expanded their territory, the Cold Crush began to realize the potential Chase and Caz had dreamt of when they joined forces. According to Chase, people were recognizing the six group members in the streets and telling them about the last show they saw them at, whether it was in Harlem, Brooklyn, or around the corner in the Bronx.[3] The Cold Crush might not have achieved the international fame of the Sugarhill Gang, but they were celebrities in their own world. Grandmaster Caz referred to their style as more "blue collar."[4] They might have looked the part, but musically they might as well have had doctorates. The Cold Crush gained a ravenous following through their use of familiar songs and melodies with new, updated lyrics (such as their "We Will Rock You" routine). Easy A.D. and Almighty Kay Gee originated the idea of using the well-known melodies, and Caz ran with it.

"The thing that's so catchy about [those routines] is that these were songs we used to call 'white boy songs' when we were growing up and a lot of people didn't listen to them on purpose, but you heard that shit," Caz said. "We listened to one radio station back in the day. Radio wasn't segregated that way where this was the Black station, you gotta turn the dial and here's the white station. Nah, we heard Motown, we heard Al Green, Simon & Garfunkel, Three Dog Night, I know the lyrics to all that shit."[5]

As Caz and the other emcees started generating more complex routines, Charlie Chase grew excited about what he heard. "I'm hearing these routines and now my mentality is that I'm not a DJ anymore," Chase said. "Now I'm a band, I was an arranger. What I mean by that is when we'd get to certain parts of songs and if I heard something where I knew we'd need a drumroll, I'd scratch it in. If I heard a really smart line coming up, I'd put a downbeat on it and stop the music so [an emcee] could put a punctuation on it."[6]

* * *

Meanwhile, the Fantastic Five had exploded in popularity and found themselves, along with Cold Crush, atop flyers in all five boroughs. If the Fantastic was performing, they were headlining. They were a machine, performing their classic routines and constantly adding to their repertoire. They were a great-looking group of young men as well, so much so that their style became part of their identity. Kevie Kev and Master Rob knew that being at the forefront of street fashion would help the group achieve their goal of being looked up to by the guys and fantasized about by the girls. "No one else cared about how they looked, that's why we dressed so well every night," Kevie Kev said.[7]

In reality, hip hop did have a specific look to it—albeit one which shifted throughout the years. When LL Cool J and Run-D.M.C. reigned over hip hop in the mid-1980s, track suits and Kangol hats were all the rage, along with thick-rimmed Cazal glasses, which were informally known as gazelles. In the late 1970s and early 1980s, the early era of rap, there were two schools of thought about hip hop fashion. Groups like Grandmaster Flash and the Furious Five went for the flashiest appearance possible: leather gloves, leather suits, cutoff shirts, cowboy hats. Anything they could do to appear more like the glam rockers such as Queen and Aerosmith who dominated the charts at the time. Cold Crush opted for T-shirts or sweatshirts and jeans in an effort to appear more relatable to an audience who dressed the same way. Caz loved to perform in a flat-topped baseball cap. For the most part, Cold Crush wore street wear—everyday clothes not selected for a particular performance. Fantastic employed this idea but took it up a notch, wearing the nicest clothes they could get their hands on, even when they weren't performing. For Kev and Rob, this was an important part of projecting Fantastic's suave image to the entire community.

"We said if they spent three dollars to get into the concert, four dollars, we were going to give them *more* than their money's worth," Master Rob said. "We gave them a great show. We were gonna dance, we were gonna rap, we were gonna harmonize, we were gonna get crowd participation, we wanted people to feel like they were a part of us, and we did it well, too."[8]

With the Fantastic Five rolling along and taking over the scene with their impeccable live show, the members brainstormed ways to take their act to the next level and secure the undisputed top spot in New York once and for all. Success would come, they thought, from making an even bigger fashion statement. According to Theodore, they took inspiration from a tuxedo shop near Prince Whipper Whip's house, on the Grand Concourse: "One day we decided to go in there and get fitted for our tuxedos and everything and we just started wearing tuxedos and just being uniform to try to bring a different feel and different look when we got onstage. When we're onstage and we're rhyming and stuff like that, we want you to be able to look at us uniformly. We loved all the groups, like the Stylistics, and Blue Magic, and Gladys Knight & the Pips. All these groups had the same outfit on, they were dancing, the Jackson 5 with the moves, we wanted to bring that to hip hop. By doing so, I think it made us more unique."[9]

Along with the change to matching tuxedos, Theodore and the group added a single word to their name that completely shifted the dynamic when they appeared at clubs. They became the Fantastic *Romantic* Five, a not-so-subtle nod to the young women who made up so much of their passionate fan base. According to Theodore, the group always had girls around—including the girlfriends of other emcees, which said emcees didn't appreciate. Luckily, no one really bothered his crew, partially because there were six members and partially because they surrounded themselves with so many friends.[10]

"We had the swag, man," Theodore said. "We knew how to treat the ladies. All of us were living at home with our mothers. We respected our mothers, and it showed. We had respect for ladies, period. The ladies loved to hang out with us because we were always doing something."[11]

Theodore and his crew were very visible around New York at fine restaurants like Tad's Steaks in Times Square and casual dining establishments like Tony Roma's. The crew especially got the celebrity treatment at a movie theater where some of their friends worked. According to Theodore, Fantastic and their lady friends would occupy the entire first row of the cinema, making plenty of noise and puffing a giant cloud of marijuana smoke, much to the chagrin of families with young children who thought they'd get a quiet afternoon out at the movies. Rather than kick them out, the crew's friends would bring them popcorn and drinks. "Everybody's like, 'These guys got the ushers bringing popcorn and drinks to them? Who are these guys?'" Theodore said.[12]

Kevie Kev and Master Rob said that many times, women offered to pay their friends for their phone numbers or followed them home from parties.[13] But the best story of the Fantastic Romantic Five's connection with their female fans involved the whole crew.

According to Grand Wizzard Theodore, the crew was playing at the Bronx club T-Connection—their unofficial home—one beautiful night. Normally they would've taken cabs to the show, but they had met at Dot-A-Rock's place at the Police Athletic League, which was right across from a bus stop. The driver was a Fantastic fan, recognized the crew, and offered to drop them off at the club. The six artists and their entourage boarded the bus and quickly noticed a woman and her boyfriend were having a fight. The man was getting physical, slapping and kicking his girlfriend. Even worse, her sister was sitting next to her and trying to stop him, but to no avail.

"We looked at each other like, 'Woah,'" Theodore said. "'We can't stand here and let him do that.'" Fantastic intervened; they got between the man and the woman, then asked the driver to open the door before unceremoniously forcing the abusive boyfriend off the bus. "We took the two girls with us to the T-Connection, and we just partied all night." Theodore said the crew bought drinks for the two young ladies and put them in a cab after their show, turning an awful night into an unforgettable one.[14]

* * *

Ladies loved the Cold Crush Brothers as well, but their fan base also consisted of all sorts of New Yorkers looking for more relatable lyrics that reflected their everyday lives. Caz's rhymes were always charismatic, even in a made-up story like the Yvette verse. That exact scenario might not have been based on his own experience, but it's a totally feasible situation that could've happened to anyone walking the streets of the South Bronx.

Another Cold Crush song, which contains a line about "Crazy Joe on the seven-o," set its sights on the scourge of the rebellious teenager: the local cop on the beat. "[Caz] was talking about a cop who used to hassle people in the neighborhood," said Joe Conzo. "It turned out to be a famous cop, one of the most decorated cops in New York City. Who had the ingenuity to write about Crazy Joe, the cop in the neighborhood, harassing the kids and shit?"[15]

It should be pointed out that in the early 1980s, radio hip hop music was mostly focused on partying, bragging, comedy, and more bragging. It hadn't transitioned into a place of real social consciousness like it would a few years later. However, Cold Crush helped leave their mark by appealing to the widest audience possible. They shared a mutual lifestyle with their fans, which they expressed both through their music and their stage personas. Quite frankly, people knew that they didn't put up with any shit. They weren't flirty on stage, and they rarely coordinated their outfits. Cold Crush's fans adored them, but not because they tried to gain their devotion by getting too flashy or adding innuendo to their routines. They were just *real*.

"Some of these motherfuckers would kill for us, literally," Charlie Chase said. "We had diehard fans, and they loved us. A lot of these fans were hardened motherfuckin' criminals and gangsters and murderers and all kinds of shit that we knew from the street, and these motherfuckers loved us. Like, 'Yo, y'all are *real*.' They related to us and vice versa, and we portrayed that in our music and the things that we said and the things Caz wrote. The way we presented it, man, they were like, 'Yo, hit me with a bucket of water, man, drench me in that shit.'"[16]

A great example of Cold Crush's "realness" came in the form of a premade rhyme Caz had written for anyone who dared to heckle the group while they were onstage. According to him, the rhyme was so famous among the hip hop community that very brave men in the crowd would heckle him intentionally just to hear it.

Troy Smith, a native New Yorker and respected collector who acquired more than three hundred hip hop tapes in the late 1970s and early 1980s, has a 1981 recording which captured Caz's lyrics. You can clearly hear someone shout "I'll give you a dime if you get off the stage" right after a singing routine ended. Caz asked the crew to point the heckler out. Then you can hear JDL tell Caz to "Go on him." And Caz did, for a minute or longer, completely a cappella, with the occasional ad-lib from the other three emcees.

Paid five or six dollars to get inside
No girl wants your ugly ass, so you sit and hide
Wait for an opportunity to scream out "Boo"
Then leave like a sucker when the jam is through.[17]

The bravado in the verse makes the tape Smith's favorite.[18] "Caz does a rhyme on the crowd and that joint was so hot that I had to listen to it twenty times, of course, to find out who had the gall to say something in the crowd that would make Caz snap on him like that," said Smith. "It all started with hecklers, that's why I call it the heckler rhyme. That's one of the reasons I dug Cold Crush so much. Because of Caz and JDL's sense of humor."[19]

Caz snapping on a member of the crowd was a much more deliberately obtuse and rebellious act than spitting the sort of rhymes the Fantastic Five were saying at the time. This confrontational verse captured the imagination of a different sort of fan who was looking for something more raw from their hip hop.

* * *

The Fantastic Romantic Five were hitting their all-time peak of popularity with Flash's crew out of town. They knew it, too, as they started to develop new routines for their show that played to their constantly growing crowds. Most famously, they added an iconic call-and-response portion to their routine that asked the crowd to yell back if they liked sex. Then they'd have the crowd repeat, "And more sex!" This popular chant was even a part of their Christmas routine one year (as was mentioned in chapter 3, to make it extra festive, they also rapped about "Always sniffin' blow").[20] They knew what would get the crowd going.

"Rest in peace, Dot-A-Rock, he had a rhyme about sex, and I think that kind of inspired us too," said Master Rob. "And who don't like sex?"[21]

Sex is the thing everybody needs,
sometime you do it slow sometime to speed.

To some people it have them on cloud nine,

to work up a sweat, to have a good time.

. . . .

It's nice to show each other's affection,

but it ain't no fun when you got protection.

That's one thing that's really crazy,

you had fun one day, now you got a baby.

A father with a son, look what you have done.

then you claimin' you ain't due and then you're on the run.[22]

The crass lyrics, which were well received by Fantastic's fan base, go on to disparage the LGBTQ community. Unfortunately, such homophobic verses were common in hip hop during the early 1980s, and resurfaced as a major social issue in the late 1990s with the rise of Eminem. The routine was a hit at Fantastic's parties.

* * *

Dot-A-Rock said that Fantastic was the first group to wear tuxedos and hump the floor: "Doin' all the wild stuff that people are doin' today, that's no problem," he claimed. "But when we did it back in the days it was a big thing." Those candid details were all in response to interviewer Bill Adler, who began an interview by saying, "Let people know what your names are, and, and uh you know who you're affiliated with, and we'll just start that way."[23]

Dot-A-Rock is clearly proud that Theodore and the five emcees made themselves into the genre's first sex symbols. To be fair, Fantastic wasn't *just* interested in sex at that time. They also wanted to project a stylish image to the community. Even when they weren't performing, they dressed impeccably in the newest jeans, the finest sneakers, and the most expensive hats. According to Kevie Kev, they often spent more money getting dressed than they would make at their parties.²⁴ Rap was their profession. They took pride in setting a positive example for everyone in the neighborhood.

"When I say the fellas loved us, I mean they loved us in the way they looked up to us," Master Rob said. "The guys hustling on the corners, the guys going to work, we were more or less like role models."²⁵

At the time, groups like the Fantastic Romantic Five and Cold Crush Brothers were completely reliant on being able to play to a live audience to maintain their popularity. They didn't have hit records out, got no play on the radio, and gave no TV performances (although the Funky 4 + 1 famously appeared on *Saturday Night Live* in February 1981). Even without any commercial success, the groups were blowing the minds of those who were lucky enough to pack into their shows. There was nothing to sing along to, but crowds still erupted during Fantastic's dancing or after one of Caz's amazing lines. Even though the Sugarhill Gang found amazing success using Caz's lyrics—success that should've belonged to him—it didn't deter the Cold Crush. They kept soldiering on, trying to establish themselves as the premier group in New York, as did Fantastic.

Amazingly, the live hip hop scene stayed intact even after Sugarhill's success. It was almost a completely separate entity from what was being played on the radio, and fans still sought out the underground groups. That is a direct result of the recording industry being such a far cry from what the founders of hip hop had envisioned for the genre, but hip hop historian Kevin Kosanovich believes that had the original groups been able to predict the success Sugarhill would have, they would've plunged into the recording world headfirst. "I'm always sort of hesitant to say 'keeping it authentic' or 'selling out,'" Kosanovich said, "because I think Cold Crush or these early groups absolutely would've jumped at a chance for [a record deal]. But also, at the same time, they're young enough and they're passionate enough about what they're doing. They're local celebrities, tristate celebrities in terms of parties. For a lot of this first generation, the idea of recording something that just felt to be a very live party phenomenon, it hadn't clicked in yet. We're performing at these different clubs and these places with these shows and that's what hip hop is. It's not going into the studio."[26]

*   *   *

With Grandmaster Flash and the Furious Five and the Funky 4 + 1 away, it was clear that the two top crews in New York were the Cold Crush Brothers and the Fantastic Romantic Five. Although each had their own unique style and their own fan base, there was only one spot available at the very top of the scene. Naturally, competition ensued, especially given how intertwined the groups were. In the Bronx and Harlem, the spark of competition existed within the community for decades before hip hop even existed, according to Paradise Gray.

"Battling was an important part of Black culture," he said. "African Americans come from a long tradition of warrior spirits and we always challenge each other. Rap was always competitive. Everything we do is competitive. We're competing with everyone else so we can get the attention. So we can get the money. So we can get the girls. We competed with everything. Before we rapped in competition, we sang in competition. We did the same ciphers, and we battled other singing groups in our community. We were little kids, seven, eight, nine years old, and we battled crooning before we battle rapped. We'd do the Stylistics, Blue Magic, Delfonics, Smokey Robinson and the Miracles, and we'd battle other crooners the same way we would with rap."[27]

As New York hip hop started to take hold at parties and parks in the 1970s, there would be dance battles between individual b-boys and, later on, crews. DJs would compete to see who could get more people on the floor and moving to the beat. However, it wasn't until the early 1980s that emcees started to seriously battle to see which crew was the best. In modern media, rap battles are portrayed as personal slugfests in which the goal is to insult or "diss" your opponent in the nastiest way possible. There is truth to that modern portrayal but in the early days of battling, the goal was simply to put on a better performance than your rival, to be judged by a crowd reaction. Whoever got the loudest screams when it came time to pick a winner walked away with the prize.

* * *

The seeds for a battle between Fantastic and Cold Crush were planted years before Flash's tour. The crews came up at around the same time, had the same number of members, and knew each other well from their grade school days. In fact, flyers advertising the L Brothers "vs" the Chase Crew date back to 1979,[28] but there's no evidence that those were formally judged battles with a winner and loser. These flyers were more designed to promote a show where the two crews put their best work on display. A rivalry between crews didn't mean everyone in the groups were mortal enemies out for blood. This was a far cry from the gang activity that infested the neighborhoods of the Bronx and Harlem. That being said, given the connections and history between the two crews, there was plenty of friendly competition to be had. For example, Caz and Theodore were very friendly and had a high level of mutual respect for one another.

"Theodore's never had a rivalry with nobody," Grandmaster Caz said. "He's one of the coolest dudes you'll ever want to meet. And we were friends as kids before we became who we are in hip hop, so we didn't have any animosity."[29]

Still, no matter how friendly Caz and Theodore were, or the fact that Caz regarded Whipper Whip and Dot-A-Rock as his "little brothers,"[30] tension ratcheted up between the two groups as spring turned to summer in 1981. Charlie Chase said that he was still cool with Dot-A-Rock and Whipper Whip during that period, but when Fantastic started running their mouths about how they were the best, Cold Crush needed to respond. "We really didn't have a lot of beef with anybody," Chase said. "But when you start climbing that ladder, people start having a little bit of resentment, a little bit of jealousy, a little bit of hate."[31]

Despite not having "beef" with anyone, Chase was quick to admit that there was a competitive rivalry between the two crews. As time went on, the trash talk escalated more and more. "The streets were like CNN for us," he said. "And girls will always be the trigger. They'd say, 'Those Cold Crush guys are this and this,' and Kevie Kev was like, 'Fuck them, they can't do that and they can't do this,' and the girls would come back to us with the feedback! We were like, 'Really? They said that?!' That was the shit that catapulted that whole situation. Next thing you know we're hearing more stuff from other people. So at some point they were playing what we were playing, we were playing what they were playing. Their crew was starting to come up, we were both coming up together, and one thing led to another."[32]

Caz remembered the escalation of tensions much like Chase did. He said Master Rob and Kevie Kev lacked respect for other crews back then and were constantly talking trash, saying Cold Crush was wack and the guys in the crew were "bums."[33]

"Kev and Rob, they come from a spoiled household," Caz said. "I know their mother, I love her to death. She spoiled the shit out of them growing up, she'll tell you herself. They had everything. All the new gear. All the new clothes. They was attractive, light skinned, nice hair, afros. They was little pretty boys. Kev had that attitude like, 'We better than any and everybody.'"[34]

From a neighborhood in which street basketball and football were king and gang life bled into the fabric of the community, calling a rival crew out meant that a score needed to be settled. Of course, battling would be the best way to see which crew was really the best, and there had been talk of it for a while. According to Charlie Chase, some jawing in the street (the first of a few incidents) was enough to really set the wheels in motion.

"We called them out and we said, 'Fuck y'all, you're wack,' and this and that, and, 'We'll battle y'all!', and I think [DJ] Randy [Sanders] from Harlem World may have had a hand in that because he was like, 'Yo, we know y'all don't like each other, we know y'all are always talking about battling, let's do it at Harlem World,' and that's what did it."[35] For what it's worth, Caz recalls local hip hop promoter Ray Chandler being the one who came up with the idea for the battle.[36]

Master Rob and Kevie Kev remember the lead-up to the battle differently than Chase does. They didn't see things as being personal between the crews, they just enjoyed trash-talking Cold Crush as if the two groups were on the basketball court. The brothers maintain that the rivalry was all in good fun and that it was Cold Crush and Cold Crush alone who took it seriously.

"You know the streets talk, these were the best two crews in the streets at that time," said Master Rob. "Grand Wizzard Theodore and the Fantastic Five. Charlie Chase, Tony Tone, and the Cold Crush Four. So people start talking, 'These guys think they're better than y'all,' 'These guys think they're better than y'all,' 'These guys *know* they're better than y'all.'"[37]

"I'm like, 'Where they at? Where they at?!'" Kevie Kev added. "We liked battling."[38]

Rob and Kev both said the Cold Crush Brothers were good friends of theirs while pointing out how both crews essentially grew up together. Still, that didn't stop the competitive juices from pouring out of the young men. Kevie Kev still pulls no punches.

"Them n*ggas was putting it out there like they wanted us to find out [about their talk] and we was happy to hear it because we wanted to crunch them anyway," he said. "They're all acting up like they're gonna do something, but them n*ggas was bums, but they're our people. They was bums back then in the '80s, man."[39]

As Chase mentioned, the crews used beats from one another's routines at parties. Meanwhile, the talk in the street only intensified, both between the crews themselves and their loyal fans.

"We don't really like to relive it," said Master Rob. "Those are our boys. We would have friendly competition in the street. We'd pass them and they'd say, 'We're better than y'all,' and we'd say, 'We know we're better than y'all.' 'OK, let's take this to the stage. Let's do this.' It was just a lot of hype going back and forth. Like boxers before a match. That was it. It would never get physical, because we all grew up together. It was friendly competition."[40]

Ultimately, both parties agreed that the rivalry should be settled and that the people should decide who really was the best. The battle was scheduled for July 3, 1981, at Harlem World. The anticipation escalated as flyers went up. They advertised "The Super Showdown" for that Friday night and listed a relatively expensive ticket price for hip hop—"guys $6, gals $5." The show's subtitle was a nod to the long buildup: "It Had to Happen."[41]

* * *

The crews began intensely preparing for battle. According to Master Rob, the Fantastic Romantic Five put their pens to paper to develop brand-new lyrics and routines.[42] For the Cold Crush Brothers, the preparation focused on developing a more theatrical show—something they hadn't done much of before—and picking out the best routines in their giant arsenal.[43] There was a decent amount of lead up time before the show; it was a big July Fourth weekend showcase. After the battle was announced, the crews continued their verbal jabs at one another, including during some very public confrontations that only drove the hype for the party further. Charlie Chase was involved in one.

"We had an argument in the street, which became a spectacle," Chase said. "We just bumped into each other, I think it was on the Grand Concourse somewhere, and we were talking shit to each other and the crowds got bigger—both crews were known and popular, they knew who we were in the streets. The people were gathering and listening to our shit and we were like, 'Fuck y'all!' and 'We'll fuck you up in the battle' and all this shit. It was all with the music, though. I mean, you ever get angry at a guy and you just want to snuff him like 'Poof'?! [*punching the air*]. All of us might've had that little inclination of wanting to do that but we never took it there."[44]

While the confrontation on the Grand Concourse might've been entertaining for fans of both groups, it paled in comparison to an incident Grandmaster Caz described that took place right in front of his building. He says that in the days leading up to the battle, he was home sick when he heard shouting from his first-floor window.[45] He stumbled out of bed and looked out the window only to see Kevie Kev and JDL jawing at each other in the street.

"I jumped up, I put on something, I ran outside, and I was like, 'Yo, what the fuck is y'all doing?' He was like, 'Yo, y'all n*ggas is wack,' and such and such. I said, 'Yo, we gonna bust y'all ass at fuckin' Harlem World, man.'"[46]

Caz took the challenges to the Cold Crush's supremacy more personally than anyone else involved. He wasn't a target of Fantastic's verbal jabs, but he was quick to rush to the defense of all of his fellow emcees.

"Some of the guys in the group didn't dress as well as them or didn't have the newest sneakers or the newest gear or whatever, but they could never say shit about me," he said. "They could never say shit about me. So [Kev's] whole thing was, 'Y'all n*ggas is bums, your crew is bums. Y'all n*ggas is this and this and that.' I ain't no bum, n*gga. I got everything you got and more. You might say that about one or two of us but that ain't what it's about anyway. That ain't what this shit is about. It's about us busting your ass on that motherfucking microphone.[47]

Caz tied this passion to the group's general approach, which prioritized the members having each other's backs no matter what. He said that, face to face, members of the Fantastic would often say that *he* was great, but the rest of the Cold Crush were bums. He hated that kind of talk.

"We ain't the Cold Crush Crew, the Cold Crush Clan, we're the Cold Crush *Brothers*, we go out together," Caz said. "That's the issue and that's where a lot of the shit started."[48]

Perhaps the biggest reason for all of the smack talk and tension was the prize that was on the line on July 3—an unheard-of one thousand dollars.[49] Battles didn't typically award that kind of cash, but the Cold Crush and the Fantastic matchup wasn't a typical battle. It was hip hop's first Super Bowl, and the groups were pushing one another to reach their full potential.

Battles were judged by the crowd at the end of the night, so having as many of your fans in the room as possible was key. That led to attempts to stack the club with people coming in from the Bronx and other boroughs. For Fantastic, that meant a concerted effort to get the ladies across the river. Cold Crush, on the other hand, needed to round up as many blue-collar guys as they could find. It was an arms race of advertising. The easiest way to get your crowd in the building was to promote the battle at parties and jams already on the schedule, which both crews had plenty of in the busy summer months.

"We really didn't ask no one to show," Grand Wizzard Theodore said. "We just know that the people that support us will be there.

Once the flyers were put out and everything—it would've been cool to text everybody, but there were no phones or internet or anything like that. Each party we gave up to the battle, we were just telling everybody, 'You gotta come, you *gotta* come, Harlem World, y'all should be there.' Once everybody sees the flyers and once word of mouth gets around we know that our people are gonna show up."[50]

Whipper Whip pointed out how, at that point, Fantastic was sometimes playing up to three shows each night, so their followers were able to stay very informed.[51]

Caz and the Cold Crush didn't talk to individual people, either. According to Caz, the battle had been brewing for more than a year at that point, so when it was announced, everyone in the hip hop crowd wanted to cram into Harlem World. Rather than convincing people to give up a Friday night to show up, the focus was just on getting the word out about the date and location where the long-awaited contest would finally take place.[52]

"The anticipation that was going on for this battle was crazy, and everywhere you go people were talking about it," Caz said. "Everybody in hip hop in the Bronx, Harlem, everybody everywhere was talking about it."[53]

As July 3 drew closer, Caz and company were feeling very confident about the show they had put together, but there were doubts about whether they could actually win the battle. As Caz openly admitted, the Fantastic Romantic Five had more fans. "It was nerve-racking because I knew that we were better," he said. "But I knew they were more popular."[54]

Charlie Chase, on the other hand, felt differently. He said the Cold Crush were riding a winning streak into the showdown and they were ready to kick ass like they'd been doing that entire year.

"We got so used to winning these things that we were already planning on spending the money we were getting from the contest," Chase said. "I remember one day we had a party, I think it was in Jersey, it was a battle with four or five groups. At this point we had already won fifteen, twenty battles. It was part of the night for us. We had other shows to do. As soon as we walked in through the rear stage door I remember this one cat said, 'FUCK MAN! SHIT! THEY SHOWED UP MAN, I FUCKING KNEW IT, MAN!' They already knew they lost."[55]

Fantastic considered the battle to be more of a showcase where they could bring new routines and rock the crowd harder than they ever had before. The Five spent the days leading up to the battle writing new lyrics and choreographing new dance routines, then practicing them for hours.

On the day of the battle, an event took place the details of which remain hotly disputed. What is agreed upon is that there was a meeting between the two battling crews, the Harlem World Crew, and promoter Ray Chandler in the spacious greenroom at the club before the party got underway. It must've been quite a scene given the costumes, props, and cannabis that would have been amassed before such a monumental event. The conversation centered around how to divide the $1,000 prize. According to Caz, the promoters offered both groups the chance to agree to a split where each would take home $500 and the audience would be told the battle was winner take all.[56] Theodore remembers the offer involving the winner taking $700 and the loser leaving with $300.[57] Regardless, neither scenario ever happened. Theodore and Caz both agreed that Fantastic were the ones who insisted on keeping the prize winner take all. Theodore said, "If we lose, y'all take the thousand dollars, if we win, we'll take the thousand dollars. None of the seventy-thirty stuff. Winner takes all."[58]

"If I remember correctly, more so it was them like saying, 'Yeah, fuck that,' they knew they was going to bust our ass," Caz said. "I think they felt confident that they were going to win, but they also knew that they weren't better than us. They knew they had the edge because they were popular."[59]

Kevie Kev remembers the meeting slightly differently. "We were smart enough to know that they were just trying to be like us," Kev said. "They wanted what we had. They knew we owned the streets. The Furious Five was on tour. There wasn't nobody around but us and them. They took a chance on trying to win that. I told them from the beginning, 'Listen, the winners take $700, the losers take $300, everybody will have some money.' 'Oh no! I'm battling, we going for it all!' I said, 'You sure?' and they said, 'Yeah,' and I told Ray Chandler, 'They said $1,000, man,' and that's how it went into the thousand."[60]

Regardless of whose idea it was, the terms were set. The top spot in New York's hip hop scene was up for grabs. One thousand dollars was on the line, and both crews were in prime form. That hot summer night would be one of the most consequential in the history of the hip hop genre. All that was left to do was get the party going.

The Cold Crush Brothers performing onstage at the battle against the Fantastic Romantic Five at Harlem World, July 3, 1981. Photo by Joe Conzo Jr.

Chapter 7

Tough-Ass Four Emcees

July 3, 1981, is significant for a couple of reasons. It was the day the *New York Times* printed the first reference in a major newspaper to "GRID"[1] (gay-related immune disorder), which would go on to be called AIDS (acquired immunodeficiency syndrome). Chris Evert won the Wimbledon Women's Championship without losing a set for the duration of the tournament. The next day, John McEnroe would secure the men's title. Ronald Reagan had settled back into his presidency after his attempted assassination that March, and *Superman II* dominated the box office, outclassing *Raiders of the Lost Ark*.[2] MTV was still four weeks away from its August 1 launch. New York reached a comfortable high of 82 degrees, but the 8:31 p.m. sunset did little to move the mercury. It was still 75 degrees during the battle.[3]

As Master Rob said, "The streets talk."[4] They screamed ahead of this night. This wasn't just a regular hip hop show. These were the two best crews in New York performing, no, competing against one another for a serious prize and even more serious bragging rights. That was reflected in the gigantic crowd that packed into Harlem World. Grandmaster Caz said one thousand people could be squished into the club, and the people in attendance claim there were likely even more fans there that night. Just to get from the subway to the club involved a perilous journey through stick-up kid territory, but once fans arrived, they were in hip hop heaven.

The night was already electric by the time the battle started. Grandmaster Flash, who was briefly back in town, performed a DJ set, and Busy Bee Starski, who was briefly a member of the group that would become the Fantastic Five, helped get the evening going. The room was already abuzz by the time the battle began, so Starski must have had a great time with his engaged audience (no tapes survive of that performance).

Grand Wizzard Theodore and the Fantastic Romantic Five were the most popular group in New York at the time of the battle. They had every reason to believe they would win. Theodore felt as though Fantastic were the rightful heirs to the throne left behind by Grandmaster Flash and the Furious Five because of the connections the two groups shared.

"Everyone knew that we were the only competition for the Furious Five, because we were all from the same camp," he said. "Grandmaster Flash, my brother Mean Gene, Keef Cowboy was down with us, we were all from the same camp. We were basically all close together."[5]

Theodore would normally be supremely confident—he had every reason to be—but that wasn't the case for the battle. The coolest DJ in the city was nervous for the entire day because of the magnitude of the occasion and what was on the line. "When we got there, I could feel a tension in the room that I'd never felt before," he confessed. "That's how serious this battle was. I felt the tension because you had people from Manhattan that was Fantastic fans and you had people from Manhattan that were Cold Crush fans. Then you had people coming in from Brooklyn, you had people coming in from Queens, and you had people coming in from the Bronx because the train station was ten feet away from the entrance of Harlem World. There was a little bit of tension in the room and I'd never felt that kind of tension before."[6]

Even Master Rob and Kevie Kev, who had talked the most trash before the battle, weren't doing great in the hours leading up to the monumental clash. The stakes were so high that even the well-dressed, smooth-talking emcees were feeling the heat generated by the moment, especially as a massive hip hop crowd flooded onto the dance floor.

"That night, let me tell you, it had to be like a boxing match going on," Kevie Kev said. "The club was *crowded*. The club was a baller's crowd. Everywhere you go there was so many people that came to see this battle."[7]

Meanwhile, in Cold Crush's camp, the pressure was having its own effect on the group's leaders. Charlie Chase gave the rest of his guys a raucous, profane pump-up speech as they prepared their routines in the greenroom. "I was the Vince Lombardi of the group," he said. "We'd always come up, I'd always be the one to pep-talk them and shit. We're getting ready, we're looking fly, and I was like, 'Yo, we're gonna crush these guys. It's been building up to this, we're finally here, and we're just gonna smash these motherfuckers and just fucking put them in their place and show [the] fucking city who the fuck we are.' There was tension because, although it's a little street thing, we didn't take battling lightly. The Cold Crush didn't take that shit lightly."[8]

According to Chase, the Cold Crush practiced heavily for the battle and added new elements to their existing routines, including a break from Edwin Starr's "I Just Wanna Do My Thing." The main focus of their performance, though, was going to be the "greatest hits"—popular routines and songs that would be sure to generate the most buzz from the crowd, thereby getting the Cold Crush their much-desired win during the final vote at the end of the night.[9] Cold Crush went the extra mile in preparing their set, even donning white suits and gathering up props, most notably plastic machine guns, to go along with the theme they'd chosen for their performance, "The Gangster Chronicles."[10]

Caz and the emcees knew that this would be the most theatrical show the Cold Crush had ever done. The idea was to infuse routines and lyrics that had been proven winners with the showmanship that some criticized them for lacking (in comparison with Fantastic).

Before hitting the stage, Caz and JDL shared their ritual "nervous cigarette."[11] The battle didn't start until about 1:00 a.m., and the crowd was at a fever pitch. Cold Crush took the stage first. Caz knew this was his moment. "It was nerve-racking. We had our chests out and our bravado, but shit, we was nervous," he said. "Shit, to us it looked like Madison Square Garden. It was epic. It was packed. Front to back, side to side. There's a staircase that leads from the upstairs of the Harlem World down the floor and that's where we made our entrance, from the staircase. It's like walking to the boxing ring. We walked through the crowd and shit. To make our way to the stage we had to walk through the audience. That shit was epic, like we was in fucking Vegas or something."[12]

While the four emcees exited the dressing room, Charlie Chase and Tony Tone loaded themselves into the DJ booth, which sat high up in a different part of the club, far from the stage. DJ Randy from the Harlem World Crew started off the festivities with an iconic introduction:

> What's up fly guy?
> Hello, fly girl
> It's the big throwdown, at Harlem World
> The Cold Crush Four
> versus Fantastic Five
> They ain't no comp

We'll eat 'em alive

Because we're the best

When it comes to rappin'.[13]

On tapes of the battle, you can hear the crowd sort of shuffling into position and getting ready to experience the epic show. Caz and company had them up and moving even toward the end of a long night of dancing.

"We had a scenario set up," Caz said. "We had a skit, fucking sound effects and everything. Everything didn't work exactly on point but the fact that we had all that and we did all that, came out in gangster suits and shit and machine guns on some *Godfather* shit. I mean come on, come on. What's fucking with that?"[14]

After Charlie Chase's first few scratches on his turntables, all four emcees joined in in unison to unleash one of Cold Crush's most memorable lines ever, which electrified the crowd.

We don't need tuxedos, because what we're gonna do

Is dog Kev and Dot, Master Rob and Whip

Just like we always do.

We battle Fantastic, and here's a little gift

To let you know, before you go

Just who you're fucking with.

It's Charlie Chase, Tony Tone, and . . .

The cold, crushin', mother, fuckin'

Tough-ass four emcees.[15]

That line blew the roof off the club and segued straight into Charlie's first beat drop— "Action," by Orange Krush. The beat was everything Cold Crush claimed to be: tough, thoughtful, uncompromising, and slick all at the same time. Oddly enough, the person in the building who may have enjoyed the line the most was behind enemy lines, watching Cold Crush from high above the dance floor. "That was the shit," said Whipper Whip. "That line right there was the shit. They did have some of the best routines."[16]

That line was far from the only reference to Fantastic in Cold Crush's nearly half hour on stage, but it set the tone for the competition and conveyed how seriously the group was taking the performance. The focus shifted in the "Yes Y'all" routine that followed, where the emcees introduced themselves.

That routine culminated with the first DJ Hollywood–style "Throw your hands in the air" moment of the night ("If you're on the go because the four told you so, everybody say 'ho!'").[17] The crowd was loving the performance. Even though the Cold Crush didn't have a record out, many fans were familiar with the Brothers' classic routines because they'd frequented their shows. These routines were instantly recognizable, although Cold Crush was throwing in some more flair that night to really impress.

At one point, for example, Tony Tone, whom Charlie Chase credits with naming the show "The Gangster Chronicles," played dead after a mock shooting. As part of the skit, Chase came down from the DJ booth wearing a doctor's coat and stethoscope. According to him, "Caz said, 'Did he make it?!' and I put my stethoscope down there and looked up [*shaking his head*] and said, 'They didn't make it, yo.' We got into the theatrics of it. That was what it was all about."[18]

As the crowd was rocking to the performance, Joe Conzo worked his way around the club to get good shots. He stood on top of the bar, made his way to the upper level, and of course pushed his way to the front of the stage.

"If you notice some of my photos, there's girls running around with Cold Crush sweatshirts," Conzo said. "They had a huge following. We'd stack the crowd as best we could. We'd bring out the smoke machines, whatever it took."[19]

* * *

When Charlie Chase put on one of his and Caz's favorite beats, Cerrone's "Rocket in the Pocket," things reached a new level. Chase sped up the scratchy, robotic sound with the heavy bass line so the titular lyrics were pitched up and sounded very funky. Cold Crush launched into one of Caz's all-time favorite routines and one of their best, "Other Emcees." In fact, this routine is so memorable that Caz and company still perform it when they get together. The routine started with Caz asking the crowd if they knew about other emcees, then ordering Chase to keep "Rocket in the Pocket" going. The crew then echoed Caz as he went through the following list:

> Now first of all, we not talking 'bout your sister (Your sister)
> We not talking 'bout your uncle (Your uncle)
> We not talking 'bout your father (Your father)
> And not your mother, or other, or other other other.[20]

What really stands out on tapes of the battle is the vocal melody that the group picked up after that—the chorus of "Cat's in the Cradle" by Harry Chapin.[21] It was an example of the group's genius: taking a classic soft-rock song from the 1970s and refurbishing it with new lyrics over a cut hip hop beat. No other groups were thinking on that level at the time. The crowd was delighted. Even though they may not have been Chapin fans, it was impossible to *not* know that song by 1981, it was so ubiquitous. Caz ran with it, starting with a hook that the four emcees harmonized on.

"I don't remember spending a lot of time on that," Caz said. "I was so enamored with the song ever since I was a kid that I just followed the melody and put us in it. The hook was simple. 'Other MCs can't deal with us, because we are the Four known as the Cold Crush./Putting fellas on the jock, making fly girls blush./You know we got a funky song, so won't you come and sing and dance along?'"[22]

Following the melody, each emcee had their own short verse. The crowd erupted as more and more people realized what was happening. The verses were simple in nature—just basic braggadocio—but the melody, with the "Rocket in the Pocket" break underneath it, was very special and unique.

After the raucous start, the crew spoke on stage and slowed things down a bit to let everyone catch their breath. They were killing the crowd in the early hours of July 4. Then they brought out a dance routine. There is no video of the battle, but on audio recordings it can clearly be heard how much the fans dug it. They screamed louder and louder with each move.

"We danced about as much as the Fantastic Five," Caz said. "They wasn't no flappers, either. They had a couple of moves, we had a couple of moves, you know?"[23]

Which crew had the better dance moves is debatable, but this routine wasn't about dancing. It was all about lyrics and delivery. About eight minutes into their performance, JDL stopped the dance routine and opened up a short skit, which involved the other emcees asking him what he had to say. "A lot of people be telling me stuff, man, but hold up, let's find out now," he rapped. With that, the emcees started a modified call-and-response act that was very on-brand for the Cold Crush: rough and rude. The four screamed into their microphones, their voices so loud they sound distorted on the tape.

Is it them?

NO!

Is it them?

NO!

Well who is it, is it, is-is it, is it?

Who is it, is it?

It is us, you know it's us

The Cold Crush, you know it's us.[24]

With Spoonie Gee's "Love Rap" playing underneath, the crew sped through a classic braggadocious rap, talking about how they "rock it well" and how they want everybody to get up and move their butts. Caz incorporated his old standard "Young ladies, isn't he the sure shot?" line into the end of everyone's verses.

Cause it's Kay Gee, A.D., the L, the L

And me, Grandmaster Caz (Huh, huh, huh)

I got the most pizzazz, I'm ranked number one in my social class

And when I rap on the mic, it gets the girls hot

Young ladies, isn't he the sure shot? (Who, me?)

Fly guys, isn't-isn't he the sure shot? (Huh!)

The L, the L, the one who rocks 'em well

Taking all the fly girls to the motel

I wanna rock the side, I wanna rock the side

I wanna, I wanna, you know I'm gonna

Wanna rock the side when I rock shock the top

Young ladies, isn't he the sure shot? (Who, me?)

Fly guys, isn't-isn't he the sure shot? (Huh!)

I'm rock shock rolling, I'm rock shock rolling

I'm rock— I'm rock— I can't be stopped

I'm rock shock rolling 'cause I'm in your block

Young ladies, isn't he the sure shot?

Fly guys, isn't-isn't he the sure shot? (Yeah baby) (Huh!)

Almighty with the capabilities

Guaranteed to conversate with all you jazzy ladies

And green means go (Yeah baby) and red means stop

Young ladies, isn't he the sure shot? (Who, me?)

Fly guys, isn't-isn't he the sure shot? (Sure shot.)[25]

The routine was well executed and a great show of skill, but it's truly significant because Cold Crush takes the unusual step of mentioning other crews by name toward the end while still bragging about how they're the best. They said the audience must have heard of the Funky 4, the Furious Five, Fantastic, and even Busy Bee Starski (he was literally everywhere), but that those performers were old news and a new era had dawned in hip hop: "Gentlemen and ladies, these are the eighties/And it's all about C.C. [Cold Crush]."[26]

In one fell swoop, the Cold Crush Brothers called out the most successful New York hip hop group to date; the first hip hop group to ever perform on *Saturday Night Live*; their opponents that evening; and the very respected hip hop innovators Lovebug Starski and Busy Bee Starski. That took some serious cojones, even by Cold Crush standards.

"This is all a street thing, this is all at a street level," Chase explained. "In the streets, doing what we're doing, if you got shown out or showed down, you were wack. All of a sudden it was like, 'Oh man, they were wack, man, they got outdone by this or that.' We weren't about to let that happen. We were too fucking arrogant. We were too prideful in what we did. We didn't want that to happen. We had fragile egos, man. If we would've got fucked up, we would've been hurt, we were not about to let that happen."[27]

No one would've called Cold Crush's performance that night wack. They moved off the braggadocious rhymes to show off Caz's lyrical dexterity with some more meaningful and complex poetry. Aside from "Yvette," which was not a part of the performance, one of Caz's best writing jobs incorporated all of the emcees in harmony, while still allowing him to flex his unique writing muscle.

> Ashes to ashes and dust to dust
> We are the brothers known as the Cold Crush
> Not one, not two, not three, but four
> We keep your arms in the air, your feet on the floor
> We're guaranteed to give you what you paid your money for
> 'Cause the Cold Crush Brothers got rhymes galore.[28]

That rhyme is a great indicator of just how far the genre had come less than a decade after Kool Herc's first parties. Recycling a phrase from the Book of Common Prayer (one that also brings to mind the nursery rhyme "Ring Around the Rosie") and using it as a commentary on the forever bond of the group still sounds fresh and interesting more than forty years later. The four emcees stood in a row on stage, each with their own microphone, and delivered the rhyme, jumping in and out and filling in each other's sentences—the result of the countless hours of practice that Cold Crush put into this performance as they tried to win over what they perceived as a Fantastic-friendly crowd.

One of the tactics that Cold Crush used, which was rare at the time, was to try to build a narrative against the emcees in the opposing group. The insults weren't particularly biting or personal, but they were there. But the barbs at Fantastic also gave Cold Crush a chance to show off their skills, thus keeping the spirit of the battle intact.

Caz started off their next routine by asking Almighty Kay Gee who he wanted to "go for"; after a bit of hesitation, the captain of the crew assigned him Rubie Dee. JDL was given Dot-A-Rock, Easy A.D. was given Kevie Kev, and Caz assigned himself both Whipper Whip and Master Rob. Chase and Tone played the break from Funkadelic's "You'll Like it Too" as each of the emcees took a turn calling out their target.[29] Caz's verse was the sharpest. The great lyricist chose to point out the perceived disparities between the groups and actually turned one of Fantastic's most favorable qualities against them in an eight-bar verse laced with gritty vocal tones. This was a pissed-off Caz, putting considerable energy into what he was saying: "Some people seem to think that to be an emcee/You need a closet full of clothes and a lot of jewelry . . . "[30]

Caz's shot at how the Fantastic carry themselves is a nice peek into his attitude regarding the rival group. As he said in chapter 6, dressing well or looking a certain way was meaningless in his eyes in terms of whether you were a talented hip hop act. While he called Fantastic out with his lyrics here, he did so in a clever way to show his skills, rather than strictly trying to bring them down.

"I went under the assumption that when I battle you, you're not the focus, I'm the focus," Caz said. "Me being dope is the focus, and you being dope is the focus. And then you show your dopeness, I show my dopeness, and then somebody judges who's the dopest. For me, it wasn't personal, it was about 'You can't rhyme as good as me, you ain't got as good a show as me, you ain't the n*gga that I am on this mic.'"[31]

Charlie Chase and Tony Tone also took pride in showing what they could do. They were competing directly against Theodore, who was one of the best-known DJs in the city and a worthy opponent. Some of their beats were classics, but when Chase reached into his rock n' roll Rolodex and pulled out Billy Squier's "The Big Beat," it proved to be an unorthodox showstopper.[32]

The all-important crowd vibed well with everything Cold Crush was saying. Shockingly, when the group asked how many people were from the Bronx, they didn't get a big reception. When they asked how many in attendance were from "money-makin' Manhattan," however, the club erupted. Even though Cold Crush called the Bronx home, their influence had spread far and wide, and the Harlem crowd loved them. In a memorable moment from late in their show, the Cold Crush summarized the story behind their battle succinctly, as Caz explained the rivalry with Fantastic.

"Us and the Fantastic Five started out about the same time," he said. "And they done tore shit up where they went, and we done tore shit up where we went. But now we tearing shit up where they go, you know? So we come to find out the real deal right about now."[33]

From there, the crew did their "We Will Rock You"–inspired "Cold Cold Crush" routine, which dates back to their earliest days with Caz and JDL in the fold. It was a signature routine, so it made sense for the group to end on it, especially considering the clapping and foot stomping from the original song were so universally known and loved across fans of all musical genres.

> I say we are the four, guaranteed to give you more
> Keep your two hands clapping, keep your feet on the floor
> Say you can look around for a better sound
> But a badder bunch of brothers could never be found
> Could never be found, could never be found
> Could never be found, could never be found.[34]

After that effort, Chase and Tone reached even further into their bag of tricks. They played the unique, double-time piano beat from

Billy Joel's "Stiletto" as the crew began their final sign-off, asking the crowd if they could get the thousand dollars (which, surprisingly, received a lukewarm response). The last "Throw your hands in the air" lines of the show once again drew thunderous roars from the packed crowd, even as the clock passed 1:30 a.m., with another half of the battle remaining.

> Throw your hands in the air,
> And wave 'em like you just don't care,
> Throw your hands in the air
> And wave 'em like you just don't care
> And if the Cold Crush Brothers are really a must
> Everybody say "Cold Crush."[35]

Cold Crush managed to perform a powerhouse show that lasted nearly a half hour and pushed the crew to places they'd never been before. The sweaty, exhausted emcees left the stage in great spirits, and Chase and Tone climbed down from the DJ booth having executed the routine as well as they could've hoped (every DJ will tell you it's impossible to perform break beats perfectly). Perhaps it wasn't the best they'd ever done, but it was close. When Caz and his fellow emcees left the stage, they did so to a massive ovation. "We felt like stars," he said, pleased with the memory. "We was dressed like stars, we performed like stars, and we was treated like that."[36]

"We was bad, dude, we were like James Brown bad," Charlie Chase added. "We rocked. You know, like, 'Those cats are bad, you can't fuck with them, man.' We liked that, we worked for that, we wanted that, and when we got it we were holding onto it like a fucking GI Joe with the kung fu grip. We were not letting go of that."[37]

Cold Crush's connections agreed that this was one of their finest hours. "It was electrifying, it's a battle. You're either with [Fantastic] or with us," said Joe Conzo, whose photos remain some of the best documentation of the matchup, alongside the audio tape. "It wasn't like coming to see a show with four or five groups on the bill and you come and support or see them perform. This was money on the table, bragging rights, you were either on the Cold Crush side or the Fantastic Side."[38]

Even the opposition had to give Cold Crush credit for what they managed to put together, but that didn't cool off the heat of competition. Whipper Whip, for example, came up under Caz and was a big fan of many of Cold Crush's routines, especially the "Cat's in the Cradle" concept and the first lines dissing Fantastic, but he said hearing them live only served to fire him and the rest of the crew up more.

"We wanted to beat their ass and let them know, and let the world know. Like, 'Yo, shut the fuck up. Stay in your lane,'" he said. "They have some joints that I love, but looky here, man, don't fuck with me."[39]

Theodore had watched Cold Crush's performance from a room on the upper level that overlooked the club. He was impressed by how loud the crowd was but he didn't see any threat to Fantastic's chances of walking away with the money. He also knew that the Fantastic faithful had shown up to the party in droves. He recognized many faces in the crowd.

"When they went on, we could actually hear their show and look down on stage and see them," Theodore said. "Once we seen their show, we was like, 'We got this, no problem, we got this.'"[40]

Gearing up for a career-defining performance, Theodore, one of the premier DJs of his era, spent the last few minutes before climbing into the booth taking in the atmosphere and soaking in the intensity. It was past 1:30 a.m. at this point and, as Theodore said, if you're not at the party at 1:00 a.m., "you probably ain't coming."[41]

"The crowd was like half and half," Theodore said. "Half was for them and half was for us and we was like, 'Woah, this is serious' because their crowd was just as rowdy as our crowd."[42]

After a short break, it was time for the self-proclaimed most popular group in the city to take their turn and step onto the Harlem World stage. Theodore climbed the rungs of the ladder and took his spot in the DJ booth. The ultimate hip hop bragging rights would be decided in a matter of moments.

The Fantastic Romantic Five at the
Sugarhill Rapper's Convention, 1981. *Back
row*, Kevie Kev, Master Rob, Whipper Whip,
Dot-A-Rock. *Front row*, Grand Wizzard
Theodore, Rubie Dee. A crowd stampede
occurred midway through this performance.
Photo by Charlie Ahearn.

Chapter 8

Somebody, and Anybody, and Everybody Scream!

While Cold Crush decided to bring out their best-known routines to the Harlem World showdown, Fantastic wrote all-new ones. In typical Fantastic Romantic Five fashion, they strove to ignite the crowd with an all-encompassing show instead of blowing their minds with the most amazing lyrics. With that in mind, they didn't start their show with a crazy confrontational line like "We battle Fantastic . . . " Instead, they whipped the crowd into a fervor with an a cappella call-and-response routine.

Fantastic introduced themselves as they came down the stairs one by one. They had the room going off before Theodore even dropped his first beat:

Everybody say "Fantastic"

"Romantic"

Everybody say "Theodore," everybody say "Theodore"

Everybody say "We gonna rock"

"We gonna rock"

Scream!

Scream!

Scream!

Everybody

Everybody, everybody, everybody

Throw your hands in the air

And wave 'em from wall to wall

And if you're in the house and you're having a ball

Everybody say "Yes yes, y'all"

To the beat y'all.[1]

The old-school intro did the trick, especially when Fantastic asked the crowd to scream. They were ready to shake Harlem World, despite dancing and screaming for a half hour with Cold Crush on stage. The Fantastic Five might as well have been the Beatles on *Ed Sullivan*. They captured the imagination of their diehard fans and had them eating out of their hands right away. In their signature tuxedos, the Fantastic Five knew their people made the trip from the Bronx and the other boroughs in droves.

"There was a line drawn down the middle of Harlem World," Theodore said. "One side was for Fantastic, one side was for Cold Crush. The crowd was really, really into it. They were really excited about this battle, they were pumped up."[2]

When Theodore cut up the very funky and hard-driving "Square Biz" by Teena Marie, the crowd popped once again, this time louder than ever before. The emcees broke into one of their best dance routines. The energy is palpable even on the audio recordings of the battle. Theodore said he picked "Square Biz" because he'd noticed that girls loved to dance to it, so he thought it would appeal even to fans who didn't love break beats.[3] That was a giant moment, when the anticipation for what the five emcees would do turned into a reality for everyone in attendance. When the inventor of the scratch used his technique to pop in the line "Everybody get up" or repeat one of Teena's "Wooooo!"s a few times, that was among the night's big climaxes. In fact, according to Whipper Whip, a second climax came when the emcees threw glitter in the air, and he did a full split with his head on his knee on the second "Woo!"

"I was more nimble back then," Whipper Whip said. "The crowd went be-fucking-zerk, just on the intro."[4]

Theodore said that he elected to play the most popular records at the time because he knew those would excite the crowd. He also thought it was important to use records that people could immediately identify with Fantastic because there was a lot of overlap musically with Cold Crush, seeing as the groups knew each other's routines and beats so well. On that night, he decided to bring in some Michael Jackson cuts and records that allowed each individual in the crew to show off their skills. "We just basically reminded them that we are the number one crew. We is, we always was. We just had to convince y'all and y'all fans that we're the number one crew out there."[5]

For Fantastic, the party was the key to a successful routine. They knew who was judging that night and understood that the trick to winning the battle would be getting them to dance and scream and make out and have a great time. The party was roaring during their introduction, even after Theodore cut off "Square Biz" early to allow for some more ad-libbing. Part of Theodore's skill set was to know when *not* to play.

Whatever the emcees and Theodore did that night, the crowd loved. They could've stopped the show, sat in a circle on stage, and sipped lattes and their fans would've erupted. It's what allowed them to perform with such confidence. According to Theodore, there was never a doubt that they would win the battle.[6] Master Rob agreed, especially when considering what he believes is the X factor for Fantastic's successes going back to the earliest days of the crew.

"Fantastic Five knew how to command a stage," he said. "If you come to a Fantastic Five show and you spend three bucks to get in, we give you a show like you spent twenty-five dollars for a ticket. We actually put on a *show* and we command that stage. Our stage presence was awesome, not to be bragging or anything but it was what it was. We knew how to cover every angle of a stage; we were not only emcees and rappers, we were entertainers. That was an advantage that we had."[7]

He was right. During Fantastic's show, it sounded like the crew was standing right among the crowd partying with them. However, one moment during a crucial juncture in the performance threatened to derail the Five's hip hop dreams. It took place during a fairly simple routine where the emcees introduced themselves by their real names:

> The way the Cold Crush look, they should be ashamed
> You know our slangs, now here's our real names
> I'm Kevin
> I'm Darryl
> I'm James
> I'm Rubin.

At that precise moment, Master Rob was supposed to say, "And my real name is Robin," and the beat would drop to keep the routine going. But the mic didn't work![8] For an act that required coordination like Fantastic's did, this could've spelled death and sent the entire battle into a spiral. However, the Fantastic Romantic Five weren't beginners. Led by Kevie Kev, who deftly saved the routine, the seasoned performers literally didn't miss a beat.

"Hold up now, the mic, let's do it one more time," Kev said. "One more time . . . let it go, put that shit back, share it with him, share it with him, share it with him. We gonna do it again, fuck a mic, we don't need mics, we need y'all. That's what we need."[9]

The mic started working once again, and the show was back on track within thirty seconds. It's not a moment without controversy, however.

"We felt great about the show, except for the one time when Rob's mic didn't come on," Whipper Whip said. "That was like the peak of the shit, and that's the reason the Cold Crush have given themselves leeway to talk shit. But that was a technical problem, that had nothing to do with us."[10]

Kevie Kev didn't blame a technical error, however. He had a far deeper conspiracy theory that involves straight-up sabotage.

"When we got to a real point that was gonna hurt them, they pulled the plug," Kev said.[11]

"Not Cold Crush, per say, but somebody for sure," Master Rob added.[12]

"Someone backstage had to pull that cord," Kev said. "Lil' Rodney Cee [from the Funky 4 + 1] used to do it at a lot of clubs and parks."[13]

It's unknown what led to the microphone failure but no matter what, it did nothing to slow down Fantastic. The fans barely noticed there was a problem at all because of how quickly Kev addressed it. He took his role as the leader of the group seriously.

"It was already out of whack; that pulling of the mic disordered everything. I had to save it," he said. "Y'all don't even know we're going through it. After that, it was a wrap. Our dance steps, man, it was a wrap, our gear, we was fly that night, and we did what we had to do."[14]

Once the show was back on track, Theodore dropped the pounding drums of "Love Rap," by Spoonie Gee. It was the second time that night the crowd had heard that break; Chase and Tone used it early in Cold Crush's routine as well. Theodore (obviously) deployed the scratch more. This is perhaps the best example of how, during their rivalry, the crews were so heavily influenced by one another. In

Fantastic's style, however, they all rapped together and harmonized their voices for a more soulful, Motown feel instead of a display of lyrical dexterity.

> And like a four-leaf clover, when the party's over
> Cold Crush'll be starvin' Marvin
> Romantic Fantastic Five, ha ha
> Each one is qualified
> To make a dead party come alive, ooh
> And make the girls gather up like flies
> Other emcees want our rep
> We got Theodore on the set
> To keep those other emcees in check
> And do us the most respect.[15]

That "starvin' Marvin" dig was one of only a few that Fantastic hurled at Cold Crush in their show. Kev said Cold Crush upset some of the crew with their callouts and open challenges, so there were a few lines slipped into the routine at particular moments to shake their confidence a bit. Theodore reiterated that Fantastic's focus was simply to outclass Cold Crush rather than put them down.

"If somebody came up to us and said we were going to battle in thirty minutes, we'd be like 'BOOM!'" he said. "All we gotta do is get up on the stage and be Grand Wizzard Theodore and the Fantastic Five. That's all we have to do, it just so happens that we wrote a rhyme or two with their names in it, but we didn't try to make the whole routine and everything about them. We made our show about us. We're not going to put anyone down to make ourselves look better. We're just going to go out and perform and show you guys that we're the better crew. We don't gotta say y'all names not even once."[16]

Many who listen to the tape decades after the fact don't realize or have the ability to visualize the level of coordination and skill it took for the five emcees and Theodore to stay together through the show. They are always surprised to learn that the guys couldn't see their DJ from the stage. According to Whipper Whip, all they could see was the top of Theodore's afro bouncing up and down.[17] Theodore, however, could see them. Because of his experience playing hundreds of shows with the emcees, plus the practice they put in to refine the new elements of the performance, he nailed the transitions.

"We hung around each other every day," Theodore said. "We know the routines. We know the pace of everything, let's go out there and just do it."[18]

Theodore maintained that he approached the battle exactly like he would any other Fantastic show, but with so much on the line, that's hard to believe. One thing that's indisputable, however, is how good Fantastic must have felt while they were performing. They were rock stars that night. Just five minutes into the performance, Theodore dropped "God Made Me Funky" by the Headhunters, and the crew asked the crowd if they had won.

> Now throw your hands in the air, everybody
> Throw your hands in the air
> So if you're having fun, this battle we won
> Everybody say, somebody say
> Everybody say, everybody say
> "Fantastic's number one."[19]

Shortly after that, Fantastic took one last shot at their opposition. They wouldn't be completely shut out from the insult game. Interestingly enough, their shots at Cold Crush took aim at exactly those personal traits that Caz claimed didn't matter in a battle, such as physical appearance.

When other MCs try to rock like us

They give no respect, just like the Cold Crush

We dress so fresh and that's no lie

You'll see no bums in Fantastic Five

. . . .

We're number one and that's a known fact

The Fantastic Five on top of the list

And you provoked us y'all, you provoked us y'all

And you provoked us y'all to rock it like this.[20]

And then Theodore dropped the famous break from the Commodores' classic "The Assembly Line," and the emcees broke into another electrifying dance routine before launching another round of introductions, which included Whipper Whip singing "I'll give the world to you, young ladies, I'll give the world to you."[21] They counted down from ten—one of their most popular techniques to keep the crowd engaged—and then danced again. Even the Fantastic don't remember their exact moves, but whatever they were, the ladies in the front row really loved them.

Rubie Dee asked the crowd how many of them like to get high; those that did were asked to wave their hands from side to side. Master Rob asked the crowd to put a finger up if they thought Fantastic was number one. The audience banter continued when Master Rob said, "And everybody in the house knows how to tongue kiss, say, 'And you know this.'" He got a great reaction. Kevie Kev got one, too, when he asked the crowd to yell "Win the G"[22] (that is, the grand, a reference to the $1,000 prize at stake during the battle). Everything was working for the crew that clearly had the louder fans, even though Theodore claimed the crowd was evenly split. Dot-A-Rock went back to an old favorite to keep the energy up.

All right, now how many people like sex?

If you like sex, put your hands in the air

Put two arms in the air

And somebody somebody somebody say

Makin' love!

Like heavens above!

Like it's good!

Like you know it should![23]

After asking who in the crowd was from Manhattan (by the sound of it, at least half of them), Kevie Kev led a really interesting call-and-response. He asked the crowd to say "Black" and then "power" a few times, and received a massive ovation.[24] Rubie Dee had recieved an enthusiastic response earlier in the show when he mentioned he was Puerto Rican, perhaps in an attempt to prove the group's appeal was more universal than Cold Crush gave them credit for.[25] That reference to heritage stood out among the sex- and money-obsessed lyrics (at one point, Fantastic even asked the crowd to repeat "Sergio Valente," the designer jeans brand[26]). Fantastic also did a separate call-and-response for the "ladies and the fellas." When they asked all of the guys in the club to say "Oh!" they got a very robust response that proved the Fantastic Five appealed to everyone, even with their "pretty boy" image.

"We were a little flamboyant, but the one thing we made sure of is that we would enunciate, pronunciate, we made sure everyone heard every fucking syllable of what we were saying," Whipper Whip said. "We weren't that far off from everybody else. We roamed the streets just like everybody else. We were fly everywhere we went, that gave us our cockiness, being dressed to a T every time. And that shit ain't cheap."[27]

All of the group's work paid off that night. Each emcee had a chance to show off, but perhaps the most flamboyant moment of the performance was when Theodore donned handcuffs for some of his scratching and needle dropping. He was competing against Charlie Chase, another top DJ, so he wanted to do something definitive. He furiously scratched his records to get some up-tempo dancing going.

"We said 'Charlie Chase, we got something for you,' and Theodore put on handcuffs and was cutting the shit out of some records," Whipper Whip said. "He was spinning around, you know how [DJs] do, show-offs. I could only see his head from the stage so I couldn't see what he exactly did but he tore shit up."[28]

To close out the show, the Five emcees took turns asking the audience more questions, such as "Who likes sniffing blow?"[29] and "Who thinks we won the thousand dollars?" and of course, "Who thinks the Cold Crush lost?" At the end of the routine, Whipper Whip said, "Fantastic Romantic rocked the house and everybody knows it," and Kevie Kev hilariously did a mid-song question-and-answer session with some young women in the front row. He qualified his question with, "I don't even know you, do I know you baby?" before asking her if she thought the Five won the battle. She replied that she thought they did. He swung the mic over to her friend, and she said Fantastic had won as well.[30] That was a good note to end on for the crew, who had poured their hearts out on stage in a fast-paced tour de force. Weirdly, the last line of the performance was Whipper Whip saying "I got an 'S' on my chest, I got the most finesse." That sounds more like the beginning of a rhyme than the end of a show, but it wasn't important. The Fantastic Romantic Five had completed their mission of getting the party going and keeping it red hot.

* * *

Cold Crush performed for twenty-nine minutes and Fantastic performed for just under sixteen, and a lot of that time was spent dancing. However, Fantastic clearly elicited bigger reactions from the
crowd during their time on stage, partly because of the playlist Theodore brought and his cutting skills, and partly because of the emcees'
enthusiasm and their trendy call-and-response routines. You also
can't discount the fact that they simply knew more people.

But none of that necessarily meant they'd win the fan vote and the
thousand dollars (although it seemed likely). The winner was still to
be determined when DJ Randy from the Harlem World Crew stepped
onstage and invited both crews to join him. The crowd quieted as he
explained the instructions. He was going to ask if they thought Cold
Crush won, and then if they thought Fantastic won, perhaps multiple
times if necessary.[31] It was very important that there was a definitive
winner. Both crews had put on the best performance they could and
there was so much on the line. With the rest of the Harlem World
Crew on stage to help draw a conclusion, Randy first asked about the
Cold Crush.

"He said, 'Right now I wanna hear it for the Cold Crush Four!'"
Kevie Kev said. "And it was so fucking loud, I thought we lost, that's
how loud this shit was."[32]

Cold Crush did have a loud, strong contingent of amazing fans.
When judging the battle, photographer Joe Conzo admitted that he
was biased because he could sing along with all of the Cold Crush
routines, even though he knew the Fantastic Romantic Five well and
had hung out with them in the past. You simply didn't go against
your squad, however. Conzo used an analogy from *West Side Story* to
encapsulate his allegiances.

"It's like the Jets," Conzo said. "When you're a Jet, you're a Jet all
the way. When you're Cold Crush, you're Cold Crush all the way."[33]

One special thing about the early hip hop era, however, is that there was so much respect and admiration for both crews, even from each other's fans. Not a single boo can be heard on the tape, and based on the volume, it's clear that many Fantastic die-hards cheered heartily for Cold Crush in recognition of their half-hour effort.

"What did it for me is just the overall performance," said DJ Baby D from the Mercedes Ladies, who was in the crowd that night and vigorously supported Cold Crush even though Theodore had taught her how to scratch. "Everything they did: the rapping, the whole nine yards. I mean, the Fantastic Five was good in their own right, but Cold Crush did it for me a little bit more."[34]

But when it came time to gauge Fantastic's support, the crowd's roar likely registered on a seismograph somewhere in Newark.

DJ Randy barely got the word "Fantastic" out of his mouth before the crowd erupted into a fervor. He actually had to yell "CALM DOWN!" which the Five got a kick out of.[35]

"The whole fucking place went bananas," Kevie Kev said. "'Let's hear it for the Fantastic— CALM DOWN!' haha."[36]

"The girls in the front were screaming like crazy," Theodore said. "The girls were screaming mostly for us. There were a lot of females in there that night, and they were screaming, and screaming, and screaming, and Randy had to say, 'OK OK OK, calm down, calm down, OK OK OK,' he was like, 'Yo, we've got to give it to the Fantastic,' and everybody was like, 'Wow, they deserved it.'"[37]

It was a decisive victory for the Fantastic Romantic Five. They had won the thousand dollars, and their spot atop the hip hop scene was secured.

"It was overwhelming," Whipper Whip said. "It wasn't just like, 'Yeah, they won by a little bit,' no, the dude was like, 'CALM DOWN!'"[38]

Baby D said a multitude of factors led to the win for Fantastic, even though she personally supported Cold Crush that night. She said the number one catalyst for the win was her mentor, Theodore. "I think Fantastic won because of Theodore actually, because of the way Theodore was playing and everything," she explained. "I liked Cold Crush more because of their rapping and their style and how they did it, yet the Fantastic won that night because they gave a *little* bit more. For me, both of them were phenomenal, Fantastic just gave them a little bit more. What I also noticed is if this is your 'home turf,' as they say, those people are coming out for you even if the other guy is so dope. They're coming for *you*. And they were cuter."[39]

According to Kevie Kev, Cold Crush cried on stage, and the Fantastic Five gave them the handkerchiefs out of their pockets.[40] That is disputed, but whether there were tears or not, the Cold Crush Brothers were beside themselves. They had curated their best routines, played their most innovative breaks, and added theatrical elements to their show. Charlie Chase wondered what more they could have done. "Call me Cleopatra, because I was in denial," he said. "I was in fucking denial. I was not fucking having it because we KNEW we didn't lose. Not because we were hurt or anything. If you saw the show, you would think we lost because of how the crowd was cheering. But when you heard it without the visualization, you would see we didn't fucking lose. I knew that deep inside and so did the rest of the crew and we were fucking HEATED. We were pissed and there wasn't shit we could do about it."[41]

"[Fantastic] are more Hollywood," Caz added. "I just don't think their show had the substance that ours did. That's my argument. My argument has never been 'We dress better than y'all,' my argument has never been 'Our braids is longer than y'all's are.' My argument is that you can't do this better than we can. You pale in comparison to us and if you take all of those other things out of the game. I even wrote a rhyme about it, this ain't about your clothes, this ain't about your outfit, and if that's what you think, take that shit off and let it perform for you."[42]

There would be heated debates about the battle to come—it remains a popular topic of conversation among old-school hip hop heads. But for that night, Fantastic had a chance to celebrate their triumph over their rivals. The party kept going for hours after the battle concluded. Theodore and company stayed for about an hour afterwards, dancing and buying drinks for some of the ladies in the audience. At about 3:00 a.m., the victors made their move and left Harlem World with the thousand dollars and the same feelings a basketball team gets after winning a World Championship. But there would be no parade. No champagne spraying. In fact, Dot-A-Rock had to go to work the next morning. The crew decided a more low-key celebration was appropriate.

"There was this spot in the Bronx near 170th Street near Jerome Avenue where everybody goes and you can have a burger and fries or you can have some breakfast," Theodore said. "It was called Munch Time. That was the spot. That's what we did after the event. We just went and had some breakfast, and kept it moving."[43]

One of the most important nights in Fantastic's history didn't end with cocaine and sex (as they rapped about onstage), but rather burgers and eggs. As the first glimpses of sun popped over the morning horizon on July 4, there was so much aftermath stemming from the battle to unpack, and a new era of hip hop was about to grow from the roots laid down at Harlem World that night. For the Fantastic Romantic Five, the win just represented one show, one summer party where they did what they needed to do. They'd be back at it right away. The rest of the hip hop world, however, would dissect the battle for the days, weeks, and years to come.

Cold Crush's Jerry Dee Lewis (*left*) and Grandmaster Caz (*right*) performing at Harlem World, 1981. Photo by Joe Conzo Jr.

Chapter 9

Traveling Tapes

When the battle was over, the Fantastic Romantic Five thought that their rivalry with Cold Crush was definitively settled and they were on to the next phase of their careers. They had won fair and square, after all. There really wasn't anything left to prove. However, as the aftermath of the legendary party played out, it became exceedingly clear that the conversation surrounding the battle was going to continue for weeks and weeks.

And that's all because of one particular piece of technology. The truth is, the battle would likely be a completely forgotten event had the cassette tape never been invented. Along with Joe Conzo's photos and a few promotional flyers, the tape recorded that night remains the only documented evidence of the party even happening.

The development of the cassette tape runs parallel to the development of hip hop music. In the early 1960s, the first cassettes began to appear in Europe and Japan, but they were too bulky, at more than six inches across, to become popular consumer goods. Early cassette recorders actually recorded onto giant tape reels like those found in professional studios. The later, smaller versions were lacking in audio quality. However, as the 1970s rolled on, improvements were consistently being made to the technology and the recorders shrank to become smaller and smaller. The tapes themselves became a booming industry. They were either sold as blanks that anything from a professor's lecture to an Ayatollah's revolutionary musings could be recorded on, or as "musicassettes" with releases from artists in the same shops that peddled records or 8-tracks.[1]

Of course, a cassette is completely worthless without the technology to play it. And the boombox, which was also introduced in the 1960s, became an iconic fixture of hip hop culture as a result. Typically dark in color with sleek chrome accents and covered with as many lights as the manufacturer could fit, the gadgets look tough and futuristic, and sat proudly on the shoulders of at least one hip hop head on every block. In Spike Lee's iconic 1989 film *Do The Right Thing*, there was even a moment when Billy Nunn's Radio Raheem and some of his Latino neighbors competed to see whose box could blast the loudest. When Raheem won out, his competitor turned his boombox off, looking dejected.

"The boombox was instrumental," said Fred Braithwaite, who took on the name Fab 5 Freddy in the 1980s.[2] Born in Brooklyn in 1959, Braithwaite was one of hip hop's most crucial early ambassadors. He helped link underground hip hop culture with the mainstream.

"In the beginnings of hip hop," Braithwaite explained, "the way the music was spread around the city was on cassette tape. Many great DJs recorded their sessions at parties in the Bronx. The way most people in the city first got any inkling of this new music was by cassettes, which were either recorded from the actual mixing board from the party, or somebody in the party with a boombox recording live in the party. If you didn't hear it there then somebody you knew, if they were cool enough, might have had a tape from one of these parties."[3]

Regan Sommer McCoy, a hip hop historian who focuses on the impacts of the cassette tape, claimed that the tape was the only way for many hip hop fans to experience the new movement, considering they were either too young or too far away to get into parties at the time.

"It was the tape at that time," she said. "It wasn't vinyl because they weren't *on* vinyl. They were live to tape. The tape could be dubbed. You could make copies of it. The tape was monumental not just for hip hop, for music in general at that time because it was an affordable way for you to record a show, you could be your own DJ at home. You could do whatever you wanted."[4]

In a *20/20* special report about hip hop that aired in 1981, reporter Steve Fox pointed out how the "big box [sic]" had become such an integral part of rap music that rapping was used in commercials for companies like Panasonic to sell their newest models.[5] While the image of a group of young people surrounding one all-important bringer of the boombox came to symbolize summer for so many people who grew up during the 1970s and '80s, that didn't mean it was particularly popular among the older generation. Those who weren't fans of hip hop considered the boombox a symbol of being forced to consume music that wasn't of their taste.

"People have traditionally been offended by noise, or what they perceive of as noise," said noted music journalist Lisa Robinson in that *20/20* special. "People hated rock n' roll fifteen years ago. It's outside of their experience, it's not something they really understand. It is very Black, and very urban, and people are scared of that."[6]

That was in 1981. In 2009, twenty-seven years later, hatred of the boombox still ran deep through many people who were interviewed on the street for NPR's story about the device's history. They were shown a picture of a boombox and then asked what immediately came to mind.

"Loud noises on the subway."

"Noise, rap."

"The only thing I remember is that people only had one volume and that volume was 'loud.'"

"There's too much noise in the streets as it is. It's so noisy and why do people have to walk around listening to music out loud?"

"'I'm really annoying you with this music that I *know* you don't like but I dare you to stop me.'"[7]

Such always seems to be the case when young people are on to a cool new trend: it's misunderstood, especially if those young people come from an ethnic minority. According to Fab 5 Freddy, the prevalence of cassette recordings on New York streets led to racially charged complaints about "noise pollution," as it was dubbed.

"I want to say that as we traveled, as young inner-city kids—African American and Latino—moved around the city in our little crews or posses and enjoyed life in the city in the summertimes, you could see there were people that weren't into us as people," he said. "They weren't into our music or our culture, and then as a result of that developed what I considered a racially tinged backlash, you know, like, 'I don't want those people and I definitely don't want to hear their music.'"[8]

It really didn't matter that some people took a disparaging view of the boombox and the tapes. The cassette tape wasn't going anywhere. In fact, the format's popularity exploded through the early 1980s. Even if a rap group didn't have a record deal, people were able to hear their routines, lyrics, and breakbeats away from the party. People were even empowered to record their own raps and bring those tapes down to the street, getting their rhymes and messages out to a block-wide audience. There were hip hop records out but they were made more in the Motown R&B style, often with a live band.[9] The lyrics and call-and-response routines were about partying, but the *energy* of hip hop hadn't yet been pressed on vinyl. Not to mention, record players weren't as portable.

* * *

The cassette and boombox captured the imagination of many young hip hop fans who couldn't get into places like Harlem World. For them, aside from the occasional block party, bootleg recordings of shows were the only way to authentically experience the new genre they loved. For Harlem's Troy Smith, tapes became an obsession that continues to this day—as was mentioned in chapter 6, he's amassed a collection of well over three hundred cassettes.[10] Smith recalled that when he first started becoming a serious hip hop head, he didn't have the equipment required to copy tapes, so all he could do was just borrow cassettes from people who had already procured or copied them.

"The strange thing is, tapes were going in the streets for like ten or twelve dollars," Smith said. "At that time, I wasn't getting no money, so I would just listen to them [in the street] but sooner or later my friend—God bless him—me and him were the same age and his momma allowed him to go to the jams. Somehow he would always get the tape and one thing I have to say about my good friend: he would allow me to listen to those tapes. He would put them in my hands, and I would get it and I would go upstairs and I wouldn't come out for the remainder of the day as I'm listening to it from side A to side B, back to side A back to side B."[11]

Tapes became so popular among young people in the five boroughs that a sort of miniature cassette economy popped up. In school cafeterias, kids traded tapes they were done with for those they hadn't heard. Sometimes Smith and his buddies would even break into schools to steal blank cassette tapes (mainly used for recording foreign-language projects) that they could repurpose to make recordings. Often, they would just record right over their old homework.[12]

Grandmaster Caz saw the potential of the cassette early, well before he joined the Cold Crush. In fact, he made a business out of it, taking advantage of his first-floor apartment. "I decided to start taping because I wanted to listen to myself," he said. "I wanted to practice and be able to go back over it, and I saw the value of having records of stuff other people didn't have. People had to go to parties to hear the records I had in my crates. So I'm like, 'Well shit, I can just make you a b-boy tape right here, or a breakbeat tape, and get paid.' That's where my entrepreneurial spirit kicked in. I started actually making people mixtapes in my house. Like one person at a time. 'Come to my house, sit down, I'll make you a tape. What's your man's name? What school do you go to? Who's your girlfriend?' That type of shit. I'd say that shit on a tape and that's their own original tape, it's got their name in it and everything."[13]

According to Caz, he sold those first mixtapes for ten bucks each. Not bad.

In the early 1980s, the premium shows—the kind to feature Cold Crush, Fantastic, the Furious Five, etc.—took place in clubs in the middle of the night, often on a school night, so the kid with the boombox and a tape sort of became a miniature DJ for his squad. Having a boombox and a cassette of a great show became the equivalent of standing behind the ropes at a park jam a few years earlier.

"You was a bad man if you had something dope," Troy Smith said. "I remember I was listening to someone playing Flash, the live party at T-Connection . . . this dude puts it in his radio and there's like four guys guarding his box. And people are just standing there and nodding their heads. But it's dope, because it was right at that time when it came. When you're standing by the box, you know, you feel like you're down with the crew."[14]

The first group to realize the cassette's potential to help grow a following was Smith's favorite one, the Cold Crush Brothers. They enlisted the help of friend Elvis Moreno, a friend of Caz and JDL who predated their time with the group and went by the name "Tape Master." Moreno recorded every Cold Crush show he could get to and he didn't need to rely on a fuzzy "speaker to speaker" recording by putting his boombox near the stage and hitting record.[15] He got access to the mixing board at most of the shows he went to and was able to make quality tapes—or at least tapes where you could distinguish the lyrics. Most of the recordings have been lost to history, but some survive to this day, serving as the only audio record of the Cold Crush's best shows. The exact number of tapes is unknown at this time, but some speculate that there are a few that remain undiscovered. Perhaps they are sitting in the possessions of late Harlem World Crew members like DJ Randy or Son of Sam. Troy Smith was quick to point out that he only has ten to fifteen tapes from Harlem World, but people were partying there nearly around the clock, seven days a week. He said he's been told there were microphones in the ceiling that recorded the happenings in the club to tape reels, but those reels haven't surfaced at this point.[16] So fans are left with Conzo's photos and Tape Master's recordings until a new discovery is made.

"Tape Master became the main person to get tapes not only of the Cold Crush Brothers but anybody who performed with the Cold Crush Brothers," Caz said. "We had a good relationship. He helped to spread the gospel of the Cold Crush and pretty much all hip hop, and he turned it into a little business."[17] Tape Master would sell his tapes at a small stall at a flea market near Caz's neighborhood. From there, they were copied and disseminated all over New York.

The tape from July 3, 1981, immediately made an impact among the hip hop faithful when it began to surface days later. It was lengthy (more than forty-seven minutes long) and was highly anticipated given how many people had attended the battle and how quickly word had spread about it. The battle would also gain legendary status with the help of an unorthodox distribution system: New York car services.

Community Car Service and the OJ Car Service were early versions of today's ridesharing apps like Uber and Lyft. Luxury car owners were on call to pick up residents of the five boroughs who wanted an extra special arrival at whatever event they were going to (some very fly kids would even take them to school). What made these services unique was their integration with hip hop.

"It was Uber with hip hop," Paradise Gray said. "It was people that had fancy cars, so if you got an OJ, you didn't get a beat-up-ass Liberty Cab. You got a Cadillac or a Lincoln, you know you got a dope-ass car, and there was always a hip hop tape playing."[18]

According to Charlie Chase, the music was more of a part of the car service experience than actually getting to your destination.

"Most of these guys, when you drove an OJ or Community, the drivers prided themselves on having banging sound systems," Chase said. "A lot of guys were like, 'If you ain't got a banging system I don't want you, send me the next car.'"[19]

The OJ Service became such a hip hop icon that a rhyme about the company was included in "Rapper's Delight."

> You say if your girl starts actin' up,
> Then you take her friend
> I say skip, dive, what can I say?
> I can't fit 'em all inside my OJ.[20]

Luxury cars included cassette players at that point, so mixtapes made by DJs and bootleg recordings of performances (like the battle) became the number one source of in-ride entertainment. But where was a good driver to get the tapes? That's where the emcees and DJs themselves came in.

One of the first guys to start copying the tape of the battle was actually Charlie Chase himself. He used his first-floor apartment and a bedroom window that overlooked the street to his advantage.

"A lot of these drivers would knock on my window, 'Yo, what's the latest tape?'" Chase said. "I'd give it to them. They'd go in the car and play the shit and people would jump in and go, 'Yo, what tape is this?' and they'd say, 'This is Charlie Chase's new tape, this is Flash's new tape, this is Theodore's new tape.' That's how it started. From there, people are like, 'Yo, how can I get a Charlie Chase tape?' There's no internet. There's no cell phones, there's none of that shit. It's word of mouth. It's CNN: the streets. 'Yeah, this is where you go, this is where he lives. You can knock on his window. He sells them out his window.' That's how that became a thing."[21]

After acquiring the tapes from Charlie Chase's window or from Tape Master or another Cold Crush member, fans copied them at will and sold them, traded them, or gifted them to their friends. They spread around "the network," as Troy Smith put it, quickly.

"[The battle] is the kind of tape to make average listeners listen more," Smith said. "It was the network. The whole projects wasn't talking about it. The whole projects wasn't talking about it the way they'd later talk about the records."[22]

The tapes of the battle flooded the five boroughs. They were everywhere. Soon they'd even make their way abroad.

"You had cats who went to college and they'd share them with their buddies," Charlie Chase said. "And then you had cats who went downtown who met other kids who were foreign. Japanese, Chinese, whatever. They'd get the tapes and mail them to their brothers and sisters overseas. Now the tapes are overseas."[23]

And because of that distribution, an interesting phenomenon occurred: people kept talking about the battle. It was one of the greatest live events in hip hop history and Tape Master got a clear recording of the entire thing. Many of the fans who weren't able to make it to Harlem World questioned how the crowd there could've possibly come to the conclusion that Fantastic defeated Cold Crush. Cold Crush's set was longer, they rapped more, they had the "Cat's in the Cradle" routine. Many fans were mystified. It definitely fostered a lot of conversation between the two fan bases in classrooms, bodegas, basketball courts, and barber shops around the city. People are still judging the battle to this day, four decades later.

"They won the popular vote," Caz said. "They went on last, most of that was girls screaming, you know? They was the pretty boys, and they had the last impression. It wasn't until later on, when you analyzed it, and through the cassette tapes that people acquired just days after, that the consensus kind of changed. This isn't just me saying it. This is historically, the consensus changed. And they was like, 'Wait, hold up, these n*ggas, they didn't sound better. They might've looked better up there but they didn't sound better.'"[24]

Charlie Chase shared similar experiences as Caz, which he said made the battle loss all the more crushing, as more and more people claimed that Cold Crush should've won based on the recordings. Those people included friends of the group, but also random people in the neighborhood.

"What really compounded that even more is when we're hearing the same thing from people in the streets," Chase said. "Like, 'Y'all won that shit, why didn't you win? What happened?' How do you explain that shit?"[25]

Chase said the crews went back and forth for *years* talking trash about that night.

"For a few more years we were like, 'Y'all motherfuckers knew you didn't win!' And they were like: 'But we won, you can say what the fuck you wanna.' We said, 'Nah, you had them little bitches up in front screaming for y'all.' They said, 'But y'all didn't win!'"[26]

As Chase indicated, the Fantastic Five don't take the legacy of the battle lightly either. In fact, some members took offense to the assertions that the tapes reveal the true winner of what was, after all, a live performance competition.

"They got the nerve to say that we stacked the deck," Whipper Whip said. "'Oh yeah, y'all bringing all these girls.' We brought *ourselves* to that fucking party. If the girls come we can't help that. What's a party with no girls? And Caz has the balls to try to put a spin and twist to this shit. 'Oh yeah, we lost, but listen to the tape.' Fuck you. Fuck that tape. The tape was good and you'll hear the same shit on the tape you heard at the show. We rocked your ass. I still talk shit about it."[27]

In his own way, many years later, the quiet, kind Grand Wizzard Theodore even puffed his chest out when remembering the aftermath of the battle. When he left Munch Time that Fourth of July morning, he couldn't have known how much talk the matchup would produce, but now he relishes it.

"That battle was talked about for weeks," he said. "'Cold Crush really won.' 'Fantastic only won because they looked good on stage, they messed up a couple of times.' It is what it is," he added with a smirk.[28]

It should be noted that many neutral fans who heard the tape still judged Fantastic as the winner of the battle. Troy Smith believed so, even though he was more of a Cold Crush fan overall.

"When I went home and I heard what Fantastic was doing, I was amazed," he said. "See I already knew the Cold Crush routines, it was an enjoyable tape, but what really hit me was the ending, when they judged to find out who won."[29]

The winner of the battle will continue to be debated, but the winners of that night more than any individual crew were hip hop fans in general. Fantastic and Cold Crush had their dedicated fan bases but there was crossover between them. People who loved Fantastic tended to also love Cold Crush and vice versa, and the battle was an opportunity to highlight the greatness of two pioneering crews bringing their very best material out to one party. The tapes highlighted hip hop at its most fun, its purest—when it's not about selling records but instead is about making the crowd as happy as possible.

"I loved Fantastic's rap routines, but I loved Caz's singing routines," Paradise Gray said. "I loved Whipper Whip and Dot-A-Rock more as rappers but I liked Cold Crush more as a crew, as a synchronized group of brothers that brought it hard with the singing routines that Caz created. They were unheralded, it was dope as hell."[30]

*   *   *

Just a few months after the battle between Fantastic and Cold Crush, another tape emerged from Harlem World that represented a complete shift in hip hop battle culture and the way emcees treated one another. It sent its own shockwaves through New York.

Busy Bee Starski was one of the best party emcees of his era. In the video captured by Charlie Ahearn at the Celebrity Club in 1980, he clearly had the best performance of any emcee there (including Caz).[31] His ability to hype up a crowd was unmatched at the time. Mohandas Dewese, a member of Harlem's Treacherous Three who went by the stage name Kool Moe Dee, followed a model closer to Grandmaster Caz and the Furious Five's Melle Mel—he dazzled the people with lyrical wordplay and pure rapping skills. The skinny, tank top–wearing, bespectacled Busy Bee participated in many emcee contests around the city, at so-called "emcee conventions"—the kind that Fantastic and Cold Crush used to dominate in the group division. According to Starski, Moe Dee grew frustrated because the Treacherous Three couldn't break out against more popular and well-established groups like Fantastic and Cold Crush. Harlem's Moe Dee, a very cerebral emcee who now holds a degree in macroeconomics, was actually hosting the 1981 Christmas Emcee Convention at Harlem World, not participating in it. There are different versions of the story depending on who is talking, but according to Moe Dee, he wasn't originally planning on performing that night.

While Busy Bee was on stage posing for photos with the trophy before the competition had even begun, he boldly claimed that no one could beat him. A heckler from the crowd shouted that Busy Bee couldn't beat Kool Moe Dee, and Busy Bee responded by saying that he didn't care who was up against him—that it didn't matter. Busy Bee carried on, saying he'd be back soon to claim his prize, to which the heckler once again suggested he couldn't beat Moe Dee.[32]

"I don't even know what I expected him to do," Moe Dee said. "Like was he supposed to turn around and say 'No, I can't beat him'? Because that's not machismo, that wouldn't work. So he did what he was supposed to do, but my ego was just out of whack at the time. So I said, 'I can't believe that he didn't acknowledge that he couldn't beat me in a battle.' So I go up to the guy in Harlem World and I said to put my name on the list. He said, 'You're getting in the battle?' I said, 'Yeah, and put me on right after Busy Bee.'"[33]

Busy Bee, in his typical fashion, totally rocked the party. His signature "ba-ditty-ba" routine (which would eventually become fodder for Kid Rock's 1999 smash hit, "Bawitdaba") drew great reactions and call-and-responses from the crowd.[34] In Busy Bee's mind, he did what needed to be done and went down to Harlem World's lower level to relax and celebrate a well-earned victory. He had no idea what was coming. He would only find out what Kool Moe Dee said, like most hip hop fans, by listening to the tape.

"I didn't pay [Moe Dee] no mind, he didn't bother me," Starski said. "But they said, 'Busy Bee, he was snappin' all this and . . . ' You know, it was called snappin' back then. 'Getting all over you!' I said, 'Yeah, what you mean?' They said, 'Busy Bee, man this guy just went crazy on you, man! Everybody laughin'.' So I said, 'Is that right?' So I go listen to the tape, I'm like, 'Oh, wow! He said all that? OK, fine.'"[35]

Moe Dee decided on an approach that completely turned hip hop on its head. He was not concerned with displaying his skills and letting the crowd decide who was better. Instead, he wanted to "snap on" or insult Busy Bee as many times as possible using an array of lyrical assaults that would've floored even the most poetic emcees of his era. Joined onstage by his Treacherous Three group mates, he tore into Busy Bee: "Hold on, Busy Bee, I don't mean to be bold/But put that 'ba-ditty-ba' bullshit on hold."[36]

That grabbed the crowd's attention, and for the next five minutes, Kool Moe Dee wouldn't let it go. According to Moe Dee and his Treacherous Three group mate Lamar Hill (L.A. Sunshine), most of the rhymes were freestyled off the top of his head.

"He didn't really write it," said Sunshine. "If you really listen to the Moe Dee versus Busy tape, you hear Moe fumbling through all that shit. All of it was [freestyled] until the very end."[37]

Moe Dee accused Busy Bee of stealing his name from Lovebug Starski, buying rhymes from Spoonie Gee, and only being able to win shows at "celebrity clubs," which he referred to in his lyrics as "the kind of shows that everyone knows," adding "those are the kind you can win/They're all set up before he comes in."[38] The leather- and dark sunglasses–wearing, bombastic emcee made it clear through his rhymes that he wasn't trying to beat Busy Bee at his own game, but was changing the object of the game entirely. Gone were the days of trying to outdo your opponent with a sheer display of skills—it was now about putting him down.

"Anybody who knows any background on Moe Dee, Moe Dee takes emceeing and his lyricism very seriously," L.A. Sunshine said. "So once he was kind of like called to the table, you can't fuck with Moe Dee. 'I don't give a fuck, I'll bust everybody's ass.'"[39]

Moe Dee didn't try to get a call-and-response going from the crowd. He didn't care about getting the party going or getting the loudest crowd reaction—the previously stated goals for winning a battle. He wanted people to listen to precisely what he was *saying* which, in 1981, was revolutionary in its own right.

"That's a testament to who Moe Dee is," L.A. Sunshine said. "When Moe Dee heard that he was like, 'I'm not going to say my rhymes,' because we were always more analytical than the average emcees in terms of our lyricism. Moe knows that Busy is just gonna get up there and say 'Bawitdaba bi dang bi dang . . .' We know that. To make the point, Moe would be like, 'I know he's gonna do this and I know he did that but I want you to *hear* what I am saying. I want you to hear my rhymes and tell me his rhymes are better than mine.'"[40]

According to Sunshine, Moe Dee went to the bathroom and planned out the basic structure of the rhymes before bringing them to the stage. Sunshine joined in a bit toward the end because Moe Dee used some familiar Treacherous Three routines that he already knew, drawing especially from "Fast Rhymes," one of their staples. When Kool Moe Dee spat out:

> Very, very merry, merry
> Every time I bust a cherry
> Oh my god, it's fame and glory
> Thought I'd never tell this story
> Only time I'm from the mic
> Because it's something that I like
> To reassure, the rhymes are low
> I always keep some sex in store.

L.A. Sunshine followed it up with:

> The baddest bad, superbad
> Never sad, always glad

Rhymer that you'd rather have

If you fail, I never have

Sleek, sleek so unique

Guaranteed to move your feet

So ladies rock without a doubt

Guaranteed to turn it out.[41]

The two-on-one double-team was just the icing on the cake, and by the time Moe Dee left the stage, the crowd was stunned. Some were screaming as if they were on a roller coaster. Others sat in silence like they had just witnessed a crime. L.A. Sunshine remembers the immediate aftermath well.

"It was a buzz, it was thick. It was thick in there," he said. "Emcee battles are thick to begin with because it's a show in there. It's *Showtime at the Apollo* when you have two emcees going at each other. Moe was so into himself in terms of his lyricism that he would not grace the stage regularly as much as the average cat would. Just seeing Moe on stage is a delight to begin with. 'Oh shit, Moe Dee's gettin' on? We're going to be treated.' So to get that and then to get 'Hold on, Busy Bee, I don't mean to be bold/but put that "ba-ditty-ba" bullshit on hold,' oh shit! It just swept the air out of the room. Everybody was like, 'Oh shit, what the fuck?'"[42]

That night, the crowd wasn't just filled with your average hip hop revelers. There were many well-known emcees in the audience watching their friends perform. Among them, there was an impression that the hip hop game had changed even before Moe Dee finished his rap. The Fantastic Five, for example, were just feet away from the stage that night.

"It was disrespectful," Kevie Kev said. "Had it been Moe Dee talking to us, someone would've been fighting. You wouldn't have been able to talk shit to me like that, you didn't even know me like that."[43]

Grandmaster Caz, who remains a good friend of the Treacherous Three to this day, was standing right in front of the stage when Moe Dee performed. He said his mouth was agape, like everyone else's in the room. He claimed that he knew the basics of Moe Dee's plan but had no idea to what extent he'd be eviscerating Busy Bee. He also disputed L.A. Sunshine's claim that Moe Dee freestyled the majority of the rap.

"Busy Bee was bragging every week like, 'Yeah, I'm gonna be knocking out all bums, and that trophy's going home with me,' and such and such," Caz said. "You know how Busy did it, that braggadocious style. It wasn't nothing to be threatened by because everybody knew Busy was no real rap n*gga. Moe Dee just took offense to it and I guess he knew a few things and was like, 'You know what? I'm gonna shut this n*gga up once and for all.' So that was a premeditated thing he did. It wasn't like he did it on the spot and it was a freestyle. From Busy's early bragging, Moe went home and concocted that rhyme and then was like, 'Aight, I'm gonna get him in the contest and do this shit.'"[44]

Caz noted that the Christmas battle changed everything about the relationship between emcees and their crews from one of respectful, sporting competition to real feuds laced with animosity. Moe Dee had forever altered the dynamics between hip hop artists.

"I was fucking shocked," Caz said. "I was like, 'OH SHIT!' I was like, 'Oh he didn't.' I was dumbfounded, I was stunned. I was just like the rest of the crowd. Because up to that point, if we battled somebody it was a battle of skills. It wasn't personal. It wasn't 'Fuck you' and 'You ain't shit' and 'You're a bum' and this and that. It wasn't like that. It was 'I'm gonna say a better rhyme than you.'"[45]

Although the rules had been permanently altered, Caz made it clear to Moe Dee (and other emcees) that they'd better not try that with him, or their public perception would never be the same.

"I wish a n*gga *would* come at me like that," Caz said. "Moe Dee will tell you himself that he wouldn't do that to me. He said, 'You don't know how Caz can come back at you. He's funny, he's smart.' Any way somebody comes at me I'm coming back at them even worse, it's not a consideration."[46]

L.A. Sunshine remembered that the majority of the people in the crowd congratulated him and Moe Dee for a great performance instead of ridiculing them for violating some unwritten rules of emceeing. Still, they're occasionally criticized to this day for picking on Busy Bee, who was regarded as a party-starter in the spirit of DJ Hollywood and not considered lyrically dexterous enough to put up a strong fight.[47] However, the compliments have far outweighed the critics. The culture was still embryonic at that point and the standards were still being set, and many people consider that performance to be crucial in determining what it meant to be a superstar emcee.

"You hear me saying, 'Shut up, shut up,'" L.A. Sunshine said. "I'm telling people I want you to *listen* to what he's saying. Then there were two guys that were saying, 'You're a fucking cheerleader, you're on Moe Dee's dick, blah blah blah.' After it was over, these same two cats are high-fiving each other, going, 'Yeah that shit was crazy,' 'Yeah, see, that's what I'm talking about.'"[48]

Obviously, word of that performance rippled far beyond the walls of Harlem World thanks to the tapes. The popularity and impact of Moe Dee versus Busy Bee rivaled only Fantastic versus Cold Crush— and for some fans, it was even more important. Troy Smith, who was too young to be in Harlem World that night, was in disbelief when he heard the tape (on loan from a friend) for the first time. There was literally nothing like it; even seasoned hip hop heads were at a complete loss.

"The Cold Crush battle with Fantastic didn't really hit me the way the Busy Bee and Moe Dee's battle hit me," Smith said. "Busy Bee and

Moe Dee's battle hit me where I was looking at the radio going, 'Oh shit. Moe said that? And he said that? And he kept saying *that*?' That's one of those tapes I didn't want to give back. It's not that I didn't want to give it back to [my friend]. It just took a long time, I had to keep listening to it. That's just one of those joints where I kept rewinding it and rewinding it."[49]

Many, many fans had the same reaction when they heard both the Cold Crush versus Fantastic tape and the Busy Bee versus Moe Dee tape. As a result, the bootlegged, fuzzy-sounding, cheap cassettes became just as popular as the latest hip hop records in New York, which would be critical for the next phase of the genre. The proliferation of tapes was key in keeping the original hip hop sounds alive and not allowing the recording industry to swallow up the underground phenomenon.

*   *   *

It was with the help of the tapes that hip hop gained exposure to a larger audience, especially in one critical subset of the city: Manhattan's thriving punk rock and avant-garde art scene. The relationship between hip hop and punk was so natural. Punk was an alternative to the over-the-top, ultra-capitalist glam rock that had overtaken the industry in the 1970s, and hip hop offered an alternative to mass-produced, monotonous disco. Both genres were all about sticking it to the man, and the "man" was the mainstream music industry, which had tried to clean up hip hop and present groups like the Sugarhill Gang and even individuals like Kurtis Blow as extensions of R&B that belonged on the ritzy *Soul Train* stage rather than the streets of the South Bronx.

Pop artist Keith Haring and Fab 5 Freddy brought graffiti culture to trendy downtown galleries—the first facet of hip hop culture to cross over between the scenes.[50] As an exceptional graffiti writer, Freddy's mission was to take what many considered just street vandalism and elevate it to a higher place.

"I was trying to hook up with people that I felt would have a sensibility in terms of what I was trying to do," Freddy said. "Because nobody was saying, 'Hi, I'm an artist.' Graffiti artist or whatever you want to call it at that time, that was not happening. But I felt like the people that were doing punk rock, and I had read a lot about what was going on with that."[51]

"There was graffiti and then there was this new music being developed," he added. "And I felt that they were connected. So I was moving in terms of making connections with the people and an audience that would understand what my point was, or the argument I was trying to make."[52]

Fascinated by the artistic style, significant power players in the scene gravitated toward Freddy and company, and they embraced both visual and musical artists from the hip hop movement. "Master of Records" Afrika Bambaataa started playing DJ sets soon afterward in galleries and downtown clubs.[53] It was in this way, coupled with the movement of cassette tapes, that hip hop became popular among students at New York University, Columbia, Fordham, and other local schools. In another significant development for the genre, it took hold among mostly white crowds who attended the punk rock clubs like CBGB and Danceteria. In fact, the new wave punk sound greatly influenced Bambaataa and Soulsonic Force's smash hit record, *Planet Rock*, which sampled new wave band Kraftwerk alongside hip hop staple "Super Sporm." *Planet Rock* is also significant because it introduces artificial drum sounds instead of breakbeats; the electronic sound would soon become a staple of hip hop.

"One of the astonishing things about the evolution of rap is how quickly it was embraced by artists in downtown Manhattan," said Bill

Adler. "That comes down to very few individuals who were ambassadors."[54]

Michael Holman, who opened Club Negril, and Kool Lady Blue, who booked hip hop shows at the Roxy, were cited by Adler as two of those pioneers.[55] In fact, Negril became a stronghold for the Cold Crush Brothers in the years after the battle. Joe Conzo has photos documenting many of their performances there. Grandmaster Flash performed at those clubs as well, taking delight in turning a fresh new audience onto hip hop music.

According to Flash, the popularity of hip hop among the college crowd allowed for a whole new market to open up. The Furious Five could expect to be booked constantly on the college circuit to play for audiences who might not have heard the music before. Flash didn't know what to expect when he played breaks like "Apache" for the first time to a majority white crowd, but when he did, "that shit went off."[56]

In addition to promoters from traditional rock clubs who were willing to go out on a limb and book hip hop artists, Adler circled back to Fab 5 Freddy as another major ambassador.[57] Before the Cold Crush and Fantastic battle even happened, Freddy would make introductions that would lead to one of the unlikeliest smash hits in hip hop history—and one of the most important.

* * *

Through his connections in the art scene, Freddy had grown friendly with Chris Stein, the lead guitarist for Blondie, which was among the most influential and popular bands from the late 1970s punk scene. Stein soon introduced Freddy to the rest of the band, including lead vocalist Debbie Harry. They immediately gravitated toward Freddy's art and entrepreneurial spirit.

"They were, like, the first patrons of my work," Freddy said. "I mean, for me being a young Black kid out of Bed-Stuy Brooklyn, there wasn't a lot of people I could talk to about these ideas, to really fully articulate them the way I was envisioning them. Who in my neighborhood knew about Andy Warhol or cared or knew about, you know, punk rock or whatever was going on and these things?"[58]

Freddy, who was an early regular of legendary rock club CBGB, soon began what he described as a "cultural exchange." He took Blondie—which had achieved massive crossover pop success at that point—to a jam at the Webster Police Athletic League in the Bronx. Among the performers were the Cold Crush Brothers and the Mercedes Ladies.[59] Stein and Harry were thrilled with the show and very excited by the whole scene in general.

"We saw this big event, this big rap event, that was super exciting," Stein said. "It was just phenomenal, it was a game-changer to me, because I saw that it was paralleling what was going on downtown but we didn't know much about it."[60]

As the members of Blondie attended more shows both downtown and in the Bronx, Freddy eventually introduced them to Grandmaster Flash, who had already made great inroads in the downtown scene. As Flash recalled, Harry told him that she'd write a song about him.[61] That song became "Rapture," a 1980 love letter to the new scene Blondie had discovered. The six-minute odyssey fuses new wave with hip hop and even some jazz elements, with live instrumentation. The beginning features Harry's soprano vocals with no indication that the song will transform into a narrative hip hop track. There is no rapping until 2:10 into the song, but the opening lines of Harry's first verse remain among the most famous lyrics of the era.

Fab 5 Freddy told me everybody's fly
DJ spinnin' I said, "My My"
Flash is fast, Flash is cool
François c'est pas, Flash ain't no dude.[62]

With those words, two of hip hop's key figures were rocketed to radios nationwide. Appearances in Blondie's music video—which featured Harry as a sort of Alice exploring a hip hop wonderland—didn't hurt either.

The video started with a Haitian man dressed in a white tuxedo and top hat who is meant to represent the voodoo *loa* [god] Baron Samedi. After dancing a bit, Samedi looked in on Harry's basement, where dozens of people were doing, quite frankly, random things. Meanwhile, the video showed Harry exploring different rooms featuring graffiti writers spraying walls. There was footage of a shirtless man wearing a Native American headdress and a tall guy dressed as Uncle Sam. A girl in a pink tutu danced ballet next to a store window display occupied by live people. It was conceptually strange and very new wave. Stein claimed the Haitian brought some girls with him, and that one of them fell into a trance during the shoot.

Lyrically, the song didn't make much sense, either, as Harry mentioned a man from Mars, eating cars, and "taking a tour through the sewer." She did have a pretty good flow to the beat, however.[63]

The song finally, mercifully, put the word "rap" on the tip of the tongues of mainstream media and Americans all over the country. Amazingly, it was put there by an artist looking to highlight the new hip hop culture and share it rather than steal from it.

"Another landmark was in '80 when Blondie did 'Rapture,'" Bill Adler said. "That was a No. 1 pop hit, and it namechecked some of the important rappers of the moment, and the video was an early smash on MTV, and it sort of codified what was going on between uptown and downtown."[64]

On February 21, 1981—six months before Fantastic and Cold Crush battled— the *New York Daily News* ran a column by Hugh Wyatt entitled "When a Rap Makes Music." In it, Wyatt claimed that "rap music, the sassy new idiom of cool, cosmopolitan street blacks, has so captivated the young white audience that it could possibly be the first form of black music since the so-called soul music of the late '60s to win mass acceptance."[65]

Acknowledging that he only felt compelled to write a column after rap caught the attention of a whiter audience, Wyatt also heaped praise on Blondie. He didn't mention any of the rappers who inspired the group.

"Punk rocker Deborah Harry and Blondie are responsible for the new mass appeal through their recording 'Rapture,'" he wrote. "For the past five years, rap music has become popular among young blacks."[66]

Blondie never claimed that they were hip hop innovators, and the attention they brought to the genre was positive, but that doesn't mean everyone was cool with "Rapture."

"The rap thing—it's more of a tribute than anything," Harry said. "It's not very good. I think it was interesting to a lot of people but I think the real rappers were a little bit uptight and pissed off about it initially."[67]

Harry's claim was contradicted by Caz, who didn't really regard "Rapture" as a rap song because Blondie weren't rappers in the traditional sense. They didn't use beats and they were from a different part of the city—a different world, even if that world shared many connections to the one Caz roamed.

"As far as her as a rapper, I was like, 'Wow, this is going to be people's first impression of hearing rap music,'" Caz said. "It was a novelty song to me. I didn't take it as if people were going to think she was the new rapper or anything like that. She already had a reputation for who she was. 'Rapture' was like an homage to hip hop. Nobody had a problem with Blondie."[68]

Regardless, it's indisputable that the true pioneers of rap like Grandmaster Flash wouldn't have ascended to the mainstream as quickly had it not been for "Rapture," much in the same way groups like Cold Crush and Fantastic wouldn't have reached their heights without the advent of the cassette tape and boombox. For example, the *20/20* special episode about the rap trend led off by saying how rap had come to people's attention through the popularity of "Rapture" before highlighting Kurtis Blow, the Funky 4 + 1, and others.[69]

Besides Blondie and other punk rockers, the downtown scene also featured a young filmmaker and artist named Charlie Ahearn who was on set while the "Rapture" video was being filmed. Unbeknownst to most people, he was already in the process of making something no one had previously attempted—a hip hop movie—and he had recruited the two premier crews from the streets to provide the music. It turned out that both the Cold Crush Brothers and the Fantastic Five would have a curtain call after their great battle, but it would play out not on stage, but on screen.

Chapter 10

———

Wild Style

By the time the landmark film *Wild Style* debuted in 1983, hip hop had changed. It had gone from a niche form of artistic expression to a national phenomenon and economic powerhouse. Still, the film is special because it preserved the original brand of hip hop—the kind enjoyed only by people in the know in the parks and auditoriums of the Bronx and Harlem—for generations to witness.

Forty years after *Wild Style* debuted, director Charlie Ahearn still has an appreciation for the pioneering hip hop artists who inspired and starred in it. One of his favorite things to do is trace the history of the various groups in New York by looking at old flyers and trying to piece together who was in what lineup at what particular time. For example, when he looks back at flyers from 1979, he sees that they were still advertising headliners the L Brothers led by DJs Theodore, Mean Gene, and Cordie-O with emcees Robbie Rob and Kevie Kev. By 1980, one of his flyers advertised "Theodore" with "The Fantastic Five Emcees" in much smaller print as the headliner, with "Chief Rocker Starski" (who had yet to take on the name Busy Bee) toward the top of the bill. Ahearn also has flyers advertising early hip hop shows in lower Manhattan and Brooklyn, far away from the South Bronx and Harlem, showing that hip hop was moving long before the popular narrative suggests.[1]

Among his flyers, Ahearn also has an advertisement for a party at the T-Connection featuring a Cold Crush Brothers lineup with Easy A.D., Dot-A-Rock, and Whipper Whip.

"I could go on and on," Ahearn said. "But in my fantasy it's kind of like, what if people discovered that the Rolling Stones and the Beatles were actually the opposite groups that you think of?"[2]

The flyers are all part of one of the prized photographs from Ahearn's career: a picture of Dot-A-Rock in his bedroom, clad in a silky red sweater and maroon leather hat, posing in front of a giant collage of flyers from shows he'd performed at, his arms up like a basketball star posing with his trophies. It's a striking image of someone who paved his own way by being part of two of the most iconic groups of the early hip hop era. Ahearn later painted the image on a giant canvas.[3] The filmmaker/artist remains passionate about tracking the history of the movement he helped fuel.

"I care. These things matter to me because these people are real and their evolution means something, I think, to hip hop," Ahearn said. "The Cold Crush and the Fantastic had this relationship and that's a really interesting relationship because they both are very close friends of mine in different ways. The first year that I was there, I was trying to understand who they were as a group and who they were as individuals. The thing I understand is that Caz is very close to Whipper Whip, they are tight. That's interesting because that seems to me almost like they could be a duo because it goes back to '79, to the beginning of this development. This is how I read the story."[4]

Ahearn is a self-described hip hop nerd and one of the foremost experts on this time period—even if he's shy to admit that. But in the late 1970s, he had no idea about any of the music. He was making a kung fu movie, *The Deadly Art of Survival*, at the Alfred E. Smith housing project in Manhattan, just across the bridge from Brooklyn. It was while making this movie that Ahearn was first exposed to the music that would inspire his next, much more celebrated project—the first ever hip hop movie.

"I spent 1978 making a kung fu movie by the Brooklyn Bridge where Lee Quiñones lived," he said. "I incorporated some of his handball courts as part of the thing and it was shot on Super 8 and I spent about a year shooting the film. I've been thinking about those days in the Al Smith projects by the Brooklyn Bridge and how the L Brothers and Grandmaster Flash were coming down to that weird spot and it just shows you that hip hop was traveling." As he studied another flyer, he said, "We're talking April of '79, but by April '79 I had already made the movie and left. I preceded this. I'm just saying I was involved in this."[5]

But just being in the presence of hip hop wasn't the only factor that led to Ahearn's appreciation for the movement. He would cross paths with Fab 5 Freddy, much in the same way Blondie did. According to Debbie Harry, Freddy was always thinking about how he could continue to expand hip hop culture beyond its current boundaries. "He's a very entrepreneurial character and just was adventurous," she said. "He likes connecting the dots. He was all over."[6]

Charlie Ahearn was in the same New Wave art scene as Harry and Chris Stein, and he had met Freddy while Freddy's group was putting on their Times Square show. Freddy was introduced to Ahearn at the show, where he told him he was a big fan of the posters Ahearn had made for *The Deadly Art of Survival*, especially one featuring a silkscreen image of a man's bloody face behind a fence. He suggested that he and Ahearn work on a movie together about hip hop music and graffiti.[7]

"By that point I had figured that [it would be good] if a film was made that showed all of these elements together, because at that time nobody saw all these different things as one thing, you know?" Freddy said. "It was like people doing graffiti were just doing graffiti. Rapping, people were rapping. The breakdance scene would go on at hip hop parties, but it was pretty much like a Latin thing, so there were Latin clubs that would happen where breakdancing would go on, you know, much more like developed form or whatever. And you know, of course the DJing thing or whatever. And I had this idea to bring these things together, and Charlie was like, 'This is cool.' So that's when we began to come together and develop the ideas that became *Wild Style*."[8]

Ahearn was fine with the idea, but he wouldn't give the project his full buy-in unless Freddy could bring one special individual aboard.

Lee Quiñones was and still is an immensely talented artist who lived in the same Alfred Smith projects where Ahearn filmed his first movie. Over the course of the filming, he met a high school–aged Quiñones and asked him to appear in the film. Although Quiñones originally said "bet" (slang for "for sure"), he left on his motorbike, his giant afro bouncing in the wind, and Ahearn didn't hear from him again. Ahearn, with his cleft chin and constantly furrowed expression (at least from pictures back then), didn't exactly ooze warmth and friendliness from every pore. Luckily, Quiñones's no-show didn't dissuade Ahearn from wanting to work with the quirky but ultra-talented young man.

It just so happened that Freddy was also a giant fan of Quiñones. In fact, according to Ahearn, he was so taken with Quiñones's spray-can skills that he took drastic measures to track him down: "Freddy made his way to that area where Lee Quiñones was working and basically came to Lee Quiñones's high school and went to the main office and they brought Lee Quiñones to him. That's how they met, like he was a cop."[9]

When Freddy proposed a movie about hip hop, Ahearn said he knew Freddy was in touch with the elusive Quiñones and he didn't want to make the movie without him: "I said, 'Well, the thing that I'm most concerned about is Lee Quiñones, because I wanted to work with Lee on this other movie so I know that Lee's kind of difficult. Bring him here, to this place tomorrow morning at 11:00, and we will talk about making a movie.' That's how I said it, I know that's crazy, that sounds like a movie, but Freddy showed up with Lee Quiñones. I cashed a check for fifty dollars and I consider that the first expenses for *Wild Style*, and I gave them some cash and said, 'Here's some bank, get some paint, and let's do something in front of this wall.' We're talking about Times Square in the daytime and these guys knocked out a large throw-up which just said 'Fab 5.'"[10]

"Fred and I were like white on rice," he added. "The way I am, I'm like very distant, but once I'm on something, I'm all over it, and Fred was the same way, so we just met constantly."[11]

Before the script was set, or even the full concept for the movie, Freddy took Charlie to experience his first park jam in the North Bronx, where he met numerous influential hip hop figures who would later appear in his film. Among them was the first rapper to be cast in the film: Busy Bee. The party starter and "Chief Rocker" didn't need much convincing.

"The Funky Four were performing, and Busy Bee was waiting to go on stage, and I had never met him. I was standing there and Busy Bee said, 'What's up?' and he told me later that he was sweating bullets because he thought I was a cop and I was gonna bust him because he had a lit joint in his hand. I said, 'I'm Charlie Ahearn and I want to make a movie about the hip hop scene,' and he put his arm around me and he walked me out onto the middle of the stage and he took a microphone and he says, 'This is Charlie Ahearn and we're making a movie about the hip hop scene.' So it took him two minutes to cast himself, and I never regretted that."[12]

Because of his presence at the old-school park jams Freddy was taking him to, Ahearn built the film around the early innovators of hip hop like Starski, who helped provide the classic sound and aesthetics the movie leaned on so heavily. What made *Wild Style* such a unique movie was its lack of professional actors. Ahearn believed that, to make the most authentic movie possible, he should cast figures directly from the hip hop scene rather than getting actors to portray the characters. Only Patti Astor, who played Virginia, the suave music reporter, had previous film experience. The rest of the cast consisted of discoveries and revelations from the same hip hop scene Ahearn was trying to capture. For example, Lady Pink, the pioneering graffiti writer, played Rose "Lady Bug," and Lee Quiñones played the main protagonist, the mysterious graffiti writer Raymond Zoro.[13]

For the talented and very cool Astor, the film was very appealing. She had known Charlie and his twin brother John since they were twelve years old; both families used to spend their summers in Binghamton, New York (she recalled hitting Charlie one time with a canoe paddle).[14] Originally, though, Charlie and Freddy had intended on casting Debbie Harry.

"Charlie starts getting this whole thing with Freddy," Astor said, "and I hear that they're making a movie and there's a part for a blonde, punk rock reporter. It wasn't pitched to me. I had to go to them and I said, 'Charlie, I hear you're making this movie and you're looking for a reporter, that's my part!' And he said, 'No, no, no,' because they were looking for Debbie Harry, and so Charlie basically lies and said, 'We want someone more mousy, it's not the part for you.' I said, 'Yes it is! Doesn't Freddy already call me Lois Lane? That's my part.'"[15]

It turned out that Harry couldn't do the movie, so Astor got the role she wanted. Perhaps that was lucky for Ahearn; as Astor pointed out, it would've been difficult to shoot on location in the Bronx with Harry because Blondie had erupted into superstardom prior to the start of production. Astor hadn't had much exposure to hip hop before she met Fab 5 Freddy and Lee Quiñones through the downtown club scene, but now she was invited to their studio to watch them paint.

She hadn't even seen many graffiti-covered train cars because her East Village location allowed her to walk to her favorite spots rather than ride the subway.[16]

Astor was going to get an up close and personal crash course in hip hop from the best possible sources.

* * *

The movie that Ahearn and company ended up releasing wasn't particularly plot-driven. It was more of an amorphous look at all aspects of hip hop, one that resembles a documentary at many points. Basically, the eighty-two-minute film depicts a conflict involving graffiti artist Raymond "Zoro" (played by Quiñones), who is emphatically against a faction of graffiti writers who work in broad daylight to beautify their Bronx neighborhood by painting commissioned murals on local businesses. The film also focuses on the romance between Zoro and Rose "Lady Bug" (played by Lady Pink). Rose is a leader of the commissioned mural painters, the Union Crew.[17]

Rose's crew attracts the attention of local music reporter Virginia, played by Astor. Tall, blonde, and white, clad in a long-sleeve green dress, Virginia represents the collision between hip hop and punk rock that was taking place in the Manhattan college scene. The individual who connects the two worlds is Phade, played (of course) by Fab 5 Freddy. Phade takes Virginia around and introduces her to the graffiti community. He also introduces her to hip hop music and b-boy culture.[18]

Later in the film, Phade and Virginia team up to bring street art to the attention of wealthy art collectors downtown. Sticking with his casting philosophy, Ahearn asked art collector Niva Kislac, who had a Lichtenstein in her bedroom, to play that role. She had also been collecting street art for some time, so she had an intimate understanding of the sort of art that Phade and Virginia were talking about.[19]

Meanwhile, Phade gives Zoro a massive canvas to spray—a run-down amphitheater that hosts a giant hip hop concert at the end of the movie. Zoro manages to finish the project in time and the film concludes with a long jam featuring many of the most notable performers from the era.[20]

Ahearn and Freddy needed hip hop performers to appear in multiple scenes of the film. In fact, it was their search for compelling performers that led Ahearn to shoot video at the Celebrity Club in Harlem in 1980. (Interestingly, he claims this footage, which he used to make casting decisions, is the earliest video ever shot of a live hip hop show.) That footage of an emcee convention, which Ahearn also took to develop his hip hop show–filming technique, showed the same kind of raw, no-frills hip hop that would flow through the film. Hosted by Kool DJ AJ, the convention featured individual emcees who took turns rocking the crowd, straying away from their groups. Grandmaster Caz, JDL, and Almighty Kay Gee all performed their own individual sets. Kay Gee and a nineteen-year-old, skinny, mustachioed Caz had the crowd going nuts. Caz sang over the beat at first before launching into one of his more lyrically dense verses. The best performer of the night by far was Busy Bee, whose character would be credited as the "Chief Rocker" in the film.

"The most interesting people to me were Busy Bee, who just killed it, and Grandmaster Caz, who I thought was an amazing artist," Ahearn said. "I would say I was already friends with both of these people in some way, but also there was Kay Gee, who I thought killed it that night. They're not coming on as the Cold Crush Brothers. They're battling as single emcees, and I thought that Kay Gee seemed to have rock and roll by the tail. He was really good."[21]

Sadly, that night at the Celebrity Club was cut short before Ahearn could record much footage. According to him, "It got to a certain point and the whole thing broke. The video equipment had already been put into boxes and all of a sudden a gun went off and you had a room that was like a basement, with like five hundred people in a basement, suddenly the room just cleared, people were screaming and running in every direction. And I'm standing there and I see the chairs are all broken, people's shoes are on the ground and everyone's gone. I can't explain it beyond that but I will say that this seemed to be a pattern I witnessed a lot in hip hop."[22]

As was the case with the July 3 battle, the circumstances surrounding the appearances of Cold Crush and Fantastic in *Wild Style* were rooted in the absence of two groups: Grandmaster Flash and the Furious Five, and the Funky 4 + 1. According to Ahearn, the Funky 4 + 1 were having major trouble staying together at the time, so having them appear in the movie wouldn't have been sensible. Ahearn actually shot a scene featuring Flash and the Furious Five, but there were questions about their availability given their tour and how each of the individuals in the group were beginning to branch out on their own.[23] The need for two groups to appear and perform in the movie led Ahearn to the top crews in the streets of New York.

"The idea that there was this rivalry between these two groups," Ahearn said. "I didn't know they were friends in junior high school. That wasn't the idea. The idea was that the Funky 4 and Flash were starting to travel. Even the Treacherous Three were starting to travel because they had records out. That created a whole different vibe. The Cold Crush and the Fantastic I saw as homegrown, superhero neighborhood kids. That was the movie I was trying to make. I didn't want to make a movie about the record business or stardom."[24]

Both Fantastic and Cold Crush agreed to appear in the movie well before the battle.[25] Interestingly, Ahearn didn't attend the battle. He said around that time he would've been thinking he was completely ruined because his plan for a summer movie hadn't come together fast enough to begin shooting.[26] Filming wouldn't commence until the fall.

For Grandmaster Caz, the decision to appear in the movie was an easy one, even though he claimed he wasn't particularly close with Charlie and Freddy prior to the start of the filmmaking process. That distance, as far as he was concerned, stemmed from a feeling of being disrespected for years.

"Charlie didn't have to say much. I mean, you're talking about the beginning of something that people are still denying," Caz said. "You're talking about a time when you said 'hip hop' and a lot of people looked on it with disdain. They saw no value in it, intrinsic or otherwise. They were like, 'What the fuck is this? Why should I lend any credence to it?' Eventually hip hop grew on everybody, its importance, its relevance, its history, and everything. When Charlie approached us it kind of validated what we were doing because outsiders said, 'Oh shit, this shit is cool, we should document this, people need to know about this,' and I was like 'See? SEE?'"[27]

Fantastic jumped at the chance to do the movie as well. Theodore was integral to the planning and production of the film's background music, and the emcees were pleased to have an opportunity to show off their skills to a wider audience.

"I felt good to be a part of *Wild Style* because that's the first rap movie," Master Rob said. "It's an honor to be in that movie. I feel great."[28]

Rob's brother, Kevie Kev, was also pleased to be in the movie, but doesn't love how it has since further intertwined his group with his archrivals in the Cold Crush. "Why does everybody keep us together?" he asked. "Why does everybody keep talking about us and they bring up Cold Crush? For what? It's one story, everybody's been fed off of it, they ate off of it. Ask us something else. Them n*ggas ain't the only thing in our career."[29]

It might just be cosmic fate that the two crews aligned once again for the film, or it might be the fact that they were the best two crews for the job, but regardless, they are connected, and the movie helped lock that connection in even tighter.

Cold Crush and Fantastic (who changed their name to the Fantastic Freaks for the movie) had a few iconic scenes in the film. They were the main performers chosen to show a potentially uneducated audience what hip hop was supposed to look and sound like, strictly using breakbeats instead of the new, more electronic sound popularized by Afrika Bambaataa and Grand Mixer DXT, among others.

Early on in the movie, the crews face off against one another on a Bronx basketball court. Fantastic looks fresh as usual; each member of the group is dressed in matching navy blue sweaters with white lettering.[30] The scene has a *West Side Story* vibe, as each crew member rhymes a line and stands nose to nose with their counterpart.

"I think the only lyric that I tried to write in my life was when [we shot] the basketball scene in *Wild Style*," Theodore said. "That's when I tried to write my own rhyme. 'Well I'm the T [Theodore] all dark my face/And when I get you on the court, I beat Charlie Chase.'"[31]

That scene is among the only footage ever captured of the two crews together, and it gives the viewer an idea of just how much they really had in common. Kevie Kev and Kay Gee both make big, drastic hand gestures as they trade lines about how the other can't ball. Whipper Whip and Caz both puff their chests out and tower over the other emcees and DJs. The rivalry is played up in the beginning of the scene when three young women credited as "Fly Girls," including Zulu Queen Lisa Lee, are in the park talking about how Cold Crush and Fantastic don't get along and how the two crews' performances later that night will be a "serious throwdown." They also add in some lines as the crews play basketball. Lisa Lee, for example, raps, "We have to come to an agreement, who's gonna survive, the Cold Crush Four or the Fantasy Five?"[32]

The really interesting thing about this scene is that it's actually a duet. The crews work together to deliver lines in the proper cadence and on beat, which is what makes the song come together so well.

"We're talking high-level hip hop," Ahearn said. "It's a very complicated web, and even that single lineup when they come out like they're in *West Side Story*, they come and face each other, I didn't make that. I made it structurally and said do whatever you can do with it, but they knew exactly what they were doing. If you watch that scene, the two groups are trading rhythmic patterns and echo each other. It's not just that one is saying something against the other. The Cold Crush and Fantastic are working together to create that song that you hear, and I think it's phenomenal."[33]

Caz said he wrote many of the one-liners for that scene and that it wasn't as complex as Ahearn stated, but that the challenge was not having the scene look too preplanned. The crews wanted to avoid going full Broadway and maintain the unpredictability and grittiness that hip hop was known for.

"It had to be kind of simple," Caz said. "It was kind of a no-brainer. We were freestyling, basically. It couldn't look like it was too unnatural. Even the way it came out, it came out a little unnatural."[34]

Caz also made sure to call out his rival, Kevie Kev, for changing up the flow with his line, which didn't follow the same cadence as everyone else's.[35]

When Phade takes Virginia to meet Raymond in a train yard so she can see the great artist in action, Raymond is afraid to continue working on his piece, especially after Virginia suddenly snaps a photo of him.[36] The three of them leave the yard and drive to the Dixie Club, where the Fantastic and Cold Crush are performing that night. Everyone in the room for that shoot offered fond memories of that evening because it wasn't shot in a sequence or in multiple short takes. Rather, Fantastic and Cold Crush performed some of their familiar routines as if they were giving a concert for a room lit up in a glowing red stage light. The Rock Steady Crew showed off their breakdancing on the floor and Busy Bee appeared in the scene as well, but the performances from the two crews were the main attraction. It remains perhaps the best footage captured of the Fantastic Five and the Cold Crush. When Virginia, Raymond, and Phade enter the club, Virginia draws plenty of weary looks from the fans in the audience, perhaps mirroring what Charlie Ahearn experienced himself when he went to his first few jams. Also perhaps like Charlie, Virginia's eyes grow wide when she sees the performers on stage.[37]

Both groups performed their classics. Kevie Kev and Master Rob claimed the routine Fantastic did in the film is their favorite ever.[38] It starts with "We're the Fantastic, five emcees, and we're pleasing all the ladies," and contains Rubie Dee's famous line, "Rubie Dee is my name and I'm Puerto Rican, you might think I'm Black by the way I'm speakin'."[39]

The emcees looked impeccable as usual on stage. Whipper Whip sported a fedora and Dot-A-Rock wore a gold and purple T-shirt, but, according to Kevie Kev, Ahearn asked them to dress down a bit and appear more street, so the tuxedos stayed in the shop.[40] On multiple occasions, the camera cut to a gold necklace–wearing Grand Wizzard Theodore, with one headphone ear on and his hand pressed up tight against it. An overhead shot showed him sticking perfect scratches and needle drops on his turntables. It's great rare footage of an artist deep in the midst of his craft.

Cold Crush's performance started with Caz's "ashes to ashes" routine. Charlie Chase had a stance similar to Theodore, but he was dressed down a bit in a white crewneck sweatshirt. Tony Tone stood next to him wearing a leather baseball cap and a red windbreaker. The four emcees looked much more serious than Fantastic. Almighty Kay Gee wore a hooded zip-up jacket with the hood raised and a bucket hat on top of that. JDL sported a leather jacket and a black turtleneck. Easy A.D. rocked an overcoat, a leather hat similar to Tone's, and leather gloves. Caz looked very cerebral, wearing thick-rimmed glasses, a sideways baseball cap, jeans, sneakers, and a red jacket similar to Tony Tone's, opened to reveal a plain yellow T-shirt.

The glasses came off when Caz took his big solo: a thunderous version of the "Yvette" verse, which was rocking enough to finally get Virginia out on the dance floor, although she didn't attempt the dazzling head spins or slick moonwalks demonstrated by the Rock Steady Crew.[41] Ahearn rightfully pointed out how that part of the scene wasn't realistic: real b-boys wouldn't be dancing like that when Caz busted out a solo. They were more likely to perform when the DJ was playing a set or just left the music running rather than while Caz or another world-class emcee was dropping a heavy verse full of incredible lyricism.[42]

Interestingly enough, Ahearn was working only with ten-minute rolls of film, meaning that anything the crews, dancers, or actors did after that didn't make it into the movie. When it came time to switch out the film, Ahearn would simply cut the scene and tell everyone to relax. For him, it didn't feel like a concert, as he was focused on getting the right shots.

"I didn't direct talent," Ahearn said. "We're working and I told them, 'OK, we start.'"[43]

The performance scene that appeared in the film is actually the second attempt, taken in 1982, according to Ahearn. He said the first one, which featured Lisa Lee, is no longer in his possession.[44]

Patti Astor is one of the few individuals lucky enough to have been in the room for that shoot. She drew parallels between her training as a professional actress and the emcees being seasoned professionals by the time the movie started shooting. "We were there *all* night," she said. "That's the great thing about *Wild Style*: when it's 2:00 a.m. in the Dixie, it's 2:00 a.m. outside in New York; we were right there. It must've been a two-day shoot because there was a whole train track thing and everything. That had to have been a two-day shoot but it must have just seemed like one giant shoot. The other thing too, though, is that with my film training, it's one take, because that's film. So by the time I made that movie it was like my eleventh movie; you couldn't do all this bullshitting around and flubbing your lines and stuff. You didn't stop unless the camera fell over. You learn to get your shit done in one take, and the music guys were the same way."[45]

"That scene was incredible," Astor added. "That's the kind of movie that I wanted to make. I'm very lucky in my career that I've been able to make the kind of movies I wanted to make. That's why that movie endures. I had seen rap performances but not really full-on, and those guys were really the cream of the crop."[46]

In the subsequent scene when Raymond and Virginia waited for Phade outside the club, they were to be accosted by a stick-up kid. There was just one problem: Ahearn hadn't cast one. Luckily, the young director was resourceful, and he once again relied on the street characters who would comprise the vast majority of his cast.

"When Charlie was doing the movie and trying to get people to be in that scene, he was just this one white boy and everybody was wait-ing for this big producer to pull up or something, and Charlie couldn't get anybody to sign contracts," Astor said. "Finally he just said, 'ALL RIGHT, I GOT A HUNDRED DOLLARS HERE FOR ANYBODY THAT WANTS TO SIGN A CONTRACT AND BE IN THE MOVIE,' and then everybody signed and we got rolling."[47]

Ahearn had asked some local young men to stick a gun in Astor's face, only for Phade (played by Freddy) to interrupt the robbers and cool down the situation by telling them that Virginia and Raymond were his friends. There was no script.

"Pooky is the guy who ends up pointing a gun at my head," Astor said. "We go outside and Charlie is like, 'OK, now we're going to do the stick-up scene.' He found these three guys just hanging out by the Dixie. These guys were recruited because they looked just like stick-up guys. Guess what? They were. Great casting."[48]

Having just watched Cold Crush tear up the room, Astor and Quiñones were in for a roller coaster, partly due to Ahearn's hilariously botched prop choice. Astor remembers that saga fondly. "We were about to do this scene and Charlie comes up beside me and pulls out this little gun, it was a starter pistol or something like that, and he says, 'This is the gun that I'm gonna use for the scene, do you think it's all right?' and I said, 'Oh my god, Charlie, that gun is so tiny, you can't even show them that.' He did because we didn't have anything else, and Pooky said, 'I ain't holding up nobody with that pussy-ass gun. Hold on, let me go get my gun, I'll be right back.' So then we all get in the van which had a generator because it was freezing and the other two stick-up guys get in there so it's me, Lee, and the two stick-up guys and whoever else could fit in the front. The other guy, the really light-skinned guy, was sitting in the van and Lee's in the corner and I was talking to him, and he said, 'See, I don't even need no gun, I have this,' and he pulls out this box cutter and clicks it open and I'm like, 'Oh, really! That's like, so interesting!' and he goes, 'Yeah, see . . .' and he turns around and pulls up his shirt and his back is all covered with box cutter scars. I thought Lee was gonna wet his pants."[49]

After a considerable wait, it was time for action, and Pooky whipped out his much more formidable shotgun. According to Astor, it was a "one-take wonder," which must have been a relief for the already petrified Quiñones.

* * *

For Lady Pink, who was just sixteen at the time, the whole experience was new. She was used to lurking around rail yards in the early morning hours, with the goal of painting her trains and never being caught in the act. Charlie Ahearn, already a friend from the art scene, was thrilled to include Pink in the film. A starring role in a movie was far from her comfort zone, but she was at least encouraged to play a version of herself: a cool but quiet graffiti-writing young woman full of unspoken swagger.

She did say that one element of her character was unrealistic. "The movie was loosely written and they did write the love story in there of myself and Lee, but I was still a youngster, still a toy, I was sixteen. They cast me as the leader of the crew of these older guys, who I'm still friends with today, and they just laughed and laughed at the idea that I would remotely be their leader because they're older and better and had been around longer and all of that."[50]

Upon its release in 1983, *Wild Style* drew major attention in New York. According to Ahearn, it was the second highest-grossing film in the city the week of its release, only behind *Terms of Endearment*.[51] Pretty good for an indie art flick with very few prints in circulation and only one trained actor. Ahearn was thrilled. "I sweated bullets when I first showed the film to people," he said. "I would have sweat down the back of my head. I was like, 'Is it grabbing them?' 'Is it working?' 'Do they get what it is?' 'Are they going to think it's a movie?' To this day, everyone calls it a documentary. It's not. It's meant to document hip hop, so let's call it whatever it is. There's no doubt that I made it for one reason and that was to document the culture. To document the people that made this so important. And I had those people in the movie. It's not a documentary. Lee Quiñones is not . . . that. But it's documenting Lee.[52]

Reviews of *Wild Style* were mixed. There was a consensus that Freddy and Quiñones were very fascinating and very cool. "The subjects are appealing, especially Mr. Quiñones, a graffiti artist in real life, and Frederick Brathwaite as a very cool artist/promoter, who attempts to transform Raymond's midnight talents into fame and riches," wrote

Vincent Canby in the *New York Times*. "The film includes one rap contest, which goes at such a clip that it may leave you exhausted."[53]

That same review, however, suggested that Ahearn couldn't keep up with the furious pace of his subjects. "['Wild Style'] never discovers a cinematic rhythm that accurately reflects and then celebrates the rare energy and wit of the artists within the film," wrote Canby. "Too often 'Wild Style' has the effect of dampening the enthusiasm of its amateur actors or of not being able to keep up with their nonstop pace. It always seems to be trailing them, as if it were a little brother who can't run as fast as the others."[54]

Perhaps more significantly than what the review actually said was the fact that Canby went out of his way to *properly* define rapping for his audience, even referring to his potential readership as "uninitiated" at one point. The review was enough to generate some solid interest in the film around the city, but Ahearn had a tried-and-true, battle-tested method of advertising which he knew would fill theaters.

"It was not a slam-dunk affair of 'Hip hop being so great and people love hip hop and this movie's going to be so huge,'" he said. "We handed out flyers. I gave a lot of teenagers that I knew a certain amount of money and a sack of flyers and sent them off to high schools all over New York and they flyered those places just like [Kool DJ] AJ did and people in hip hop. It was done exactly like it was 1979 and we were doing a party. That was my attitude, and we didn't have a lot of budget for advertisement, but that theater was packed so much that they put it on two screens."

The movie ended with a triumphant final jam at the amphitheater Raymond painted. The image of God's hands wielding lightning bolts loomed over the massive party. Fantastic (featuring Rubie Dee in a sheer blue mesh shirt) gave a red-hot performance. The Treacherous Three were there as well (although they were the 'Treacherous Two' the night of filming, according to Ahearn, and therefore weren't included in the movie).[55] Busy Bee and "Double Trouble," which was made up of K.K. Rockwell and Lil' Rodney Cee from the Funky 4 + 1, performed as well. In fact, Rodney Cee was from the neighborhood the film was shot in.[56] Double Trouble's routine was very similar to Cold Crush's at the battle, right down to their white suits and hats and the toy guns they waved at the audience. Cold Crush appear at the end of the jam when all the acts are together on stage, but there is no footage of them performing at the amphitheater.

While it's impossible to know for sure, it's so easy to imagine the energetic crowd from the movie resembling the one at the battle that took place a few months prior to filming. An enthusiastic bunch of people—most of whom shared connections with one another—taking in amazing music that didn't exist a decade prior is why *Wild Style* was such an exciting film. It captured the hip hop that very few people were ever able to see. The hip hop shown in the movie was raw and gritty. It was rebellious and dangerous. It was *real*. It was still party music, but party music that meant something. It wasn't made with the intention of selling millions of records, but instead of entertaining the tight community where hip hop incubated.

Also, it's worth noting that even though the hip hop that groups like Cold Crush and Fantastic performed could be considered "party music," performers like Kevie Kev were able to blend a socially conscious message into all of the funkiness. In the Dixie Club scene, much like during the Harlem World battle, Kevie Kev led a call-and-response in which he asked the audience to repeat "Black" and "power," "Black is beautiful," and "I'm proud to be Black."[57] Those lines got the party going, but more significantly, further cemented hip hop as a Black cultural cornerstone in an era where African Americans were showing more racial pride.

"It was a movement, it was about getting Black people together," Kev said. "It wasn't nothing malicious, no. It was just opening up a door. Just like when I first started saying 'Puerto Rico, ho!' What I was doing was trying to get the unity."[58]

Kev and the rest of the crew were very successful in that way. That call-and-response routine grew to the point where Kev gave shout-outs to Dominican and white audience members as well.[59] It predated *Wild Style*, which is still a beloved cult classic to this day.

The film is often screened in museums and at various festivals, where a new generation can experience the Cold Crush, Fantastic, and other stalwarts of early hip hop. While Kevie Kev's routine was innovative and successful, it was only the tip of the iceberg considering what Grandmaster Flash and the Furious Five brought to the world in 1982. Hip hop was about to have its big moment—the explosion that would propel it like a rocket to the upper echelon of American art forms: a "Message."

Epilogue

———

"The Message"

Hip hop had already evolved massively since DJ Kool Herc first played at the park in the early 1970s, but the one thing that wouldn't budge was the genre's general classification as party music. There was nothing intrinsically wrong with that—everyone loves parties. However, it was hard for the music to be taken seriously as an art form, one that required physical dexterity, incredible wit, and crafty lyricism. That changed suddenly in July 1982. Unlike "Rapper's Delight," the new defining hit of the genre came from a group that had cut their teeth at Harlem World, in the parks, and at the Bronx clubs right alongside the rest of hip hop's pioneers.

"The Message," by Grandmaster Flash and the Furious Five, was a perfect crossroads hip hop song. It was delivered by Melle Mel (born Melvin Glover), one of the original innovative emcees and a peer of Caz, Kool Moe Dee, and many others. The beat is in the newer, electronic style, using synthesizers and special sound effects in place of breakbeats.[1] It was catchy and very danceable, even though it featured a slower tempo than the vast majority of hip hop songs to that point. What was far more significant, however, was that this song was not meant for parties. It wasn't meant to be danced to. Much like Moe Dee at Harlem World in 1981, Melle Mel and his co-writer Duke Bootee wanted audiences to listen to the intricacy of the lyrics and the story they were trying to tell. The song was about urban decay; it touched on everything that poor New Yorkers had tried to convey to Ronald Reagan in 1980 when he visited the Bronx. Bootee and Mel described broken glass, junkies, rats, and horrible smells.[2] They weren't offering any hope through the lyrics. The song wasn't about improving the borough or all coming together, it just laid out the issues.

The famous last verse of the song began with the line, "A child is born with no state of mind,/Blind to the ways of mankind."[3] From there, Mel told a story about how that child could grow up to idolize drug dealers and pimps and drop out of high school. According to Mel, a boy like that could expect a future as a stick-up kid and, with it, prison time. This kind of social criticism was groundbreaking; it ushered in a new era of hip hop music that was topical and concrete. It's worth noting, of course, that Mel recites some questionable lyrics in the verse and uses homophobic language.

Ironically, the group was very reluctant to make the record when the idea was first presented to them by Sylvia Robinson, according to a *Los Angeles Times* profile. Flash was concerned that the serious and dry approach the song would require would conflict with the group's well-established reputation as party starters who helped fans celebrate good times.[4] Mel admitted that even he didn't know what to make of the song.

"Nobody believed in that song except for Sylvia Robinson," Mel said. "Just like probably nobody believed in 'Rapper's Delight' except for Sylvia Robinson. Duke Bootee had written two songs. One was called 'Dumb Love' and the other one was the 'The Message.' He liked 'Dumb Love'; I didn't think too much about either of the songs either way. Sylvia was so fixated on doing that song, she told him, 'We'll put out "Dumb Love" on you, but I want to do "The Message" for one of the groups.' We had a song out at that time, so Sugarhill Gang was supposed to do 'The Message,' but *they* didn't like the song, so she had a song that basically nobody wanted to do. I did the song because I knew she was so fixated on doing the song anyway, so we might as well go for the ride."[5]

Mel said he didn't believe the record would be successful even after recording it. However, millions of people outside of the core hip hop community would gravitate toward it.

"It didn't resonate [with] nothing that was going on in the basic hip hop world," Mel said. "It wasn't a hip hop song, there were no beats in it, you couldn't breakdance to it, but it resonated in the general public basically. 'Don't push me cuz I'm close to the edge, I'm trying not to lose my head.' That could be anybody."[6]

Besides the scores of new fans of rock and new wave pop who loved the song, the mainstream music world, which had treated hip hop odiously prior, responded favorably. While other hip hop songs had achieved great popularity, "The Message" was the first of its kind to earn critical acclaim.[7] It was clear that this was far from a gimmick song or some passing fad people would party to.

"Like a spray-painted mural down the side of a New York City subway, or a ghetto blaster carried on a shoulder broadcasting 130 beats a minute all over a Bronx street, this subculture, nicknamed hip hop, is about assertiveness, display, pride, status, and competition, particularly among males," wrote Jay Cocks in a feature for *Time Magazine*'s March 21, 1983, issue.[8]

The same article described the platinum-selling track as one of the best singles of 1982. *Rolling Stone* agreed. In their "Year in Review" for 1982, for which Christopher Connelly selected winners and losers for the year in music, they listed "cassettes and 12-inch singles" as a "winner," commenting on how the formats were rebounding from the collapse of disco in 1980. Cassettes were behind not only the success of pop singles like "Rock the Casbah" by the Clash but massive-selling hip hop tracks like "Planet Rock" and "The Message," which clerk

Steve Wilson from Kief's Record Store in Lawrence, Kansas, claimed to be "selling the shit out of."[9]

"Even still to this day, that is the single most important song in hip hop," Mel said. "People have to understand the true meaning of the word 'important.' You can say anything is important but it's up to anybody's discretion. That was when hip hop actually grew up."[10]

The *Los Angeles Times* made a bold statement in 1983 when reporter Robert Hilburn wrote, "Grandmaster Flash and the Furious Five have done as much—on record—to jolt pop as any other group in the '80s."[11] Hilburn cited how "The Message" pulled a skeptical rock audience toward embracing rap because of the grit of the lyrics and the authenticity of the song's core themes.

It was impossible to call hip hop "party music" after "The Message" came out. That would have been categorically untrue. To many people, the boombox suddenly became a tool of spreading truth rather than noise and artistry instead of shenanigans.

* * *

Beyond popularizing meaningful hip hop, Flash and company also popularized a very specific look that would come to be associated with the genre until the emergence of Run-DMC a few years later. Leather motorcycle jackets and hats, studs, furs, chains, panties worn on the shoulder, and just about every other piece of flair known to mankind was on display. This style was influenced heavily by the punk rockers who Flash, Theodore, Caz, and company brushed shoulders with in the downtown scene. The look was that of an anti-establishment group, even though the Furious Five never intended to represent that kind of attitude. According to the *Time* article, the stage outfits were meant to represent "gusto," or show off the amount of money Flash and company had.[12] The goal was to come out onstage wearing something that the audience couldn't replicate in their everyday outfits. This often meant sporting something very opposed to the urban, humble roots of hip hop, like a sheepskin coat or a gigantic, heavy belt buckle.

The Cold Crush Brothers went through a leather and stud phase as well. In fact, in a 1984 BBC documentary entitled *Beat This: A Hip-Hop History*, Cold Crush performed a much more modern routine featuring very heavy drums and an afro-sporting Charlie Chase riding the mixer with his hand in a steel-studded leader, a ring of bullets around his wrist. JDL wore a blue leather jacket that only reached his ribcage and matching leather pants, no shirt. Easy A.D. wore a similar outfit made of red leather and a red beret to top things off. Caz's black-and-white leather ensemble is crowned with a finishing touch: a giant black wig.[13] According to Caz, by the time *Wild Style* started filming, the Cold Crush had already gravitated more toward that look, but Ahearn asked them to tone it down for the sake of the aesthetic he was looking for.

"We had gone on to that rock-star look behind the Furious Five and those guys who had been on tour," Caz said. "When Charlie filmed *Wild Style* he wanted it to look more street, like before we adopted that rock-star mentality."[14]

The footage captured in *Beat This* featured essentially the same the routines that Cold Crush performed on their tour of Japan in the aftermath of *Wild Style* (both Chase and Caz cited that Japanese tour as one of their favorite experiences from their time in the group). Video from the tour showed Charlie Chase and Tony Tone cutting up Michael Jackson's "Billie Jean" and the emcees introducing themselves one by one, draped in leather.[15] As usual, Caz and his wig stood out from the group. For the six young men from the Bronx, it was a surprising yet satisfying demonstration of how far their art had reached.

While they became known in Japan, according to Caz, there wasn't a significant rise in Cold Crush's popularity stateside. He said that was because of the movie's limited release and because it was largely seen by audiences who were already familiar with the Cold Crush.[16]

Regardless, the tour was one of the few times where the Cold Crush received the star treatment they felt they deserved. Charlie Chase appeared on national TV, and each of the members were given translators so they could interact with the Japanese fans, who had never seen anything like them.[17]

However, there was something missing from that tour: the Fantastic Romantic Five. The group had started to come apart before the tour began. It was a classic story, really—young people growing up and moving on to bigger things. Whipper Whip joined the Navy,[18] and Kevie Kev left to fill an open spot in the Furious Five.[19] Rubie Dee joined the Army.[20] The group slowly dissolved over time, without any particular drama or major issues. They just went their separate ways. Before they drifted apart, Fantastic did get a record deal. They released their lone single, "Can I Get a Soul Clap," on Tuff City Records. It was catchy and rooted in the routines Fantastic used to gain popularity in the local club scene, but it wasn't a particularly hot seller.[21]

"I didn't see no future, and I just wanted to make my family happy," Whipper Whip, who was the first to leave, said. "They were like, 'You're out there running the streets, you're doing this and God knows what else.' You have to be respectful of your parents. My dad was in the Army, my brother was in the Navy, so I said, 'Let me just do this shit.' If it's meant for me to continue being who I am afterwards, then so be it."[22]

After leaving the Navy, Whip moved out West, making it much harder for the group to convene. By that time, hip hop had moved well beyond the early party tradition that had allowed Fantastic to gain so much success. Hip hop artists were selling platinum records, with LL

Cool J, the Beastie Boys, Eric B. and Rakim, and Run-DMC leading the way. On the heels of "The Message," the genre erupted into a monster industry, but some of the most important figures in its development were left behind in the jet wash upon takeoff.

*   *   *

Cold Crush would sign a record deal as well. Like Fantastic, they signed with Tuff City Records. Their debut single, released in 1984, was called "Fresh, Fly, Wild, and Bold." Like "Can I Get a Soul Clap," it sounded good, but was a disappointing seller. Cold Crush were among the best live performers hip hop had ever seen, but they didn't find that same success on wax.

Chase and Caz both lamented the experience they had while being signed to a label. "The records had so-so success," Chase said. "Part of it was when we signed on to Tuff City Records, they didn't handle us correctly, CBS didn't handle us correctly. That was because these companies didn't know how to market and promote hip hop. When they got us, they were learning, and once they got the learning curve done and over with, they shelved us and said, 'OK, let's bring something fresh we can work with.' That also discouraged us."[23]

"We never enjoyed the record company experience, the true 'being signed to a record label' experience," Caz said. "Having a band, having a production, having collaborators, having a publicist and marketing people and booking agents and tours and tour buses and shit. We didn't experience any of that. By the time we started making records, we were already jaded with the record business by the shit that happened with the Sugarhill Gang. We really wasn't quick to jump to try to get signed. We didn't know that was going to be the standard. We were still performing in the streets. We were still the top-booked group in the streets, we was getting booked three or four shows a night sometimes. It wasn't that important to us that we jump on the back of a bandwagon; we didn't know how that bandwagon was going to expand the way it did."[24]

The bad experience with the record deal and the rise of more popular acts were a death blow to the Cold Crush's chances of hitting true superstardom. Still, the group stayed together and performed at bigger events when they were called upon. The business of playing clubs all over the city was slowing. Even the Funky 4 + 1 and Grandmaster Flash and the Furious Five didn't stay together. The system that the pioneers of hip hop worked tirelessly to build now left them in the dust.

"To be brutally honest, the rug was pulled out from under us when we realized we weren't the biggest dog on the block anymore," Charlie Chase said. "Other people were coming up, the music was changing a little bit, we're in the '90s now and other groups are emerging. Public Enemy, KRS-One, Slick Rick, all these guys were coming up and things were starting to dwindle down. When we weren't doing that many shows, there was no real reason to meet and practice. It was less and less. We were still meeting as a group but we weren't connecting as much as we used to."[25]

Charlie Chase left the Cold Crush around 2015, after more than thirty years in the group. He said that in more recent years, there was conflict between the members, and he was tired of the arguments that seemed to consume most of the conversation within the group. It got to a point where one day, during a phone call with the other members, he began going through the "Rolodex of bad memories through the years," as he described it.

"In the middle of that shit in the argument on the phone, I said, 'I quit.' They were like, 'What do you mean you quit?' I said, 'I'm done. Fuck the Cold Crush. Fuck everything, I'm done.' [They said] 'No, you can't leave,' and I said, 'I am leaving, I'm done.'"[26]

To set his decision in stone, Chase decided to craft a post on social media making his departure official, stunning fans of the longest run-ning hip hop group in history to that point. These days, he resides in Florida and mainly stays out of the spotlight. He avoids Cold Crush activities, apart from having the occasional financial conversation with Caz.[27] Cold Crush still performs at reunion shows and old school hip hop events, with Tony Tone handling all of the DJing responsi-bilities.

Aside from occasional shows with Cold Crush, their leader stays very busy as one of the best ambassadors hip hop has. Caz leads hip hop bus tours in New York for tourists who want to see the hallowed ground where their beloved music was first developed.[28] One of the stops is the site that was once Harlem World, which closed in 1985—ironically, as soon as it turned a profit.[29] At that time, the large-bill, multi-act hip hop club show was on the decline as the biggest hip hop acts suddenly started selling out giant arenas, lessening the need for plush clubs. The mosque across the street still stands.

Caz still gives interviews on radio stations, TV shows, and pod-casts around the world about those legendary nights in the '80s at Har-lem World. He even hosts his own show, alongside Sha-Rock from the Funky 4 + 1, on LL Cool J's Rock the Bells Radio station on Sirius XM.

When multi-platinum rapper Macklemore cut his smash hit single "Downtown" in 2015, he wanted the throwback hip hop sound to play a big role in the overall vibe of the record, so he decided to bring in some of the best old-school emcees for a feature. He settled on Kool Moe Dee, Melle Mel, and Grandmaster Caz. The song—about riding a moped around the city—wasn't exactly what Caz and company were accustomed to, but this track finally got the longtime hip hop devotee some mainstream exposure. The emcees also got to perform with Macklemore at the opening to that year's MTV Video Music Awards.

* * *

Fantastic still occasionally gets together to perform as well, but since 2015, they've had to do so without their best writer. Dot-A-Rock passed away in February of that year, leaving a permanent hole in the group. When Fantastic does perform, the other members fill in Dot-A-Rock's parts in their routines. Theodore and the rest of the crew are still in touch with his family, and Charlie Ahearn's giant painting of him with his flyer collection is shown all over New York. Dot-A-Rock's legacy is best preserved in the tapes of Fantastic performing, where his lyrics still dazzle the old school hip hop heads that have made sure to preserve the recordings and post them online. Former members of the L Brothers still stay in touch with their sister group, the Mercedes Ladies, as well.

Grand Wizzard Theodore, much like Caz, has remained one of the great ambassadors for hip hop over the course of his career. He teaches DJ skills to students at the Scratch Academy in New York and, like Caz, loves to tell his stories of the old days to a variety of different outlets, including radio hosts and documentarians. He is a living piece of history: someone who was a part of hip hop before it was even called hip hop. He is still one of the best DJs in the world today, even as the technology has changed and allowed anyone with a laptop to preside over a dance floor, and he has brought the hip hop sound all over the world. If there's a *real* party going down, you can bet Theodore will want to be there. He is perhaps America's foremost expert on getting a party going.

"Everybody has a gift," Theodore said. "Everybody in this world is given a gift. Me, you, everybody you see on the street, everybody we walk by. *Everybody* has a gift. My gift that was given to me was the gift of DJing. I just realized what that gift was at a certain age. That's why I feel that I'm still here, I'm still traveling around the world, I'm still doing parties and everything. I'm still going to have this gift forever."[30]

Most members of Fantastic and Cold Crush have transitioned into day jobs. Joe Conzo became a paramedic and served on 9/11.[31] Whipper Whip works as a nurse in the Detroit area; the vast majority of his patients have no clue that he was once a part of the hottest hip hop group in the streets. Sometimes, however, they wonder why he's always singing as he makes his rounds.[32] Dot-A-Rock stayed at his job at the rehabilitation facility throughout all of Fantastic's success and retired with a nice pension only to pass away a few years later. For both groups, there were some incarcerations, some near death experiences,[33] lots of children, and tons of grandchildren. Being teenage ghetto superstars can only last so long before the real world rears its ugly head.

While neither group has national household name recognition in mainstream white America or a spot in the Rock & Roll Hall of Fame, they've unquestionably made a massive impact. Their reach has even spread further than some might realize. Will Smith, for example, has consistently cited Grandmaster Caz as an inspiration for his career.[34] In his 2001 smash hit single "Izzo," the great Jay-Z cited the Cold Crush as an example of what the record industry can do to an up-and-coming artist's career.

> Industry shady it need to be taken over
> Label owners hate me I'm raisin' the status quo up
> I'm overchargin' n*ggaz for what they did to the Cold Crush.

Caz said he's never completely gotten over what happened with "Rapper's Delight," but he doesn't dwell on it. He's had plenty of other successes to take the place of that one song.

"I'll never forget it," Caz said. "I don't think about it every day. When it comes up, it comes up, it is what it is."[35]

Perhaps the best story that shows the reach of this era of hip hop dates back to the *Wild Style* Japan tour. Charlie Chase remembered a particular encounter with an individual on the street that really helped define what it meant to be an underground hip hop star. "All of us had translators," he said. "We were walking through the streets. By this time we had already done national TV, this cat recognized me. This Japanese kid with a boombox recognizes me but he doesn't speak a lick of English. He's saying something and the translator's translating and I'm like, 'Oh man, cool!' He presses play on the box and it's a Cold Crush tape, he's rocking it. But that's not the shit that fucked me up. What fucked me up is that this motherfucker doesn't know English and he's reciting it word for word. That's how big the cassette tape was to hip hop."[36]

And that, in essence, is why the underground scene and moments like the battle at Harlem World are so crucial to hip hop's story. These groups weren't mass-marketed and packaged by record companies to look a certain way or deliver a certain message. They *were* the message, and they created a whole musical movement from scratch. The movement still survives in its purest form in the hearts and minds of the individuals who started it in the first place and didn't give in to industry pressures or societal norms. Hip hop is about being unique; the organic popularity of the Fantastic Romantic Five and Cold Crush Brothers demonstrated that even after many had dismissed their music as a passing fad. In truth, hip hop was viable and strong. It remains a massive cultural force to this day, both as a mainstream, billion-dollar industry and as a countercultural idea.

Not bad for some neighborhood kids just hanging around after school.

Acknowledgments

First and foremost, my biggest thank-you goes to you, the reader. This entire crazy dream would be completely impossible without your support, and I'm forever grateful. Thank you for reading my book.

My agent, Kevin O'Connor, received a random email in his inbox in June 2021 from a stranger who had always wanted to write a book. He took a chance on me and helped turn my idea into a reality, while answering my truly infinite amount of publishing industry questions. Without him this project would never have even gotten out of my head and onto the page.

Thank you to the amazing team at Johns Hopkins University Press, especially my editor, Laura Davulis, who saw the potential of this story and gave me the chance I'd been hoping for over the past decade. Her editorial vision guided this project beautifully. Thank you to Ezra Rodriguez for keeping everything together and running smoothly. Thank you to Dr. Rachel E. Weissler for her sharp and thoughtful edits of my first draft. Hilary Jacqmin provided a phenomenal copyedit.

This project is the culmination of many years of waffling on whether to put myself out there and enter the mysterious world of publishing. My grandparents, Sol and Gloria Brenner, have encouraged me for every second of this journey and helped me muster up the confidence to pursue this dream. They're the best people I know. My uncle, Dr. Adam Brenner, provided brilliant feedback on this project at every turn, starting with my original pitch letter. He was integral in the early phases of my research and has continued to be the best sounding board anyone could ask for.

My brothers Jacob, Josh, and Jackson, and my father, Michael, all had to listen to me go on and on about Cold Crush routines and old cassette technology and they never complained; thank you.

Neither of my two best friends, Matty Dowd and Ryan Kaplan, ever told me writing a book was a bad idea. I appreciate their willingness to listen to all of my ideas (one of which actually worked!).

Thank you to Dr. Vincent Cannato, Stephen Puleo, and Dr. Laurence Jurdem for all of their guidance in helping me get my author dreams off the ground. Their books are always a joy to read and I'm honored to call them friends.

Charlie Ahearn and Joe Conzo Jr. provided their time for interviews and allowed me to license their wonderful photos documenting the individuals featured in this story. Grandmaster Caz, DJ Grand Wizzard Theodore, Master Rob, Kevie Kev, DJ Charlie Chase, Rubie Dee, Whipper Whip, L.A. Sunshine, DJ Baby D, DJ Hollywood, Patti Astor, Lady Pink, Kevin Kosanovich, Bill Adler, Dr. Steven Payne, Sule Holder, Dr. Fred Collins, Troy Smith, Ben Ortiz, and especially Paradise Gray were all so generous with their time and knowledge. Thank you!

Regan Sommer McCoy was instrumental to the success of this project. She's a brilliant hip hop scholar, the founder of the Mixtape Museum, and was so kind to me in helping me get in touch with so many of my heroes.

I wasn't able to speak with Dot-A-Rock prior to his passing in 2015, but I'd like to acknowledge the incredible contributions he made to hip hop. The events detailed in this book wouldn't have happened if not for him.

Finally, thank you to all of the baristas at the Starbucks locations in Canton and Walpole, MA, for putting up with me for literally hundreds of hours as I wrote nearly this entire story in your cafes. Thank you for memorizing my order, and asking me about the book. It's finally done, I promise!

Notes

Introduction. The Crispy Crust Pizzeria

1 Big Bank Hank and Joey Robinson Jr., interview by Jim Fricke, May 8, 2001, Adler Hip Hop Archive, #8092, Division of Rare and Manuscript Collections, Cornell University Library, Ithaca, NY, https://digital.library.cornell.edu/catalog/ss:13450502.

2 Hank and Robinson Jr., interview by Fricke.

3 *Hip-Hop Evolution*, season 1, episode 2, "From the Underground to the Mainstream," directed by Darby Wheeler, Netflix, 2016.

4 Jon Caramanica, "Big Bank Hank, Early Star of Rap, Dies at 58," *New York Times*, November 11, 2014, https://www.nytimes.com/2014/11/12/arts/music/big-bank-hank-an-early-star-of-rap-dies-at-58.html.

5 Hank and Robinson Jr., interview by Fricke.

6 Hank and Robinson Jr., interview by Fricke.

7 Hank and Robinson Jr., interview by Fricke.

8 Sugarhill Gang, "The Sugarhill Gang - Rapper's Delight," Sugarhill Records, video, 6:15, accessed May 29, 2021, https://www.youtube.com/watch?v=mcCK99wHrk0.

9 Bill Adler, interview by Jon Mael, September 30, 2021.

10 Sugarhill Gang, "Rapper's Delight."

11 "'Rapper's Delight' on the Billboard Charts Worldwide," *Billboard Magazine*, HHCBA_00214.pdf, Adler Hip Hop Archive, #8092, Division of Rare and Manuscript Collections, Cornell University Library, https://digital.library.cornell.edu/catalog/ss:13450466.

12 "'Rapper's Delight' on the Billboard Charts."

13 "100 Greatest Hip Hop Songs of All Time," *Rolling Stone Magazine,* June 2, 2017, https://www.rollingstone.com/music/music-lists/100-greatest-hip-hop-songs-of-all-time-105784/sugarhill-gang-rappers-delight-3-102826/.

14 Hank and Robinson Jr., interview by Fricke.

15 "What People Get Wrong about African-American English," June 16, 2021, in *Otherwords*, produced by Katie Graham, PBS Digital Studios, https://www.youtube.com/watch?v=1YxH43Cw6tI.

16 *Hip-Hop Evolution*, "From the Underground to the Mainstream."

17 Cold Crush Brothers, interview by Bill Adler, September 28, 1998, Museum of Pop Culture Oral History Collection.
18 Grandmaster Caz, interview by Jon Mael, December 4, 2021.
19 Sugarhill Gang, "Rapper's Delight."
20 *Hip-Hop Evolution*, "From the Underground to the Mainstream."

Chapter 1. The Sound Room

1   Andy Greene, "Flashback: Watch 'Disco Demolition Night' Devolve Into Fiery Riot," *Rolling Stone*, July 12, 2019, https://www.rollingstone.com/music/music-news/flashback-watch-disco-demolition-night-devolve-into-fiery-riot-206237/.
2   Claude "Paradise" Gray, interview by Jon Mael, July 19, 2021.
3   Fred Collins, interview by Jon Mael, September 5, 2021.
4   Collins, interview by Mael.
5   Collins, interview by Mael.
6   *Hip-Hop Evolution*, season 1, episode 1, "The Foundation," directed by Darby Wheeler, Netflix, 2016.
7   *Hip-Hop Evolution*, "The Foundation."
8   *Hip-Hop Evolution*, "The Foundation."
9   Gray, interview by Mael.
10 Collins, interview by Mael.
11 Collins, interview by Mael.
12 Collins, interview by Mael.
13 Collins, interview by Mael.
14 Gray, interview by Mael.
15 Gray, interview by Mael.
16 *20/20*, "Rappin' to the Beat," July 9, 1981, aired on ABC, YouTube video posted by Live from the Basement (courtesy of RapRadar), https://www.youtube.com/watch?v=onRKOcsf1J0&t=67s.
17 Grand Wizzard Theodore, interview by Jon Mael, August 30, 2021.
18 Theodore, interview by Mael.
19 Theodore, interview by Mael.
20 Theodore, interview by Mael.
21 Theodore, interview by Mael.
22 *Library Rap*, "Grand Wizard [sic] Theodore," interview by Tim Einenkel, posted to YouTube by OG Podcast Network, February 26, 2019, https://www.youtube.com/watch?v=SSKb1Hf1DtU.
23 *Library Rap*, "Grand Wizard [sic] Theodore."
24 *Hip-Hop Evolution*, "The Foundation."
25 *Hip-Hop Evolution*, "The Foundation."
26 DJ Hollywood, interview by Jon Mael, October 26, 2021.
27 Hollywood, interview by Mael.
28 Hollywood, interview by Mael.
29 Hollywood, interview by Mael.
30 Hollywood, interview by Mael.
31 *Hip-Hop Evolution*, "The Foundation."

32 Hollywood, interview by Mael.
33 Grandmaster Caz, interview by Jon Mael, September 1, 2021.
34 Grandmaster Caz, interview by Jim Fricke, March 22, 2001, Museum of Pop Culture Oral History Collection.
35 Caz, interview by Fricke.
36 Caz, interview by Mael.
37 "Hip-Hop History in NYC Parks," New York City Department of Parks & Recreation, accessed July 12, 2021, https://www.nycgovparks.org/about/history/hip-hop.
38 Gray, interview by Mael.
39 Caz, interview by Mael.
40 Caz, interview by Mael.
41 Caz, interview by Mael.
42 Caz, interview by Mael.
43 Caz, interview by Mael.
44 Caz, interview by Mael.
45 Caz, interview by Fricke.
46 Victor K. McElheny, "Con Edison Admits Its Operator Erred," *New York Times*, August 29, 1977, https://www.nytimes.com/1977/08/29/archives/con-edison-admits-its-operator-erred-concedes-that-he-may-not-have.html.
47 *American Experience*, season 27, episode 7, "Blackout," directed by Callie T. Wiser, written by Sharon Grimberg and David Murdock, aired July 14, 2015, on PBS.
48 *American Experience*, "Blackout."
49 Lawrence Van Gelder, "State Troopers Sent into City as Crime Rises," *New York Times*, July 14, 1977, https://www.nytimes.com/1977/07/14/archives/state-troopers-sent-into-city-as-crime-rises-some-civilians-assist.html.
50 Van Gelder, "State Troopers Sent."
51 ABC News, "7/14/77: NYC Blackout," July 14, 1977, https://abcnews.go.com/Archives/video/july-14-1977-nyc-blackout-10252811.
52 ABC News, "7/14/77: NYC Blackout."
53 Ethan Sacks, "Geraldo Rivera: 'Hip Hop Has Done More Damage to Young African-Americans than Racism in Recent Years,'" *New York Daily News*, April 9, 2018, https://www.nydailynews.com/entertainment/music/rivera-hip-hop-damage-racism-article-1.2276269.
54 Van Gelder, "State Troopers Sent."
55 Jimmy Carter, "Energy and National Goals: Address to the Nation" (televised speech, Washington, DC, July 15, 1979), https://www.jimmycarterlibrary.gov/assets/documents/speeches/energy-crisis.phtml.
56 ABC News, "7/14/77: NYC Blackout."
57 *Hip-Hop Evolution*, season 1, episode 2, "From the Underground to the Mainstream," directed by Darby Wheeler, Netflix, 2016.
58 *Hip-Hop Evolution*, "From the Underground to the Mainstream."
59 Grandmaster Caz and DJ Disco Wiz, interview by Jim Fricke, 2001, Museum of Pop Culture Oral History Collection.

Chapter 2. Routines

1   DJ Hollywood, interview by Jon Mael, October 26, 2021.
2   Claude "Paradise" Gray, interview by Jon Mael, July 19, 2021.
3   DJ Charlie Chase, interview by Jon Mael, September 28, 2021.
4   Grand Wizzard Theodore, interview by Jon Mael, August 30, 2021.
5   Theodore, interview by Mael.
6   Gray, interview by Mael.
7   Gray, interview by Mael.
8   Gray, interview by Mael.
9   Charlie Ahearn, interview by Jon Mael, November 4, 2021.
10 Anthony Riley, *308 E. 166 St., Oct. 20, 1979*, event flyer, Johan Kugelberg Hip Hop Collection, #8021, Division of Rare and Manuscript Collections, Cornell University Library, https://digital.library.cornell.edu/catalog/ss:1333885.
11 Master Rob and Kevie Kev, interview by Jon Mael, September 13, 2021.
12 Rob and Kev, interview by Mael.
13 Theodore, interview by Mael.
14 Rob and Kev, interview by Mael.
15 Rob and Kev, interview by Mael.
16 Theodore, interview by Mael.
17 Rob and Kev, interview by Mael.
18 Rubie Dee, interview by Jon Mael, November 13, 2021.
19 Dee, interview by Mael.
20 Dee, interview by Mael.
21 Dee, interview by Mael.
22 Dee, interview by Mael.
23 Dee, interview by Mael.
24 Dee, interview by Mael.
25 Theodore, interview by Mael.
26 Richard Cameron, *Famous People Who Dropped Dead* (Pittsburgh, PA: RoseDog Books, 2010).
27 Theodore, interview by Mael.
28 Gray, interview by Mael.
29 Gray, interview by Mael.
30 Theodore, interview by Mael.
31 Whipper Whip, interview by Jon Mael, October 22, 2021.
32 Whip, interview by Mael.
33 Whipper Whip, interview by Jim Fricke, 2001, Museum of Pop Culture Oral History Collection.
34 Whip, interview by Mael.
35 Whip, interview by Mael.
36 Whip, interview by Mael.
37 Grandmaster Caz and DJ Disco Wiz, interview by Jim Fricke, 2001, Museum of Pop Culture Oral History Collection.
38 Caz and Wiz, interview by Fricke.
39 Grandmaster Caz, interview by Jon Mael, September 1, 2021.

40 Ivan Sanchez and Luis "DJ Disco Wiz" Cedeño, *It's Just Begun: The Epic Journey of DJ Disco Wiz, Hip Hop's First Latino DJ* (Brooklyn, NY: PowerHouse Books, 2009).

41 Whip, interview by Mael.

42 Whip, interview by Mael.

43 Whip, interview by Mael.

44 Whip, interview by Mael.

45 Whip, interview by Mael.

46 Whip, interview by Mael.

47 Gray, interview by Mael.

48 *Hip-Hop Evolution*, season one, episode one, "The Foundation," directed by Darby Wheeler, Netflix, 2016.

49 DJ Baby D, interview by Jon Mael, November 12, 2021.

50 Baby D, interview by Mael.

51 Whip, interview by Fricke.

52 *Hip-Hop Evolution*, "The Foundation."

53 Gray, interview by Mael.

54 Whip, interview by Fricke.

55 Chase, interview by Mael.

56 Chase, interview by Mael.

57 Chase, interview by Mael.

58 Chase, interview by Mael.

59 Chase, interview by Mael.

60 Chase, interview by Mael.

61 Chase, interview by Mael.

62 Chase, interview by Mael.

63 Chase, interview by Mael.

64 Riley, "308 E. 166 St."

65 Chase, interview by Mael.

66 Whip, interview by Fricke.

67 Whip, interview by Fricke.

68 Theodore, interview by Mael.

69 Theodore, interview by Mael.

70 Caz, interview by Mael.

71 Chase, interview by Mael.

72 Notorious Two, "Notorious 2 (Grandmaster Caz & JDL) Rapping over 'Got to Be Real' Live 1979," audio recording posted by J-Lo, 2017, https://www.youtube.com/watch?v=G34ZzYMbIMg.

73 Caz, interview by Mael.

74 Chase, interview by Mael.

75 Chase, interview by Mael.

76 Chase, interview by Mael.

77 Caz, interview by Mael.

78 "New York City Hip Hop Convention," video taken by Charlie Ahearn and Fab 5 Freddy at the Celebrity Club in Harlem, 1980, private collection.

79 Grand Wizard [sic] Theodore, interview by Jim Fricke, 1999, Museum of Pop Culture Oral History Collection.

80 Theodore, interview by Mael.

81 Grand Wizzard Theodore and the Fantastic Five, "Grand Wizzard Theodore and The Fantastic 5 Tape 223," audio recording posted by Troy Smith, accessed July 19, 2021, https://www.youtube.com/watch?v=kTztYAs1yu8&t=62s.
82 Gray, interview by Mael.
83 Theodore and the Fantastic Five, "Tape 223."
84 Caz, interview by Mael.
85 Cold Crush Brothers and the Fantastic Five, "Cold Crush vs. The Fantastic Five–Harlem World 1981 (Best Edit) 2021 Redo," audio recording posted by Tape Deck Wreck, https://www.youtube.com/watch?v=IhAffvoCKgk&t=2338s.

Chapter 3. New York, New York

1 "CPI Inflation Calculator," U.S. Bureau of Labor Statistics, accessed September 2, 2021, https://www.bls.gov/data/inflation_calculator.htm.
2 Lou Cannon, "Ronald Reagan: Campaigns and Elections," Miller Center, University of Virginia, July 11, 2017, https://millercenter.org/president/reagan/campaigns-and-elections.
3 "Reagan, in South Bronx, Says Carter Broke Vow: Raises Voice Above Chants," *New York Times*, August 6, 1980, https://www.nytimes.com/1980/08/06/archives/reagan-in-south-bronx-says-carter-broke-vow-raises-voice-above.html.
4 "Reagan, in South Bronx," *New York Times*.
5 "Reagan, in South Bronx," *New York Times*.
6 WBBM Channel Two, "1980 Throwback: 'Ronald Reagan Goes to the South Bronx and Gets Heckled, Loses His Temper,'" video posted by Hezakya Newz & Films, February 5, 2019, https://www.youtube.com/watch?v=hHRSGDpMGGQ&t=154s.
7 "Reagan, in South Bronx," *New York Times*.
8 WBBM, "1980 Throwback."
9 "Reagan, in South Bronx," *New York Times*.
10 WBBM, "1980 Throwback."
11 WBBM, "1980 Throwback."
12 WBBM, "1980 Throwback."
13 WBBM, "1980 Throwback."
14 WBBM, "1980 Throwback."
15 Jennifer Bain and Bob Fredericks, "Ted Cruz's Campaign Stop in the Bronx Is a Complete Dud," *New York Post*, April 6, 2016, https://nypost.com/2016/04/06/ted-cruzs-campaign-stop-in-the-bronx-is-a-complete-dud/.
16 "How Groups Voted in 1980," Roper Center for Public Opinion Research, Cornell University, accessed September 4, 2021, https://ropercenter.cornell.edu/how-groups-voted-1980.
17 *CBS Reports*, "The Fire Next Door," March 27, 1977, video posted by Hezakya Newz & Films, https://www.youtube.com/watch?v=RQkhD-2cWwY.
18 *CBS Reports*, "The Fire Next Door."
19 *CBS Reports*, "The Fire Next Door."
20 *CBS Reports*, "The Fire Next Door."
21 *CBS Reports*, "The Fire Next Door."
22 *CBS Reports*, "The Fire Next Door."

23 *CBS Reports*, "The Fire Next Door."

24 *CBS Reports*, "The Fire Next Door."

25 *CBS Reports*, "The Fire Next Door."

26 "How Did the Boroughs Get Their Names?", New-York Historical Society, January 12, 2012, https://www.nyhistory.org/community/borough-names.

27 G. Hermalyn and Lloyd Ultan, "Bronx History," the Bronx County Historical Society, March 31, 2019, http://bronxhistoricalsociety.org/about/bronx-history/.

28 Hermalyn and Ultan, "Bronx History."

29 Hermalyn and Ultan, "Bronx History."

30 Stephen Payne, interview by Jon Mael, August 24, 2021.

31 John Braithwaite, interview by Mark Naison, n.d., the Bronx African American History Project, digital archive at Fordham University.

32 Braithwaite, interview by Naison.

33 "Immigration and Relocation in U.S. History: Migrating to a New Land," n.d., Library of Congress, https://www.loc.gov/classroom-materials/immigration/puerto-rican-cuban/migrating-to-a-new-land/#:~:text=By%201955%2C%20nearly%20700%2C000%20Puerto,more%20than%20a%20million%20had.

34 "Jamaicans," The Stories of Us, Macaulay Honors College at Baruch, Spring 2013, accessed July 25, 2022, https://eportfolios.macaulay.cuny.edu/degraauw13/jamaicans/#:~:text=The%20Jamaican%20foreign%20born%20make,native%2Dborn%20descendants%20of%20immigrants.

35 Claude "Paradise" Gray, interview by Jon Mael, July 19, 2021.

36 Kevin Kosanovich, interview by Jon Mael, August 20, 2021.

37 Oliver Wainwright, "Street Fighter: How Jane Jacobs Saved New York from Bulldozer Bob," *The Guardian*, April 30, 2017, https://www.theguardian.com/artanddesign/2017/apr/30/citizen-jane-jacobs-the-woman-who-saved-manhattan-from-the-bulldozer-documentary.

38 Kosanovich, interview by Mael.

39 "Affordable Housing: Mitchell-Lama," NYC Housing Preservation & Development, 2019, https://www1.nyc.gov/site/hpd/services-and-information/mitchell-lama-program.page.

40 Kosanovich, interview by Mael.

41 Payne, interview by Mael.

42 Payne, interview by Mael.

43 Payne, interview by Mael.

44 Sandra "Lady Pink" Fabara, interview by Jon Mael, October 3, 2021.

45 Pink, interview by Mael.

46 "About Lady Pink," LadyPinkNYC, accessed July 25, 2022, https://www.ladypinknyc.com/about.

47 "About Lady Pink."

48 "About Lady Pink."

49 "About Lady Pink."

50 "About Lady Pink."

51 "About Lady Pink."

52 "About Lady Pink."

53 Grand Wizzard Theodore, interview by Jon Mael, August 30, 2021.

54 Theodore, interview by Mael.

55 Gray, interview by Mael.

56 Gray, interview by Mael.

57 Joe Conzo Jr., interview by Jon Mael, August 26, 2021.

58 Joe Conzo, *Wales Ave. and 152nd St., Bronx*, ca. 1977–1980, black-and-white negatives, Cornell Hip Hop Collection, Cornell University, https://digital.library. cornell.edu/catalog/ss:927241.

59 Joe Conzo, *Street Vendor, 149th St. and 3rd Ave., Bronx*, ca. 1977–1981, black-and-white negatives, Cornell Hip Hop Collection, Cornell University, https://digital. library.cornell.edu/catalog/ss:927243.

60 Joe Conzo, *Unidentified Boy, Bronx*, ca. 1977, black-and-white negatives, Cornell Hip Hop Collection, Cornell University, https://digital.library.cornell.edu/catalog/ ss:927423.

61 Conzo, *Unidentified Boy.*

62 Conzo, *Unidentified Boy.*

63 Conzo, *Unidentified Boy.*

64 Conzo, *Unidentified Boy.*

65 Conzo, *Unidentified Boy.*

66 Sule Holder, interview by Jon Mael, July 29, 2021.

67 Theodore, interview by Mael.

68 Theodore, interview by Mael.

69 Theodore, interview by Mael.

70 Grandmaster Caz, interview by Jon Mael, September 1, 2021.

71 Caz, interview by Mael.

72 E. R. Shipp, "Harlem Battles Over Development Project," *New York Times*, July 31, 1991, https://www.nytimes.com/1991/07/31/nyregion/harlem-battles-over-development-project.html#:~:text=The%20project%20would%20create%20 2%2C200,and%20recreational%20and%20cultural%20activities.

73 Rosi Sellers, "Forever Beautiful: Harlem in the 1970s," *Medium*, April 12, 2020, https://medium.com/the-cool/forever-beautiful-harlem-in-the-1970s-d45523262a09.

74 Sellers, "Forever Beautiful."

75 Sellers, "Forever Beautiful."

76 Gray, interview by Mael.

77 L.A. Sunshine, interview by Jon Mael, November 2, 2021.

78 Marcia Chambers, "City Seeks to Dislodge Drug Trade by Demolishing Tenement Havens," *New York Times*, July 18, 1982, https://www.nytimes.com/1982/07/18/ nyregion/city-seeks-to-dislodge-drug-trade-by-demolishing-tenement-havens.html.

79 Chambers, "City Seeks to Dislodge Drug Trade."

80 Chambers, "City Seeks to Dislodge Drug Trade."

81 Chambers, "City Seeks to Dislodge Drug Trade."

82 Chambers, "City Seeks to Dislodge Drug Trade."

83 David F. Musto, "Illicit Price of Cocaine in Two Eras: 1908–14 and 1982–89," *Pharmacy in History* 33, no. 1 (1991): 3–10, http://www.jstor.org/stable/41111356.

84 Grand Wizzard Theodore and the Fantastic Romantic Five, "Fantastic Five Harlem World 1982 MERRY CHRISTMAS tape 16," video posted to YouTube by Troy Smith, https://www.youtube.com/watch?v=7ECk8U_NisA.

85 "1985–1990," U.S. Drug Enforcement Administration, Archive.org, accessed August 21, 2021, https://web.archive.org/web/20060823024931/http://www.usdoj.gov/dea/ pubs/history/1985-1990.html.

86 "Interview: 'Paul,'" *Frontline*, 2000, https://www.pbs.org/wgbh/pages/frontline/shows/drugs/interviews/paul.html.

87 "Interview: 'Paul,'" *Frontline*.

88 Conzo, interview by Mael.

Chapter 4. Hip Hop's Great Poet

1 Grandmaster Caz, interview by Jon Mael, September 1, 2021.

2 Caz, interview by Mael.

3 Charlie Ahearn, interview by Jon Mael, November 4, 2021.

4 Caz, interview by Mael.

5 Caz, interview by Mael.

6 Caz, interview by Mael.

7 Joe Conzo Jr., interview by Jon Mael, August 26, 2021.

8 Conzo, interview by Mael.

9 Lord Jamar and Rah Digga, "Grandmaster Caz: Origins of the 'Grandmaster' Title," 2020, in *Yanadameen Godcast*, episode 153, segment #2, video, 8:33, https://www.youtube.com/watch?v=sL_Mar1igxA.

10 Master Kid, *35 Jackson St., Yonkers, N.Y., Dec. 13, 1980*, event flyer, Breakbeat Lenny Archive, #8052, Cornell University Library, https://digital.library.cornell.edu/catalog/ss:455462; *T-Connection*, event flyer, Johan Kugelberg Hip Hop Collection, #8021, Cornell University Library, https://digital.library.cornell.edu/catalog/ss:1334099.

11 Caz, interview by Mael.

12 "Grand Master Caz and Yvette Harlem World 1982 Tape 6," audio posted by Troy Smith, 2:25, https://www.youtube.com/watch?v=px8coXW6tmI. Note that there are multiple versions of this verse, including one that appears in the film *Wild Style* and another that Caz performs in the present day. All the versions are slightly different but have the same story structure.

13 "Grand Master Caz and Yvette, Tape 6."

14 Caz, interview by Mael.

15 Caz, interview by Mael.

16 Caz, interview by Mael.

17 Caz, interview by Mael.

18 Caz, interview by Mael.

19 Caz, interview by Mael.

20 Caz, interview by Mael.

21 Caz, interview by Mael.

22 Caz, interview by Mael.

23 Claude "Paradise" Gray, interview by Jon Mael, September 1, 2021.

24 DJ Charlie Chase, interview by Jon Mael, September 28, 2021.

25 Grand Wizzard Theodore, interview by Jon Mael, August 30, 2021.

26 Claude "Paradise" Gray, interview by Jon Mael, July 19, 2021.

27 Theodore, interview by Mael.

28 Theodore, interview by Mael

29 Master Rob and Kevie Kev, interview by Jon Mael, September 13, 2021.

30 Rob and Kev, interview by Mael.
31 DJ Baby D, interview by Jon Mael, November 12, 2021.
32 Baby D, interview by Mael.
33 Rob and Kev, interview by Mael.
34 Rob and Kev, interview by Mael.
35 Theodore, interview by Mael.
36 Rob and Kev, interview by Mael.
37 Rob and Kev, interview by Mael.
38 Rob and Kev, interview by Mael.
39 Rob and Kev, interview by Mael.
40 Rob and Kev, interview by Mael.
41 Theodore, interview by Mael.
42 Dot-A-Rock, "Interview w/ Dot-A-Rock of Fantastic Romantic Five," interview by Troy Smith, 2002, Davey D's Hip Hop Corner, http://www.daveyd.com/dotarockinterview.html.
43 Rock, interview by Smith.
44 T La Rock, Special K, and Dot-A-Rock, interview by Bill Adler, Museum of Pop Culture Oral History Collection, April 11, 2001.
45 Theodore, interview by Mael.
46 La Rock, K, and Rock, interview by Adler.
47 Rob and Kev, interview by Mael.
48 Rob and Kev, interview by Mael.
49 "Grand Wizzard Theodore and the Fantastic 5 Tape 223," audio posted by Troy Smith, 10:00, https://www.youtube.com/watch?v=kTztYAs1yu8&t=280s.
50 La Rock, K, and Rock, interview by Adler.

Chapter 5. Harlem World

1 *Prohibition*, episode 2, "A Nation of Scofflaws," directed by Ken Burns and Lynn Novick, aired October 2, 2011, on PBS, https://www.thirteen.org/programs/prohibition/prohibition-women-in-prohibition-lois-long/.
2 Jerry Harkness, "Jerry Harkness Talks about the History of the Harlem Globetrotters," interview by Julieanna L. Richardson, The HistoryMakers Digital Archive, session 1, tape 2, story 5, July 12, 2000, https://da.thehistorymakers.org/story/64387.
3 "People & Events: The Rise of the Ku Klux Klan in the 1920s," PBS/*American Experience*, 2001, http://www.shoppbs.pbs.org/wgbh/amex/flood/peopleevents/e_klan.html.
4 W. E. B. Du Bois, "Criteria of Negro Art," *The Crisis* 32 (October 1926): 290-97, https://allisonbolah.com/site_resources/reading_list/DuBois.pdf.
5 Du Bois, "Criteria of Negro Art."
6 Gloria Toote, "Gloria Toote Describes the Housing Conditions in New York's Harlem Neighborhood," interview by Shawn Wilson, The HistoryMakers Digital Archive, session 1, tape 2, story 7, November 29, 2006, https://da.thehistorymakers.org/story/572891.
7 Donnie McClurkin, "Donnie McClurkin Describes His Mother's Upbringing in

New York City's Harlem Neighborhood," interview by Harriette Cole, session 1, tape 1, story 4, The HistoryMakers Digital Archive, October 6, 2016 https://da.thehistorymakers.org/story/527105.

8   McClurkin, interview by Cole.

9   Will Lissner, "Harlem Mothers Crowd Exhibit to Learn How to Spot Addicts," *New York Times*, July 17, 1965, https://www.nytimes.com/1965/07/17/archives/harlem-mothers-crowd-exhibit-to-learn-how-to-spot-addicts.html.

10 Lissner, "Harlem Mothers."

11 Lissner, "Harlem Mothers."

12 Nancy Bowlin, "Nancy Bowlin Describes the Drug Culture in New York City's Harlem Neighborhood," interview by Larry Crowne, session 1, tape 2, story 10, The HistoryMakers Digital Archive, April 17, 2007, https://da.thehistorymakers.org/story/531497.

13 Eliot Fremont-Smith, "Coming of Age in Harlem: A Report from Hell," *New York Times*, August 14, 1965 https://www.nytimes.com/1965/08/14/archives/coming-of-age-in-harlem-a-report-from-hell.html.

14 Fremont-Smith, "Coming of Age in Harlem."

15 Fremont-Smith, "Coming of Age in Harlem."

16 Malcolm X, "Malcolm X: Early Speech in Harlem," video posted by Malcolm X Files, 2018, 7:33, https://www.youtube.com/watch?v=eFqrm9I5224.

17 "Timeline of Malcolm X's Life," PBS/*American Experience*, accessed September 23, 2021, https://www.pbs.org/wgbh/americanexperience/features/malcolmx-timeline-malcolm-xs-life/.

18 *The Lost Tapes*, "Malcolm X," season 2, episode 1, directed by Tom Jennings, first aired February 26, 2018, posted by the Smithsonian Channel, https://www.youtube.com/watch?v=k7MP_h3eQ1o&t=663s.

19 *The Lost Tapes*, "Malcolm X."

20 *The Lost Tapes*, "Malcolm X."

21 Troy L. Smith, interview by Jon Mael, September 17, 2021.

22 L.A. Sunshine, interview by Jon Mael, November 2, 2021.

23 Fred Collins, interview by Jon Mael, September 5, 2021.

24 Collins, interview by Mael.

25 Claude "Paradise" Gray, interview by Jon Mael, July 19, 2021.

26 *Audubon, Dec. 8, 1978*, event flyer, Johan Kugelberg Hip Hop collection, #8021, Cornell University Library, https://digital.library.cornell.edu/catalog/ss:1333856.

27 Troy L. Smith, "Charlie Rock of 'The Harlem World Crew' and Harlem World," *The Foundation*, 2003, http://www.thafoundation.com/charock.

28 "Harlem World Club Now at Noted Corner," *Billboard Magazine*, July 8, 1978, https://books.google.com/books?id=wiQEAAAAMBAJ&lpg=PT64&ots=k6gGybwFIE&dq=harlem%20world%20club%20now%20at%20noted%20corner&pg=PT64#v=onepage&q=harlem%20world%20club%20now%20at%20noted%20corner&f=false.

29 "Harlem World Club Now at Noted Corner," *Billboard*.

30 "Harlem World Club Now at Noted Corner," *Billboard*.

31 "Harlem World Club Now at Noted Corner," *Billboard*.

32 "Harlem World Club Now at Noted Corner," *Billboard*.

33 Smith, "Charlie Rock."

34 Smith, "Charlie Rock."

35 Smith, "Charlie Rock."

36 "Harlem World Club Now at Noted Corner," *Billboard*.

37 Smith, "Charlie Rock."

38 Smith, "Charlie Rock."

39 Smith, "Charlie Rock."

40 Smith, "Charlie Rock."

41 *Harlem World, Mar. 13, 1980*, event flyer, Johan Kugelberg Hip Hop Collection, Cornell University Library, https://digital.library.cornell.edu/catalog/ss:1333950.

42 *Harlem World, Dec. 24, 1980*, event flyer, Johan Kugelberg Hip Hop Collection, Cornell University Library, https://digital.library.cornell.edu/catalog/ss:1335297.

43 Smith, "Charlie Rock."

44 Grandmaster Caz, interview by Jon Mael, September 1, 2021.

45 Joe Conzo Jr., *Cold Crush Brothers at the Treacherous Three Anniversary, Harlem World*, ca. 1981, black-and-white negatives, Cornell Hip Hop Collection, Cornell University, https://digital.library.cornell.edu/catalog/ss:927090.

46 Sunshine, interview by Mael.

47 Conzo, *Cold Crush Brothers at the Treacherous Three Anniversary*.

48 DJ Charlie Chase, interview by Jon Mael, September 28, 2021.

49 Smith, "Charlie Rock."

50 Smith, interview by Mael.

51 Grandmaster Caz, *Grandmaster Caz Opens Up about the Kool Moe Dee & Busy Bee Rap Battle*, interview by Classic Flavors, 2015, video posted by WBLS, https://www.youtube.com/watch?v=zBp5aniNa2I&t=311s.

52 Sunshine, interview by Mael.

53 "'Rapper's Delight' on the Billboard Charts Worldwide," *Billboard Magazine*, 1979, accessed July 3, 2021, Adler Hip Hop Archive, Cornell University Hip Hop Collection, https://digital.library.cornell.edu/catalog/ss:13450466.

54 Bill Adler, interview by Jon Mael, September 30, 2021.

55 Adler, interview by Mael.

56 Adler, interview by Mael.

57 Smith, interview by Mael.

58 Grandmaster Caz, interview by Jon Mael, December 4, 2021.

59 Big Bank Hank and Joey Robinson Jr., interview by Jim Fricke, May 8, 2001, Museum of Pop Culture Oral History Collection.

60 Ann Powers, "A Bit of Rock History from Five Young Guys Doomed to Repeat It," *New York Times*, March 17, 1999, https://www.nytimes.com/1999/03/17/arts/pop-review-a-bit-of-rock-history-from-five-young-guys-doomed-to-repeat-it.html.

61 Shawn Brown, *Rappin' Duke: Shawn Brown a.k.a. The Rappin' Duke*, 1984, video by Von Regan Davis, posted by djbuddyloverootsrap, https://www.youtube.com/watch?v=85G5SI5Nu3s.

62 *20/20*, "Rappin' to the Beat," July 9, 1981, aired on ABC, YouTube video posted by Live from the Basement (courtesy of RapRadar), https://www.youtube.com/watch?v=onRKOcsf1J0&t=67s.

63 Adler, interview by Mael.

64 *20/20*, "Rappin' to the Beat."

65 Caz, interview by Mael, December 4, 2021.

66 Roy Trakin, "Long Before that Creature from Mars," *New York Daily News*, February 8, 1981, https://www.newspapers.com/image/485842130/?terms=long%20

before%20that%20creature%20mars&match=1.

67 Robert Palmer, "Recordings; New Bands on Small Labels Are the Innovators of the 80's," *New York Times*, September 6, 1981, nytimes.com/1981/09/06/arts/recordings-new-bands-on-small-labels-are-the-innovators-of-the-80-s.html.

68 Palmer, "New Bands on Small Labels."

69 Claude "Paradise" Gray, interview by Jon Mael, September 1, 2021.

70 Ben Ortiz, interview by Jon Mael, September 30, 2021.

71 Master Rob and Kevie Kev, interview by Jon Mael, September 13, 2021.

72 Joe Conzo Jr., interview by Jon Mael, August 26, 2021.

73 Gray, interview by Mael.

74 Gray, interview by Mael.

75 Grand Master Flash, interviewer unknown, October 1, 1999, Museum of Pop Culture Oral History Collection.

76 Elektra Records, "Bio: Grandmaster Flash and the Furious Five," Adler Hip Hop Archive, Division of Rare and Manuscript Collections, Cornell University Library, accessed October 5, 2021, https://digital.library.cornell.edu/catalog/ss:13450410.

77 Sha Rock, interview by Jim Fricke, August 25, 2001, Museum of Pop Culture Oral History Collection.

78 *Hip-Hop Evolution*, season 1, episode 2, "From the Underground to the Mainstream," directed by Darby Wheeler, Netflix, 2016.

Chapter 6. Collision Course

1   Joe Conzo Jr., interview by Jon Mael, August 26, 2021.

2   DJ Charlie Chase, interview by Jon Mael, September 28, 2021.

3   Chase, interview by Mael.

4   Grandmaster Caz, interview by Jon Mael, September 1, 2021.

5   Caz, interview by Mael, September 1, 2021.

6   Chase, interview by Mael.

7   Master Rob and Kevie Kev, interview by Jon Mael, September 13, 2021.

8   Rob and Kev, interview by Mael.

9   Grand Wizzard Theodore, interview by Jon Mael, August 30, 2021.

10 Theodore, interview by Mael.

11 Theodore, interview by Mael.

12 Theodore, interview by Mael.

13 Rob and Kev, interview by Mael.

14 Theodore, interview by Mael.

15 Conzo Jr., interview by Mael.

16 Chase, interview by Mael.

17 Grandmaster Caz, interview by Jon Mael, December 4, 2021.

18 Troy L. Smith, interview by Jon Mael, September 17, 2021.

19 Smith, interview by Mael.

20 Grand Wizzard Theodore and the Fantastic Romantic Five, "Fantastic Five Harlem World 1982 MERRY CHRISTMAS tape 16," video posted to YouTube by Troy L.

Smith, November 22, 2012, https://www.youtube.com/watch?v=7ECk8U_NisA.

21 Rob and Kev, interview by Mael.

22 T La Rock, Special K, and Dot-A-Rock, interview by Bill Adler, Museum of Pop Culture Oral History Collection, April 11, 2001.

23 La Rock, K, and Rock, interview by Adler.

24 Rob and Kev, interview by Mael.

25 Rob and Kev, interview by Mael.

26 Kevin Kosanovich, interview by Jon Mael, August 20, 2021.

27 Claude "Paradise" Gray, interview by Jon Mael, July 19, 2021.

28 Anthony Riley, *308 E. 166 St., Oct. 20, 1979*, event flyer, Johan Kugelberg Hip Hop Collection, #8021, Division of Rare and Manuscript Collections, Cornell University Library, https://digital.library.cornell.edu/catalog/ss:1333885.

29 Caz, interview by Mael, August 27, 2021.

30 Caz, interview by Mael, August 27, 2021.

31 Chase, interview by Mael.

32 Chase, interview by Mael.

33 Caz, interview by Mael, August 27, 2021.

34 Caz, interview by Mael, August 27, 2021.

35 Chase, interview by Mael.

36 Caz, interview by Mael, August 27, 2021.

37 Rob and Kev, interview by Mael.

38 Rob and Kev, interview by Mael.

39 Rob and Kev, interview by Mael.

40 Rob and Kev, interview by Mael.

41 *The Super Showdown: Coldcrush vs Fantastic*, event flyer, accessed October 4, 2022, https://www.barnebys.com/auctions/lot/the-super-showdown-coldcrush-vs-fantastic-early-QoIWHKdehfS.

42 Rob and Kev, interview by Mael.

43 Chase, interview by Mael.

44 Chase, interview by Mael.

45 Caz, interview by Mael, August 27, 2021.

46 Caz, interview by Mael, August 27, 2021.

47 Caz, interview by Mael, December 4, 2021.

48 Caz, interview by Mael, December 4, 2021.

49 At least, unheard-of on flyers from the time or among the individuals interviewed for this book.

50 Theodore, interview by Mael.

51 Whipper Whip, interview by Jon Mael, October 22, 2021.

52 Caz, interview by Mael, December 4, 2021.

53 Caz, interview by Mael, December 4, 2021.

54 Caz, interview by Mael, August 27, 2021.

55 Chase, interview by Mael.

56 Caz, interview by Mael, August 27, 2021.

57 Theodore, interview by Mael.

58 Theodore, interview by Mael.

59 Theodore, interview by Mael.

60 Rob and Kev, interview by Mael.

Chapter 7. Tough-Ass Four Emcees

1   Laurence K. Altman, "Rare Cancer Seen in 41 Homosexuals: Outbreak Occurs Among Men in New York and California—8 Died Inside 2 Years," *New York Times*, July 3, 1981, https://timesmachine.nytimes.com/timesmachine/1981/07/03/180485.html?pageNumber=20.

2   Nash Information Services, "Weekend Domestic Chart for July 3, 1981," The Numbers, accessed October 11, 2021, https://www.the-numbers.com/box-office-chart/weekend/1981/07/03.

3   "New York City, NY Weather History, July 3rd, 1981," Weather Underground, accessed October 10, 2021, https://www.wunderground.com/history/daily/us/ny/new-york-city/KLGA/date/1981-7-3.

4   Master Rob and Kevie Kev, interview by Jon Mael, September 13, 2021.

5   Grand Wizzard Theodore, interview by Jon Mael, August 30, 2021.

6   Theodore, interview by Mael.

7   Rob and Kev, interview by Mael.

8   DJ Charlie Chase, interview by Jon Mael, September 28, 2021.

9   Chase, interview by Mael.

10 Chase, interview by Mael.

11 Grandmaster Caz, interview by Jon Mael, September 1, 2021.

12 Caz, interview by Mael.

13 Cold Crush Brothers and the Fantastic Five, "Cold Crush vs The Fantastic Five–Harlem World 1981 (Best Edit) 2021 Redo," audio recording posted by Tape Deck Wreck, September 20, 2021, https://www.youtube.com/watch?v=IhAffvoCKgk&t=2338s.

14 Caz, interview by Mael.

15 "Cold Crush vs The Fantastic Five–Harlem World 1981."

16 Whipper Whip, interview by Jon Mael, October 22, 2021.

17 "Cold Crush vs The Fantastic Five–Harlem World 1981."

18 Chase, interview by Mael.

19 Joe Conzo Jr., interview by Jon Mael, August 26, 2021.

20 "Cold Crush vs The Fantastic Five–Harlem World 1981."

21 "Cold Crush vs The Fantastic Five–Harlem World 1981."

22 Caz, interview by Mael.

23 Caz, interview by Mael.

24 "Cold Crush vs The Fantastic Five–Harlem World 1981."

25 "Cold Crush vs The Fantastic Five–Harlem World 1981."

26 "Cold Crush vs The Fantastic Five–Harlem World 1981."

27 Chase, interview by Mael.

28 "Cold Crush vs The Fantastic Five–Harlem World 1981."

29 "Cold Crush vs The Fantastic Five–Harlem World 1981."

30 "Cold Crush vs The Fantastic Five–Harlem World 1981."

31 Caz, interview by Mael.

32 "Cold Crush vs The Fantastic Five–Harlem World 1981."

33 "Cold Crush vs The Fantastic Five–Harlem World 1981."

34 "Cold Crush vs The Fantastic Five–Harlem World 1981."

35 "Cold Crush vs The Fantastic Five–Harlem World 1981."

36 Caz, interview by Mael.

37 Chase, interview by Mael.

38 Conzo Jr., interview by Mael.

39 Whip, interview by Mael.

40 Theodore, interview by Mael.

41 Theodore, interview by Mael.

42 Theodore, interview by Mael.

Chapter 8. Somebody, and Anybody, and Everybody Scream!

1 Cold Crush Brothers and the Fantastic Five, "Cold Crush vs The Fantastic Five–Harlem World 1981 (Best Edit) 2021 Redo," audio recording posted by Tape Deck Wreck, September 20, 2021, https://www.youtube.com/watch?v=IhAffvoCKgk&t=2338s.

2 Grand Wizzard Theodore, interview by Jon Mael, August 30, 2021.

3 Theodore, interview by Mael.

4 Whipper Whip, interview by Jon Mael, October 22, 2021.

5 Theodore, interview by Mael.

6 Theodore, interview by Mael.

7 Master Rob and Kevie Kev, interview by Jon Mael, September 13, 2021.

8 "Cold Crush vs The Fantastic Five–Harlem World 1981."

9 "Cold Crush vs The Fantastic Five–Harlem World 1981."

10 Whip, interview by Mael.

11 Rob and Kev, interview by Mael.

12 Rob and Kev, interview by Mael.

13 Rob and Kev, interview by Mael.

14 Rob and Kev, interview by Mael.

15 "Cold Crush vs The Fantastic Five–Harlem World 1981." Note that group members confirmed that the late Dot-A-Rock wrote this routine.

16 Theodore, interview by Mael.

17 Whip, interview by Mael.

18 Theodore, interview by Mael.

19 "Cold Crush vs The Fantastic Five–Harlem World 1981."

20 "Cold Crush vs The Fantastic Five–Harlem World 1981." Group members again confirmed that the late Dot-A-Rock wrote this routine.

21 "Cold Crush vs The Fantastic Five–Harlem World 1981."

22 "Cold Crush vs The Fantastic Five–Harlem World 1981."

23 "Cold Crush vs The Fantastic Five–Harlem World 1981."

24 "Cold Crush vs The Fantastic Five–Harlem World 1981."

25 "Cold Crush vs The Fantastic Five–Harlem World 1981."

26 "Cold Crush vs The Fantastic Five–Harlem World 1981."

27 Whip, interview by Mael.

28 Whip, interview by Mael.

29 "Cold Crush vs The Fantastic Five–Harlem World 1981."

30 "Cold Crush vs The Fantastic Five–Harlem World 1981."

31 "Cold Crush vs The Fantastic Five–Harlem World 1981."
32 Rob and Kev, interview by Mael.
33 Joe Conzo Jr., interview by Jon Mael, August 26, 2021.
34 DJ Baby D., interview by Jon Mael, November 12, 2021.
35 "Cold Crush vs The Fantastic Five–Harlem World 1981."
36 Rob and Kev, interview by Mael.
37 Theodore, interview by Mael.
38 Whip, interview by Mael.
39 Baby D, interview by Mael.
40 Rob and Kev, interview by Mael
41 DJ Charlie Chase, interview by Jon Mael, September 28, 2021.
42 Grandmaster Caz, interview by Jon Mael, December 4, 2021.
43 Theodore, interview by Mael.

Chapter 9. Traveling Tapes

1 Sound Selection, "A Brief Audio History of The Compact Cassette," narrated and edited by Michael Hudachek, September 19, 2019, https://www.youtube.com/watch?v=U7KxIq4eDDA.
2 NPR Music, "The History of the Boombox," written and edited by Roy Hurst, April 22, 2009, https://www.youtube.com/watch?v=e84hf5aUmNA&t=1s.
3 NPR Music, "The History of the Boombox."
4 Regan Sommer McCoy, interview by Jon Mael, August 27, 2021.
5 *20/20*, "Rappin' to the Beat," July 9, 1981, aired on ABC, YouTube video posted by Live from the Basement (courtesy of RapRadar), https://www.youtube.com/watch?v=onRKOcsf1J0&t=67s.
6 *20/20*, "Rappin' to the Beat."
7 NPR Music, "The History of the Boombox."
8 NPR Music, "The History of the Boombox."
9 Such as Kurtis Blow's work and the first Grandmaster Flash album.
10 Troy L. Smith, interview by Jon Mael, September 17, 2021.
11 Smith, interview by Mael.
12 Smith, interview by Mael.
13 Grandmaster Caz, interview by Jon Mael, December 4, 2021.
14 Smith, interview by Mael.
15 Caz, interview by Mael.
16 Smith, interview by Mael.
17 Caz, interview by Mael.
18 Claude "Paradise" Gray, interview by Jon Mael, July 19, 2021.
19 DJ Charlie Chase, interview by Jon Mael, September 28, 2021.
20 Sugarhill Gang, "The Sugarhill Gang - Rapper's Delight," Sugarhill Records, video, 6:15, accessed May 29, 2021, https://www.youtube.com/watch?v=mcCK99wHrk0.
21 Chase, interview by Mael.
22 Smith, interview by Mael.
23 Chase, interview by Mael.

24 Caz, interview by Mael.

25 Chase, interview by Mael.

26 Chase, interview by Mael.

27 Whipper Whip, interview by Jon Mael, October 22, 2021.

28 Grand Wizzard Theodore, interview by Jon Mael, August 30, 2021.

29 Smith, interview by Mael.

30 Gray, interview by Mael.

31 "New York City Hip Hop Convention," video shot by Charlie Ahearn and Fred Brathwaite, Celebrity Club in Harlem, 1980.

32 "Busy Bee vs. Kool Moe Doe [sic]," from *Beef*, directed by Peter Spirer (2003; United States: Image Entertainment), video posted by bazzgiar102, https://www.youtube.com/watch?v=wipb37LGe4U).

33 "Busy Bee vs. Kool Moe Doe [sic]," from *Beef*.

34 Kool Moe Dee, Busy Bee Starski, and L.A. Sunshine, "Kool Moe Dee vs Busy Bee Starski Dec 1981 Harlem World," audio posted by Tape Deck Wreck, https://www.youtube.com/watch?v=am9C2_DZ7s4.

35 Busy Bee, interview by Jim Fricke, Museum of Pop Culture Oral History Collection, March 24, 2001.

36 Dee, Starski, and Sunshine, "Kool Moe Dee vs Busy Bee Starski."

37 L.A. Sunshine, interview by Jon Mael, November 2, 2021.

38 Dee, Starski, and Sunshine, "Kool Moe Dee vs Busy Bee Starski."

39 Sunshine, interview by Mael.

40 Sunshine, interview by Mael.

41 Dee, Starski, and Sunshine, "Kool Moe Dee vs Busy Bee Starski."

42 Sunshine, interview by Mael.

43 Master Rob and Kevie Kev, interview by Jon Mael, September 13, 2021.

44 Caz, interview by Mael.

45 Caz, interview by Mael.

46 Caz, interview by Mael.

47 Sunshine, interview by Mael.

48 Sunshine, interview by Mael.

49 Smith, interview by Mael.

50 *Hip-Hop Evolution*, season 1, episode 2, "From the Underground to the Mainstream," directed by Darby Wheeler, Netflix, 2016.

51 Fab 5 Freddy, interview by Jim Fricke, Museum of Pop Culture Oral History Collection, November 11, 2001.

52 Freddy, interview by Fricke.

53 *Hip-Hop Evolution*, "From the Underground to the Mainstream."

54 Bill Adler, interview by Jon Mael, September 30, 2021.

55 Adler, interview by Mael.

56 *Hip-Hop Evolution*, "From the Underground to the Mainstream."

57 Adler, interview by Mael.

58 Freddy, interview by Fricke.

59 Freddy, interview by Fricke.

60 Red Bull Music Academy, "Debbie Harry & Chris Stein Talk '60s New York, CBGB and Rapture," May 12, 2015, https://www.youtube.com/watch?v=-veZ_WkUxA0.

61 *Hip-Hop Evolution*, "From the Underground to the Mainstream."

62 Blondie, "Blondie – Rapture (Official Music Video)," directed by Keef, Universal Music Group, 1981, posted by BlondieMusicOfficial, February 24, 2009, https://www.youtube.com/watch?v=pHCdS7O248g.

63 Blondie, "Blondie – Rapture."

64 Adler, interview by Mael.

65 Hugh Wyatt, "When a Rap Makes Music," *New York Daily News*, February 20, 1981, Adler Hip Hop Archive, #8092, Division of Rare and Manuscript Collections, Cornell University Library, https://digital.library.cornell.edu/catalog/ss:9061404.

66 Wyatt, "When a Rap Makes Music."

67 Red Bull Music Academy, "Debbie Harry & Chris Stein Talk."

68 Caz, interview by Mael.

69 *20/20*, "Rappin' to the Beat."

Chapter 10. Wild Style

1 Charlie Ahearn, interview by Jon Mael, November 4, 2021.

2 Ahearn, interview by Mael.

3 Ahearn, interview by Mael.

4 Ahearn, interview by Mael.

5 Ahearn, interview by Mael.

6 Red Bull Music Academy, "Debbie Harry & Chris Stein Talk '60s New York, CBGB and Rapture," May 12, 2015, https://www.youtube.com/watch?v=-veZ_WkUxA0.

7 Ahearn, interview by Mael.

8 Fab 5 Freddy, interview by Jim Fricke, Museum of Pop Culture Oral History Collection, November 11, 2001.

9 Ahearn, interview by Mael.

10 Ahearn, interview by Mael.

11 Ahearn, interview by Mael.

12 Ahearn, interview by Mael.

13 *Wild Style*, directed by Charlie Ahearn (1983; United States: Submarine Entertainment, https://www.amazon.com/Wild-Style-Lee-Quinones/dp/B07V818YL7/ref=sr_1_1?crid=2E2X2P3TJUVY&keywords=wild+style&qid=1641861061).

14 Patti Astor, interview by Jon Mael, October 28, 2021.

15 Astor, interview by Mael.

16 Astor, interview by Mael.

17 *Wild Style*.

18 *Wild Style*.

19 Ahearn, interview by Mael.

20 *Wild Style*

21 Ahearn, interview by Mael.

22 Ahearn, interview by Mael.

23 Ahearn, interview by Mael.

24 Ahearn, interview by Mael.

25 Grandmaster Caz, interview by Jon Mael, September 1, 2021.

26 Ahearn, interview by Mael.
27 Grandmaster Caz, interview by Jon Mael, December 4, 2021.
28 Master Rob and Kevie Kev, interview by Jon Mael, September 13, 2021.
29 Rob and Kev, interview by Mael.
30 *Wild Style.*
31 *Wild Style.*
32 *Wild Style.*
33 *Wild Style.*
34 Caz, interview by Mael, December 4, 2021.
35 Caz, interview by Mael, December 4, 2021.
36 *Wild Style.*
37 *Wild Style.*
38 Rob and Kev, interview by Mael.
39 Rob and Kev, interview by Mael.
40 Rob and Kev, interview by Mael.
41 *Wild Style.*
42 Ahearn, interview by Mael.
43 Ahearn, interview by Mael.
44 Ahearn, interview by Mael.
45 Astor, interview by Mael.
46 Astor, interview by Mael.
47 Astor, interview by Mael.
48 Astor, interview by Mael.
49 Astor, interview by Mael.
50 Sandra "Lady Pink" Fabara, interview by Jon Mael, October 3, 2021.
51 Ahearn, interview by Mael.
52 Ahearn, interview by Mael.
53 Vincent Canby, "'Wild Style,' Rapping and Painting Graffiti," *New York Times*, March 18, 1983, https://www.nytimes.com/1983/03/18/movies/wild-style-rapping-and-painting-graffiti.html.
54 Canby, "'Wild Style,' Rapping and Painting Graffiti."
55 Ahearn, interview by Mael.
56 Ahearn, interview by Mael.
57 *Wild Style.*
58 Rob and Kev, interview by Mael.
59 Rob and Kev, interview by Mael.

Epilogue. *"The Message"*

1 Although it should be noted that "The Message" does use a sample of a previous Grandmaster Flash and the Furious Five song.
2 Grandmaster Flash and the Furious Five, *The Message*, n.d., Sugarhill Records, 1982.
3 Flash and the Furious Five, *The Message*.
4 Robert Hilburn, "Rap 'Message' Jumps Out in a Flash," *Los Angeles Times*, March 27, 1983, https://digital.library.cornell.edu/catalog/ss:13450415.

5   Jay-Z, Biggie, Eminem, KRS-One, and Willie D, "Melle Mel on 'The Message,' Jay-Z, Biggie, Eminem, KRS-One, Willie D (Full Interview)," interview by Melle Mel, VladTV, 2021, https://www.youtube.com/watch?v=WxXQfkCFYCA.

6   Jay-Z, Biggie, Eminem, KRS-One, and Willie D, "Melle Mel on 'The Message.'"

7   *Hip-Hop Evolution*, season 1, episode 2, "From the Underground to the Mainstream," directed by Darby Wheeler, Netflix, 2016.

8   Jay Cocks, "Chilling Out on Rap Flash," *Time Magazine*, March 21, 1983, https://time.com/vault/issue/1983-03-21/page/90/.

9   Christopher Connelly, "1982 in Review: Who Won, Who Lost," *Rolling Stone,* February 17, 1983, https://www.rollingstone.com/music/music-news/1982-in-review-who-won-who-lost-69510/.

10 Jay-Z, Biggie, Eminem, KRS-One, and Willie D, "Melle Mel on 'The Message.'"

11 Hilburn, "Rap 'Message' Jumps Out in a Flash."

12 Cocks, "Chilling Out on Rap Flash."

13 *Beat This! A Hip-Hop History*, directed by Dick Fontaine (1984, United Kingdom: BBC), video posted by Upproxx, https://www.youtube.com/watch?v=Hd0N4NHm4xo&t=187s.

14 Grandmaster Caz, interview by Jon Mael, December 4, 2021.

15 Cold Crush Brothers, *Wild Style Japan Tour (Tokyo, 1983) 7 (The Cold Crush Brothers Live)*, video posted by DJ Shoji, 2018, https://www.youtube.com/watch?v=DuESGVPdBlE.

16 Caz, interview by Mael.

17 DJ Charlie Chase, interview by Jon Mael, September 28, 2021.

18 Whipper Whip, interview by Jon Mael, October 22, 2021.

19 Master Rob and Kevie Kev, interview by Jon Mael, September 13, 2021.

20 Rubie Dee, interview by Jon Mael, November 13, 2021.

21 Grand Wizzard Theodore, interview by Jon Mael, August 30, 2021.

22 Whip, interview by Mael.

23 Chase, interview by Mael.

24 Caz, interview by Mael.

25 Chase, interview by Mael.

26 Chase, interview by Mael.

27 Chase, interview by Mael.

28 This was true at the time of writing.

29 Troy L. Smith, "Charlie Rock of 'The Harlem World Crew' and Harlem World," *The Foundation*, 2003, http://www.thafoundation.com/charock.htm?fbclid=IwAR2Hv IVOMZKIXq4A1xNWtTTv9kaNn96k1uwgZ8T6MrY9IigAGytz_BoSGZc.

30 Theodore, interview by Mael.

31 Joe Conzo Jr., interview by Jon Mael, August 26, 2021.

32 Whip, interview by Mael.

33 Including a time when Whipper Whip was shot in the chest, but made a full recovery.

34 Caz, interview by Mael.

35 Caz, interview by Mael.

36 Chase, interview by Mael.

Index